To my mother, Kundan Kaur, to whom I owe much for her humour and compassion for (almost) all, regardless of race or religion, and to my father, Dr Diwan Singh, for his example of living true to his principles despite the difficulties and challenges he faced.

Indarjit Singh

FROM WHERE I STAND

AUSTIN MACAULEY PUBLISHERS™
LONDON • CAMBRIDGE • NEW YORK • SHARJAH

A CIP catalogue record for this title is available from the British Library.

ISBN 9781398432819 (Paperback)
ISBN 9781398432833 (ePub e-book)

www.austinmacauley.com

First Published 2022
Austin Macauley Publishers Ltd®
1 Canada Square
Canary Wharf
London
E14 5AA

Acknowledgements

My wife Kanwaljit and daughters Mona and Rema who persuaded me to put pen to paper.

Nearly expelled on my first day at school, see page 136

Table of contents

Foreword

This is both an endearing and necessary book, written simply and honestly by someone the public has grown to regard with great affection. The early struggles of Indarjit in the 1940s up until his peerage, conferred in 2011, as the first turbaned Sikh parliamentarian, reveals that the racism of the 1960s although now much diminished continues to exist in politics. Far from becoming embittered, Indarjit's characteristic sense of humour helped him see the funny side of unthinking bigotry as in the lift story he narrated in his maiden speech. He elaborates on this in Indarjit's Law, which states:' *if two or more people find sufficient in common to call themselves 'us', they will immediately look for a 'them' to look down on to strengthen their sense of common identity'.*

Lord Singh's deep interest in the interface between religion, culture and politics has been a thread throughout his life; a central part of this memoir is the Mandla court case which eventually resulted in the protection of Sikh religious identity under the 1976 Race Relations Act. Indarjit played a key role as chief witness and the transcript of the court proceeding provides a fascinating and concise insight into the history and fundamental tenets of Sikhism. If we are to be a truly interracial society, memoirs such as these provide the foundations for understanding and tolerance.

Rt Hon Baroness D'Souza CMG
The Lord Speaker (2011-2016)

PART ONE:
My Story

Chapter One
My Parents

My parents grew up in pre-partition Rawalpindi, now in Pakistan. My father's family were wealthy landowners living in a small village called Takhatpari, which its proud inhabitants referred to as 'shaar', or 'the city'. My father had his heart set on going to England to study law but, unfortunately, my grandfather lost most of the family money in property speculation so my father was unable to pursue his dream. Undeterred, Dad took a job as a government auditor in Amritsar, sending money home and studying in the evening. His ambition changed from studying law to becoming a doctor and, using his savings, he duly enrolled, and a few years later, qualified as a doctor at Amritsar Medical College.

Soon after, he found himself involved in the 1922 Guru ka Bagh movement to free Sikh places of worship (gurdwaras) from the control of government-appointed nominees. Batches of five Sikhs pledged to non-violence would go to the occupied gurdwaras to pray for the freeing of the gurdwaras. They refused to raise a hand in self-defence, despite being beaten senseless by the police and government officials. Every day, several batches of Sikhs would go in non-violent protest and inevitably would be brutally beaten. My father used to dress the wounds of the protesters.

Eventually, nationwide adverse publicity led to the government acceding to the demands of the protesters to restore the gurdwaras to Sikh hands. Mahatma Gandhi sent a telegram to the Sikhs saying, "Congratulations, first battle for India's independence won." The young Dr Diwan Singh, however, was a marked man for having given medical assistance to the protestors.

The 1919 Jallianwala Bagh massacre in a small enclosed public space close to the Darbar Sahib (Golden Temple) was still fresh in the memory of the people of Punjab. Thousands of Sikhs from Punjab had enlisted to fight for Britain in the First World War, encouraged by the promise that India would receive a measure of self-rule on the conclusion of the war. Instead, the government increased repression with legislation allowing internment of political activists without trial. The meeting at Jallianwala Bagh was called to discuss the increasing repression. The authorities decided to make an example of the peaceful protestors. Soldiers commanded by General Dyer manned the only entrance to the walled park and, without warning, fired volley upon volley of bullets at the protestors, including the elderly and children, until there was virtually no one left alive. Estimates of the number killed vary from a few hundred to more than a thousand. Unbelievably, the then Governor, Sir Michael O'Dwyer, sent a telegram to General Dyer saying: "Your action correct."

The massacre was widely condemned in the House of Commons by Winston Churchill and many others. On the centenary of the massacre, the Prime Minister Theresa May described it as "a shameful act". The Archbishop of Canterbury, Justin Welby, in a visit to the site in September 2019, said: "I recognise the sins of my British colonial history that has too often subjugated and dehumanised other races and cultures." The massacre galvanised the freedom movement, influencing the minds of my father and many others. One of the few survivors was a young lad called Udham Singh, who never forgot the cruelty and horror he had witnessed. He later travelled to England and would visit my parents and was also a regular visitor to the gurdwara at Shepherd's Bush in London. Twenty-one years after the infamous massacre, he assassinated Michael O'Dwyer at a meeting at Caxton Hall in London. Udham Singh, who had secretly nursed revenge for the atrocity he had witnessed as a child, was convicted of murder and hanged at Pentonville prison in London.

My father was a popular and well-loved doctor, but his support for India's freedom movement and his medical assistance at Guru ka Bagh incurred the anger of the government and it became difficult for him to practise in Punjab. He and his young wife, Kundan, moved to Kashmir, but his continuing support for the freedom movement meant that he was constantly under the threat of arrest. His friends decided to put him, my mother and their infant son Gurbachan (Bachan) on board a ship leaving from Bombay to East Africa; a popular venue for many young Indians at the time.

For a time, this was one of the happiest periods in my parents' life. My other older brother, Surindar, was born in Nairobi and they had a thriving practice, many friends and an active social life. They would tell us of their friends and experiences. Times were so different then – one of their servants was a reformed cannibal who was always watched with suspicion by another slightly portly servant from another tribe.

My parents, East Africa, 1928

14

My mum also described another incident when she was resting in the veranda and a leopard appeared and brushed against her sari as it walked away. My father continued to support the freedom struggle in India and, after a while, it became clear to the English authorities, who used to freely socialise with my parents, that this could not continue. He was told he had to stop his support for the freedom movement or he would end up in prison. My father proposed an alternative: "Send me to England to study for further medical qualifications." The authorities, not wanting to anger the East African Indians, agreed, and while my mother and her two small children temporarily moved back to Rawalpindi, my dad took a boat to England, the heart of the Empire.

On arriving in London, my father was told that they would not accept his Indian medical qualifications and so he had to sit all the exams again. After completing his matriculation in London, he studied at Edinburgh University and then completed his training at Queen Elizabeth Medical School in Birmingham, obtaining the UK qualifications to practise as a doctor.

Racism then, and later in my schooldays, was quite different from the racism of the 1950s and 1960s over jobs, housing and fear of difference. It was simply a recognition of the natural superiority of white people and the inferiority of others. Dad frequently experienced such racism. He also experienced kindness that he never forgot, such as his landlady in Edinburgh going out of her way to cook Indian food for him. On one occasion, he was rather glad that he wore a turban when, while walking with two Indian friends, they passed some children who remarked: "Look, there's two blacks and a Maharaja!"

Once qualified, racist attitudes meant that he was unable to secure a job at a hospital. Undaunted, my father set up his own practice. Back then, setting up your own practice simply involved putting a sign outside your house which read, 'Dr Singh'. It was then just a matter of waiting for paying customers on which he could build a practice suitable to support a family. It was not easy. There was then no National Health Service and people only used his services when they needed a doctor in an emergency, but, with his clear dedication and a growing reputation for being good with children, he slowly built up the practice.

By 1932, my father was able to bring my mother and two brothers to Birmingham, although life was still financially hard. Once settled and living in rented accommodation with Bachan and Surinder, my mother briefly returned home to Rawalpindi to welcome me into the world amongst the support of her parents and family. I made my first journey by ship at six months of age, sailing through the Suez Canal long before air travel became common.

In 1934, our youngest brother Jagjit or Kak ('baby'), as we still call him, arrived. Mum, with hands more than full, was not very pleased when I, a nearly two-year-old, fancied myself as an interior decorator and started ripping wallpaper off the walls of our rented house. This was when I was not attempting to eat coal – a 'foretaste' of my later mining career.

At one time, while my father was gradually gaining a reputation as a local doctor and building his practice to pay the rent, my mother had to pawn her jewellery to purchase basic food supplies for us. Mum, or Manji as we called her, was a remarkable woman. She was pious and principled, with a lovely singing voice and wonderful sense of humour. She also kept her wits about her. My brother Surinder recalls a time when a thief entered the house and demanded that she gave him money and jewellery. She said she had no money but there was some jewellery hidden in the larder. He went in and she promptly locked the door on him and called the police.

As a family of six we were close and somewhat separated from mainstream British life. Coming to this country, my mother, my brothers and I didn't understand much English. My mother experienced the stress of looking after four children, particularly during the war years, which sometimes resulted in spells of depression.

My father had become an active member of the only Sikh gurdwara then in England, at 79 Sinclair Road in West London's Shepherd's Bush. He would become the President for almost 20 years until the mid-1950s, and throughout this period was often approached to speak, not only as the chief spokesman of the UK Sikh community, but also for other religious communities from the sub-continent.

While Mum was picking up bits of English herself, we would speak Punjabi at home, so while us boys were naturally more fluent in Punjabi at first, once we were at school, we started to speak English more and more until it quickly became our first language.

While we were still quite young and spoke mostly Punjabi, there was one time when we could turn this to our advantage. We were entered into a competition during the celebration of the coronation of King George VI. We were told jokes and anyone who did not laugh at the jokes won a prize. I didn't understand much English at the time and sat there stony-faced. At the end, I collected my first ever award: a small tin of biscuits.

Chapter Two
School

In 1937 ,aged five, I attended school for the first time and was left with an interesting impression of what happens when you take the path less trodden.

It was my first day, and my mother had left me at the foot of the steps leading up to the school. The school was on a bit of a hill, so pupils had to walk up 15–20 steps to get to it. Near the steps was a huge mound of sand, almost reaching the top of the steps. After my mother had seen me off at the bottom of the steps and waved goodbye, I looked at the sand and I looked at the steps. The sand looked much more tempting, so I set off to trek up the giant pile of sand. I could see the faces of horrified teachers at the top of the steps looking at me as I sank deeper and deeper with each step, before finally, I arrived at the top, bringing much of the sand with me. Unknown to me, my mother had also watched horrified and then saw me being told off and warned that I would not be allowed in the school if I ever tried that again. Threatened with expulsion on my first day at school – before I'd even got through the front door! Some years later, I read some words which immediately resonated with me, 'We do not have to tread the path worn smooth by careless convention.' They summed up my independent and, admittedly, perverse nature.

Soon after, we moved out of the rented house to a newly-built, detached house at 80 Bandywood Road, Kingstanding, in Birmingham.

It had four bedrooms and looked huge and spacious to us at the time. When I went back in later life, it looked a lot smaller. At the time, it was easy to borrow money, and my father had saved and managed to buy the property for £800. There was a downstairs space for the patients, with a surgery and a waiting room, and an interconnecting door with the house which had a kitchen and two reception rooms on the ground floor.

I joined my two brothers at the nearby school on the same road. (Many years later, Kanwaljit (Kawal), my future wife, was to have her first teaching post at this school.)

At infant school, they tried to teach me to read and write. Not easy. We were told to leave a finger space between words when writing. I did this and was surprised when my teacher got cross, saying, "You're leaving too much space!" I protested that I had left a finger space! At first, the teacher did not believe me, then she looked at my larger than average hands and told me to use my little finger! At Christmas, I won a pink writing pad in a jumbled animal names competition. My parents were delighted, but I was not too pleased when they made me use it to practise sums! It didn't do me much good. When the teacher asked us to say if our dad's foot was a foot or a yard in length, I wasn't sure of what a yard was, but confident that my dad's feet must be bigger than those of 'ordinary' dads, I shouted out, "A yard!" I'm not sure if it was due to a shortage of teachers or the fear of German bombs that led to the school being closed for a few weeks, but to my dismay, my class continued in my dad's waiting room!

I fancied myself as something of a doctor when I first went to school. I would get hold of some discarded bandages from Dad's surgery and would insist on bandaging slightly injured classmates, often against their will!

In contrast to my first years at home, school was an endurance when it came to the incessant teasing and taunting. No one had seen Sikhs before, and while today young Sikhs will wear a mini turban called a 'patka', this had not yet become the fashion. As a result, before we were old enough to tie a turban, we wore little pigtails, tied at the back and tucked under the coat. It was an open invitation to other children to pull them.

One day after school, there was a group of older boys waiting to tease and bully me. I didn't know how to respond, but I soon became very angry and hit out at one of the taller boys. I was about seven or eight at the time, and he was about ten or eleven. I must have got a lucky hit at him in his stomach, because he doubled-up with pain and fell to the ground. I pretended I knew that it was going to hurt him, even though I hadn't a clue about fighting. Consequently, there was a bit of an aura about me. Other children thought that this person could take care of himself, so they had better be careful. The bullying then stopped for a while, which was fine. We had lots of adventures like that – the Singh family of four brothers against the rest of the world.

At the gates of the school there was a large roundabout with lots of trees, many of which are now no longer there. My two older brothers, Bachan and Surinder, had both moved on to senior school by the time I was nine. However, sometimes they would hide behind the trees by the roundabout as we were leaving school. That way, the bullies never knew if our older brothers were around to protect Kak and me.

I remember a time in the middle of winter when the local children decided to throw snowballs at the house. Far from being intimidated, we took it as a challenge and we'd go to the back and make lots of snowballs and throw them at our adversaries – so it was all good fun, though a little intimidating.

Junior School

I entered the junior school at Bishop Vesey's Grammar aged nine. It was then still a fee-paying school, becoming a state-funded school two years later. Old-fashioned public-school attitudes still persisted, and I was asked to be a senior boy's fag. I totally refused and threatened to hit the older boy with a slipper lying in his study. Stunned, he decided to ask someone more compliant to do his fagging for him.

Lunchtime often involved chasing and fighting some of the teasers. Once, after school, I chased a boy into the senior school. A tall guy, not in school uniform, tried to stop me. I threatened to hit him if he did not move out of my way. The next day, my brother's French teacher complained to him of how his younger brother had threatened to beat him up!

Eventually, the Singh brothers would make up more than half of the school boxing team at Bishop Vesey's Grammar School in Sutton Coldfield. This helped with managing the teasing and bullying. I enjoyed boxing, as I did all school sports, even though I wasn't particularly good at it. I would take blows from my opponents, then wait for my opportunity and hit out hard with my left hand, taking them by surprise. My father, concerned about possible injury, not necessarily to us, cautioned us to step aside from conflict, but he and my mother were secretly happy that we were able to stand up for ourselves.

At school, we discovered that the Catholic children did not have to attend School Assembly or RE classes, and so we suggested to our mother that we should have the same exemption. Our mother would have none of it – she wanted us to go into assembly and join the RE classes and learn something about other religions. At the time, we thought our parents were being unreasonable and it was a long time before we understood their respect for other faiths.

The long summer holidays were spent walking and playing at nearby Sutton Park and a small Roman settlement called Barr Beacon. The 'Red Army', a group of boys who carried a red flag taken from some roadworks, were the deadly rivals of the 'Singh Brothers', but fortunately, boasts of superiority never resulted in physical conflict. Then, one day, there was a knock on our front door. We opened it to find the leader of the Red Army standing on the doorstep with a catapult in hand. He knew it belonged to Bachan and had come to return it; peace was declared.

We would play lots of indoor games, including pontoon with matchsticks for money, often hiding aces or a royal card in our sleeves. When Kak and I played chess, we often began the game asking if cheating was allowed!

I found school a little boring. The best teachers had been called up for the war effort. The maths teacher seemed to spend forever talking about Pythagoras's theorem. I could never understand how he got so carried away about a square on the hypotenuse, or why anyone would want to put a square there. I should however, have paid more attention to the lessons on gravity and acceleration when responding to a challenge or 'dare' at school.

My elder brothers both had bikes and had been taught to ride. My younger brother Kak and I missed out because of other pressures during the war. This did not stop us secretly borrowing the bikes when our elder brothers were at school and teaching ourselves to ride by going round and round the almost grassless lawn in the back garden. One day, at the end of school, a friend challenged me, "I bet you can't ride a bike." Confident of my cycling skills, I borrowed his bike and began to go down a steep cul-de-sac which had a gate at the end leading to the playing fields. Unfortunately, I had never learnt to use the brakes to control speed and the bike began to move faster and faster and I decided that a lamppost near the bottom of the road was the best place to stop. The bike was OK, but I limped home with badly grazed knees. Dad dressed my wounds. I'm sure he spent more time bandaging us up than treating other patients.

The winter of 1947 was exceptionally long and severe and there were fuel shortages resulting in no heating in schools. In one geography lesson about Africa, the teacher told us that goats would eat the bark of trees causing what he referred to as 'forest erosion'. I was off school for about two weeks after this lesson, and by the time I came back, the geography teacher had moved on to talk about physical geography. At the start of the lesson he asked if anyone could explain the causes of erosion. I didn't know he was talking about the erosion of rocks and thinking back to the last lesson I had attended, and to everyone's amusement, I confidently called out, "Goats."

Generally, my interest in different subjects varied with the teacher. My first history teacher would look at me and mutter aloud that, "They come here, get educated and then go back to push us out." But a later history teacher, who also taught RE, made lessons so interesting that I thoroughly enjoyed both subjects.

Art was initially taught by a teacher who, despite having Parkinson's disease, could still draw beautifully. In one lesson on the top floor of a three-storey building, I found myself fighting with another boy at the back row of the class. We didn't realise the teacher was watching until he commented in a bored voice, "Throw him out of the window, Singh."

English was probably my favourite lesson. I had a good general knowledge and could remember poetry and passages from Shakespeare quite easily; something that has proved useful in my later writing and speaking. Following a lesson on the play *Julius Caesar*, we were set homework to learn Mark Antony's speech following the assassination of Caesar. The next day, the teacher said if one boy could recite the speech, he wouldn't test the rest of the class. I volunteered and became a class hero for about five minutes.

In another English lesson, a teacher was talking about an island paradise "Where no white man had ever been."

Without thinking, I said, "Is that why it was a paradise?" The teacher was not amused. I have since used John of Gaunt's speech in *Richard II* in several talks to illustrate unconscious racism built into education.

I loved sport at school. The head, Sylvanus Jones, was fanatical about rugby, but would allow soccer in the junior school. I was made a full back and still remember an odd incident when the ball came to me. I kicked it forward and chased after it, successfully dodging players on the opposing side until there was no one between me and the opposing goalkeeper, a slightly built boy called Herringshaw. When he saw me coming towards him, he burst into tears. I thought I must have broken some rule of football and, leaving the ball near the goal, walked back to my full back position all embarrassed. In rugby, I later had the distinction of playing alongside Peter Robbins, who was in the same 'Red House'. He was a much better player and later went on to captain England.

At Bishop Vesey's Grammar School

Chapter Three
The Second World War

The war had its additional problems for my parents. My father was not a person who would hide his feelings if he thought that something was wrong, and so he continued to speak out for Indian independence, even during the war, attending and speaking at public meetings. Throughout this period, he was constantly shadowed by CID officers looking for an excuse – a hint of something disreputable – to arrest him. However, when they couldn't find anything, they complained to him and accused him of … being boring!

My parents' association with Udham Singh, once close, suddenly decreased and he stopped visiting us. Concerned, my father would invite him to visit us, but Uncle Udham would simply make excuses to keep away. Prior to this, I remember him as a playful character who was particularly fond of our youngest, Kak, born in Birmingham. Udham Singh, who, as described earlier, was a witness to the horror of Jallianwala Bagh, quietly planned revenge, and to the surprise of our shocked parents, shot and killed Sir Michael O'Dwyer, the former Governor of Punjab, who authorised the brutal massacre, while he was addressing a public meeting at Caxton Hall in East London.

My parents' house was a popular one for Sikhs, Hindus and Muslims alike. As my father was constantly speaking up for India's freedom, between 1939 and 1947, our home played host to many of the leading campaigners for Indian independence. These included an uncle and a cousin of Subash Chandra Bose. During 1941, Chandra Bose had been placed under house arrest by the British, having risen to lead a junior wing of the Indian National Congress. He had escaped to try and rouse the support of Japan and Germany in the struggle for Indian independence.

Another visitor was Krishna Menon. The Singh brothers referred to Krishna Menon as 'the red Indian' because, well, he looked like a red Indian. Menon went on to become India's first High Commissioner to the UK after independence in 1947. (In 2007, hundreds of pages of MI5 files documenting their surveillance of Menon were released, including transcripts of phone conversations and intercepted correspondences with other statesmen, including Jawaharlal Nehru himself.) My father also became friends with the Irish Premier de Valera, who supported India's freedom struggle.

When war was declared in 1939, our parents found themselves with conflicting loyalties. It was a war between two European powers, one of which was still denying independence to India. Germany, on the other hand, had clearly expansionist aims and was a threat to the life and liberty of those living in Britain.

There was no travel possible, so moving back to India was not an option for my parents, even if they had wished to. Any travel would have had to have been made well in advance of 1939. My parents hoped that the war would result in Britain's victory, but would weaken the hold on its Empire, thus allowing India its independence.

As the war progressed, my parents realised that the suffering of Jews under Hitler was far worse than the then all too common antisemitism found in Britain. At the time, the word 'Jew' was sadly a frequent insult in this country, levelled at anyone who was 'different'. My brothers and I were frequently called Jews by those who wished to hurt us. Britain had very different values back then, and the press criticism of Ralph Miliband in 2013, father of former Labour leader Ed Miliband, who also had the temerity to speak out at the time, reflects how much we have forgotten about the very different values that Britain once held – and which people like my father would frequently criticise.

During the period of the Second World War, we had some fascinating experiences. At the start of the war we had to tape up all the windows with sticky paper tape, so that if there was a bomb explosion nearby, the blast would not shatter the windows and injure people inside the house. We also had to obey black-out instructions – householders were not allowed to show any light at all at nighttime and street lights were switched off. This made it difficult for my father to visit sick patients, but he somehow managed. Of course, there was also food rationing, and the whole atmosphere could be quite intimidating if you wanted to be intimidated. Fortunately, our parents seemed to have no fear whatsoever, they just took it in their stride, and because of this, we children also took it in our stride. We didn't know fear, so we didn't complain about life, and, like many others, took it as part of the background of life.

I'm sure that the positive outlook on life which influenced us as children came mostly from the Sikh ethos our parents were trying to instill in us – Sikhs are taught to be optimistic in all circumstances, and our parents certainly provided a good example of this.

At one time, our local area was bombed. There were two types of bombs used by the Germans – one was an explosive bomb which destroyed everything, and the other was an incendiary device, designed to start fires and burn buildings. One night, we had five incendiary bombs in our garden alone – three at the back and two at the front. Fortunately, the house was missed, but again we took it in our stride with my father shoveling sand onto the fires to put them out. As a doctor, he was exempt from military service, but he worked as an Air Raid Protection (ARP) Warden. All children had to carry the government-issue 'Mickey-Mouse' gas masks during this time as a precaution against gas attacks.

We had to go into bomb shelters during the nights for cover, but for us children it was good fun – we had bunk beds. It was exciting and different, even a good laugh and joke. My father had taken the trouble to have a mandatory shelter installed in the garden but dug down even deeper than the recommended levels to give us greater protection. Sitting in the darkness, illuminated by a small paraffin light, I would read my comics – *Beano*, *Wizard* and others – as the bombs fell around us.

In that sort of atmosphere, children always find something to amuse themselves. We would play in the bombed-out houses and buildings, where we could all collect bits and pieces of shells that had been fired to try and down the bombers, as well as the casings of the incendiary bombs that had been dropped. We all had our little 'museums' and would swap something for something else as we amassed our collections. There were also several clubs, such as the spotters club, to spot the planes, and we had to work out whether they were German or British aircraft flying over us.

Providing sustenance for four growing boys during the war was virtually impossible. As a young child, I didn't really notice this, although I remember my eldest brother commenting that he had never seen either of our parents eat an egg. They, of course, would pretend – "Oh, we don't like eggs," they would say, or protest that they were not bothered – although in reality, they always put us boys first. There was a terrific spirit during the war. I remember attending some function, possibly a gathering of the Indian Association, with our parents where they were offered tea with sugar, but they declined the sugar due to its scarcity, even though we knew that they would have gladly had the sugar if it had been readily available!

Throughout the war, my father was President of the gurdwara at Shepherd's Bush in London, and I have many memories of our family travelling down from Birmingham to London, six of us squashed into our father's Austin 7, to celebrate Sikh festivals three or four times a year – or as many visits as our father's determined saving of petrol coupons would allow. These journeys would take an incredibly long time, not least because there were no motorways, but also because we would invariably become lost on the way due to the wartime policy of removing all signposts and advising people not to give directions to strangers who might be German spies. However, my father would wind down the window and ask the way, and you could see people thinking to themselves, "Well, he doesn't look very German," before sending him on his way with a nod in the right direction.

In the back seat, Bachan and Surinder, by now growing teenagers, would suffer the most with travel sickness, and so the long car journeys would cause them the most discomfort. Lodged in my seat between a wriggling seven- or eight-year-old Kak and the two travel-sick brothers for upwards of five hours, I too claimed I felt sick and was instantly cured if Mum gave me a biscuit!

Once at the gurdwara, we would stay overnight with others who had travelled their own similarly arduous journeys to get there. The Sikh holy book, the *Guru Granth Sahib*, would be read continuously from beginning to end, with Mum and Dad often taking their turns in the reading.

During the early years of the war, there was widespread fear and uncertainty. The Blitz had begun, and Dad described his strange experience of being one of the few people struggling to get into London against the tide of people being evacuated, all heading in the opposite direction. He had travelled down to retrieve the Holy Books from the gurdwara, and for a year or so our family hosted the gurdwara at our house until the Holy Books were returned to London once the Blitz had ended.

In the front row, sitting in the middle of three turban-wearing boys, with my brother Kak on my left-hand side

As children, we followed the progress of the war to some extent, but more so because our parents did, and their interest was of course in the freedom of India, something intertwined with the progress and outcome of the war. At school, all that we were told about the war was very black and white – the Germans were the enemy, the British were fighting for the freedom of the world – yet we could still see a part of the world that was not free. Any move towards freedom in India was violently crushed, and suffering was allowed to continue. A devastating famine in Bengal could have easily been prevented by reducing the export of grain from India. When Churchill was told about the famine, his first remark was simply to ask whether Gandhi was among the dead. He continued that he hated Indians: "They are a beastly people that breed like rabbits."

By the time Britain erupted in a flurry of celebrations across the nation in May 1945 for VE Day (Victory in Europe) and later, VJ (Victory over Japan) Day, declaring an end to almost six years of war, I was twelve-years-old and had barely been a year at my new senior school, Bishop Vesey's Grammar School in Sutton Coldfield. Despite the street parties, flag-waving and cheering, my parents remained indifferent, and unlike other houses, ours did not fly the Union Flag. Indian independence had not yet been achieved and for my parents the struggle continued, and they felt they were not able to celebrate. As a result, my father lost many of his patients. He was known as a very good doctor, and as a father to four children himself, word had spread amongst parents that he had a wonderful way with children, ensuring that they felt relaxed. However, this did not prevent his practice shrinking. It was a difficult time with my mother increasingly affected by depression.

During the VE Day celebrations, I was sent next door to the parade of shops, one of which was owned by a certain Mr. V. Pendry, a greengrocer, whose name, later used by me as an alias, was to become well known in India. Food was strictly rationed and only issued on the production of coupons after enduring long queues. When I arrived at the front of the queue to buy my fruit and vegetables, the shopkeeper said to me in front of everyone, "You lot must be Germans because you're not celebrating." I was terribly embarrassed, as any teenager would have been, but I had learnt to keep my wits about me. With my best attempt at a German accent, I simply agreed, "Ja", and with that the rest of the queue collapsed laughing. I learnt an important lesson – that humour is often a better way to defuse tension than confrontation, and so I took my shopping back home!

Looking back on our parents' attitude to the British establishment, in today's context, it seemed unduly uncompromising, but they had experienced and witnessed cruelty and racial superiority that would be widely condemned today. The demeaning description 'heathen', still in dictionaries today, was applied to all those 'not of the Abrahamic faiths'. Racism in my parents' time was an unquestioned and an accepted norm.

The war had left its mark on our mother's health and she had periods of lasting depression. My father decided to take her to India where she could recuperate in the company of her family. To complicate matters further, Surinder had developed pneumonia and was admitted to hospital. A doctor friend volunteered to help and visit Surinder until my dad returned, so my brothers and I were placed in school boarding for a term. We soon learnt why school boarders were always hungry. Food was scarce and there was no choice other than the 'with or without' – referring to gravy and custard.

Chapter Four
Choosing a Career

Bachan had got admission to medical school and was set on a medical career. Priority for university entrance was being given to ex-servicemen and as university places in the UK were severely limited, Surinder went to a university in Salt Lake City in the USA to study metallurgy.

I thought my father's life as a GP operating from his home surgery would be too boring and thought of being an engineer of some sort and roaming the world. Energy then was mainly derived from coal, and mining had suffered in the war years due to a lack of resources. One of the first acts of the Attlee Labour government was to nationalise key industries like mining and steel. Generous scholarships were available for sandwich courses which would allow mining experience, including working at the coalface, to be gained to sit an exam for first-class mine manager. A career in mining engineering felt exciting. At home, we talked a lot about returning to India where mine managers, then mostly British, were also highly paid.

What sounded exciting turned out to be extremely tough. Even the first step of getting attached to a mine proved difficult. There were two mines which were cycling distance from home and I thought that with all the recruitment going on, I would be welcome. Not so. Miners were a very clannish group of people and they resented foreigners. They had given Italian and Polish workers a tough time and the manager of the nearest mine, fearing trouble if he employed someone with a turban, refused to take me on. The manager of the second mine in nearby South Staffordshire, a Welshman by the name of Morris, proved more helpful. He warned me of the difficulties: not only the physical dangers inherent in mining, but the ignorance and taunts of those who worked underground to anyone who looked different!

The manager was right. Miners were prejudiced and suspicious. In the event, it proved even harder. The deputy manager would send me to the more difficult areas of the mine. Anyone with any sense would have left for a different career, but my pride and youthful stubbornness made me carry on and I slowly gained the admiration of the management.

I once hurt my finger in a mining accident, losing the nail on my middle finger. A first-aid guy dressed it and I was told to report to the first-aid room back on the surface. The man in charge looked at the dressing and said, "You can't trust the people underground," and promptly removed the dressing and applied iodine all over again. When I got home, my dad said, "I don't trust the mine first-aid people," and removed the dressing and cleaned the wound all over again. There is such a thing as too much care!

I learnt a lot at the mine: something about the challenges of mining, but more importantly, about people. The miners were rough and uncouth and used language they would blush to use outside the mine. It is a reflection on the changing culture of our times that such language is now common currency of children travelling home from school.

Despite their exterior roughness, most of the miners had hearts of gold and you could trust them with your life. Many of them came from the Black Country area around Dudley and spoke in a dialect of earlier times. "Ow bin thee" translated as, 'how are you?' "Thee day?" meant 'you didn't, did you?' I got seriously worried when after a few months, the miners complimented me on my improved English! Football and cricket were common topics of conversation and I remember being taunted when England beat the West Indies. When I protested that India and West Indies were different countries, they said that I was just making excuses.

After three years' experience, and more enhanced training as a directed practical trainee, I became eligible to sit the open competition exam for a first-class mine manager's certificate and managed to pass at the first attempt. I was subsequently invited for an interview with the then National Coal Board (NCB) at which I was bluntly told to my face that miners would never agree to a Sikh mine manager and I was asked to consider a career in the scientific department of the NCB. Today, most people would be outraged and affronted if told this, particularly after nearly five years of study and hard-earned practical experience, but, at a time when there were no laws against racial discrimination, such setbacks were simply par for the course. I politely declined the suggestion that I change career direction. I decided to go to India where the mining engineers were in growing demand and the position of mine manager carried considerable prestige.

Chapter Five
India

In late 1959, aged twenty-seven, I travelled by Anchor Line on a three-week trip to India. It was an old-fashioned luxury liner, smaller, slower and less expensive, but in some ways, more luxurious than the larger, faster P&O liners. Initially, all the passengers pretended to be more superior than one another with vague connections to the tea plantations and industries of the Raj. My close companions were Onkar Singh, a newly-qualified architect I had known in England, Fazal Mahmood, a former Pakistan cricket Test captain, and a young Catholic priest, a little uncertain of his calling and the life he was going to lead. He later visited me in New Delhi. He looked as if he had been starved in the seminary and, looking at the fruit bowl on the table, his first words of greeting were: "Can I have a banana?"

The smaller boat meant it rocked more in places like the notorious Bay of Biscay. Fazal Mahmood had his own remedy for sea sickness: to drink so that the movement of the ship was, he claimed, countered by the swaying of his head and body!

The voyage took three weeks, first sailing through the Mediterranean to stop at Egypt and through the famous Suez Canal. All the ships would stop there, and the same conjuror would come aboard to entertain the passengers with the same sleight of hand tricks and illusions, pulling chickens out of ears (as opposed to rabbits out of hats)! The ship would then travel on to Aden, a port on the coast of Yemen on the Saudi Arabian Peninsula, known as a very good shopping location. There I bought an early pride and joy, a bulky tape recorder, which was very much a novelty at the time. Having travelled this route many times, I would see the changes in Aden a few years later, brought about by a greater sense of independence and bringing with it some hostility to foreigners.

Reaching India, I remember the sudden impact of the heat and disembarking with throngs of people milling around. I was met by my father and younger brother. After a long train journey, we finally arrived in Delhi, where I found my cabin trunk was too large to fit into a taxi, so I travelled with it to my parents' home in Delhi's Patel Nagar in style – on a bullock cart!

Early Adventures in India

The job of mine manager was then considered highly prestigious in India and at one time most mine managers were British. To give better opportunities to Indians, a new rule said it was now necessary for foreigners to take an Indian mining legislation exam. I was a foreigner from England and had to take this exam after six months of living in India.

Adventures in Delhi

I was in Delhi with my parents and my younger brother Kak for about four months before going on to seek a mining post in West Bengal. Kak had secured a job as a lecturer in mechanical engineering at Delhi University and had also written a book on the subject and was always chasing a shifty looking agent to get his commission and royalties.

India, which I had left in infancy, was a totally foreign country to me, and, although he wouldn't admit it, to Kak too. With our turbaned Sikh appearance, we were in the peculiar position of looking very Indian but without Indian mannerisms. Street-savvy vendors would see this and adjust prices accordingly! We spoke little Hindi, and in conversation would do what any self-respecting Englishman would do in the same circumstances – speak louder in English, or our English version of Hindi or Punjabi. We would get on a bus and the conductor would ask: "ka sey?" We were never too sure whether this meant 'where to' or 'where from', and we got lots of stares. Once, we went to the cinema to see an American comedy. The audience didn't seem to appreciate western humour and would laugh in all the wrong places. When we laughed, there was silence and stares. It was, however, a change from not being stared at for looking different.

Kak and I were saddened by the way in which people in lowlier positions were sometimes treated by others. We saw this on our way to an India–Australia Test match, in the way a group of youngsters shouted at a poor bus conductor when he had done nothing wrong. They then asked for the 'Complaints Book' and wrote comments in it that could easily have jeopardised his job. Kak and I also asked for the Complaints Book, and wrote in it our admiration for the way he had put up with gratuitous verbal abuse from a group of hooligans.

Plight of Sikhs in Punjab

I arrived in India at the time of the Punjabi Suba movement for an official recognition of Punjabi as the state language of Punjab. Other states in India had their regional languages recognised as the official state language. Strong lobbying by Hindu extremists had resulted in Punjabi, the language of the Sikh scriptures and the most widely spoken language in Punjab, being denied official status. Sikhs protested and were being arrested in their thousands and a strongly Hindu-controlled media was constantly smearing Sikhs as being anti-national. Kak and I regarded this as unfair and worse, un-British!

We knew that any letter of protest written by a Sikh would never be published. We devised a cunning plan, and in my first venture into journalism, I decided to write with an English pen name. I chose the name of our somewhat pompous greengrocer neighbour, Mr. Victor Pendry. I wrote to the two main English language dailies in India: *The Statesman* and the *Hindustan Times*. To our surprise and delight, lingering deference to the Raj ensured that the letter was published in both papers. The letter began:

Surely it bodes ill for the future of democracy in India that the government is deliberately ignoring the constitutional rights of Sikhs and arresting members of the community in thousands, rather than giving Punjab the same linguistic status as that granted to other States.

It was signed by Victor Pendry.

The letter was warmly welcomed by Sikhs throughout India. It was published and republished in the Punjabi media. Everyone wanted to know more about the Englishman who had been writing in favour of Sikhs. Interestingly, my future wife Kawal, knew of Mr Pendry long before she met me! We finally decided to tell our parents and my father insisted on taking me to the main gurdwara in Delhi to meet those in charge.

I got slightly carried away by success and thought that if the papers were prepared to publish the views of Mr Pendry, why not those of my old Head, Mr Sylvanus Jones and other people I knew? Letters duly appeared in different names. All this infuriated a Mr Vishvanathan who wrote that foreigners shouldn't interfere in Indian affairs. This led to another idea: I thought, why shouldn't the letters be supported by Hindus and Muslims? With the help of names taken from a telephone directory, further letters highlighting the plight of Sikhs duly followed.

Mining in India

Having overcome the first hurdle of a written examination in Indian mining law, I successfully applied for the post of deputy manager at Methani colliery, one of several large mines operated by the British-owned Equitable Coal Company. My first day was an eye opener.

I shared an office with four assistant managers who nominally, at least, reported to me. They were all Bengalis and it soon became evident that they resented working for a 'foreigner' whose origins lay in Punjab. I soon realised that racism is not just a western thing. They were quite fluent in English but would switch to Bengali, knowing I couldn't understand a word, as soon as I entered the office. I ignored the slights and began to talk to more junior officials in my broken Hindi to understand the detailed problems and potential of the mine. The more junior officials instantly took a liking to me and enjoyed the way I mangled the Hindi language.

At Methani colliery

I was given a huge bungalow with a large garden in front and about an acre of land at the back. I was also allocated a cook, a gardener and several part-time servants. My problem was what to do with all of them. The cook agreed to keep some chickens to avoid the need to go to the village for eggs. Despite this, he would still ask for money to buy eggs as he claimed the hens were not laying. I suggested to the part-time servants that they cultivate the land at the back and I would provide seeds to enable them to feed their families. Unfortunately, the project never got off the ground as the servants maintained that farming was beneath their caste status!

Back at the mine, I came across a more serious problem. I found I had been signing a payment book for work that had never been done. The procedure was for the assistant managers to supervise work done by contractors and sign the payment book ready for me to initial. The manager would then add his signature and make payment.

As I got to know the mine better, I began to realise that much of this work had never been done and refused to countersign for it. I naively thought that this would put an end to the false invoicing and the manager would support my action. It was the other way around. I was called to the manager's office and told I had to sign. I refused.

I was then reported to the local agent, a person responsible for the running of several mines, and summoned to his office. The agent was a Mr Malhotra, a Punjabi. He was aware that the submitting of false invoices was common practice and boosted the income of officials. He appealed to my 'Punjabiness' and advised that I go along with the system and take my cut. I refused. Eventually, the assistant managers were transferred, and I was left in my place, along with a manager who saw me as a troublemaker.

Chapter Six
Meeting Kawal

I began to take stock. I had met a nice girl on my last visit to Delhi and had continued corresponding and wanted to get married.

While I was secure in my present post, I had upset the hierarchy and promotion would be difficult. I decided to resign my job and get married. Finding another job would not be too difficult now that I had Indian qualifications and experience.

In the event, I was off work longer than I had planned. I thought it would be nice if my wife Kawal knew a little about the country I had grown up in. My parents also thought it a good idea and booked us on a liner belonging to the same company I had travelled with on my way to India.

We both enjoyed the relaxing experience, with excellent food and little to do. We also made some excellent friends. The sea voyage allowed passengers to alight at the town of Suez on the entrance to the Suez Canal and re-board later in the day at Port Said. Some of our friends decided to visit Cairo and the Pyramids and invited us to join them.

There was a problem. At that time, severe foreign exchange restrictions meant that we only had £5 each to see us to England where I had some savings. We politely declined, but our friends wouldn't have it and one of them, a Mr Andrew Edge, wrote out a cheque for £200 saying I could pay him back when we got to England. It was a wonderfully kind and trusting gesture from someone who had known us for only two weeks. It enabled us to have a wonderful time visiting the Pyramids and riding on camels.

Wedding, 22 April 1962

34

The honeymoon was already proving longer and more adventurous than planned. But it was to get more so. My first action on landing in England was to send a cheque and our thanks to Mr Edge. Then, after a short stay in our family home in Birmingham and visits to places of interest, I decided to spend the bulk of my UK savings on a three-week coach tour of the continent, visiting France, Germany, Switzerland and Italy. We returned to India after a wonderful break, sailing from Falmouth at the height of the Cuban Missile Crisis.

A bumpy ride on honeymoon, the Pyramids, Egypt

Chapter Seven
Working at Nemuria Colliery

On arriving back in Delhi , I placed an advert in a mining magazine looking for a job in management. A couple of days later, I received a telegram inviting me for an interview at six p.m. at the fashionable Gaylords Restaurant. I was met by three Sikh brothers who owned a mine in Bihar. It was the best job interview that I have ever had. I was asked no questions on my experience or suitability, given a luxurious meal and asked when I could start!

Life at Nemuria Colliery at first seemed like an extension of our honeymoon. There was plenty for me to do but also lots of free time for us to roam around, although the nearest town, Asansol, was about twenty miles away. We would travel there to eat a meal and watch a Hindi film. By now, Kawal had got used to my odd sense of humour and when she asked me which part of the film I enjoyed most, was not taken aback when I replied, "the interval".

I am not a great believer in God watching over us and intervening to help us out on routine human matters, but two near miraculous incidents are difficult to explain by the laws of chance. The first occurred when I was about ten. I had gone by bus to a library about three miles away and had enough money for my fare back home. It was Kak's birthday the next day and I saw a beautiful lead model of a soldier on horseback and, without thinking, went into the shop and bought it. It was then I realised I had no money left for the bus back home, nor was I sure of the way on foot. I started walking down the road when suddenly I heard someone in a small van shouting at me to get in. It was the owner of one of the small parade of shops next to our house.

The second incident was while at Nemuria. My mother, recovering from a bout of flu, had come to stay with us. We had taken her to Asansol for a meal out and were on the way back, about five miles from home, when the Land Rover broke down on a deserted road frequented by robbers. Kawal was pregnant at the time with our first child. We were frantically trying to get the car going again but were having no luck and it looked as if the driver and I would have to try and push the Land Rover all the way back home. Then we became aware of a distant vehicle coming towards us. It was another Land Rover and the occupants began shouting and tooting as they saw us. They were car mechanics, friends of our driver. They stopped and quickly got us back on the road.

The mine workers mostly belonged to a tribe called the Santals, who improbably still carried bows and arrows – particularly on pay day. I tried to get them to have vaccinations against the then still prevalent threat of smallpox.

Unfortunately, they were very superstitious and either refused the vaccinations offered, or subsequently rubbed dirt on the area to 'clean it'.

The owners of the mine were very kind to us and took us on frequent trips to Calcutta. They wanted me to help increase output at the mine, and after a little time I found that production was hampered by poor transport to the surface. I spent time on making it more efficient and within six months output had virtually doubled. Increased income, however, created different problems.

Awash with extra income, the Bedi family owners increased the lavishness of their lifestyle, jetting around the country with their families and pets for numerous social functions. I found it harder and harder to get them to put money back into the mine for essential safety work.

Medical facilities at the mine were poor and my wife had gone to her family home in Amritsar for the birth of our first child. I was over the moon when I got a telegram that I was the proud father of a baby girl. I rushed to a neighbour to tell him the good news. I was dismayed by what he said. It was my first encounter with subcontinent attitudes to girls. I later spoke about it in a 'Thought for the Day' on BBC Radio 4.

Extract from 'Thought for the Day', 6 November 2014

Guru Nanak was particularly concerned about the plight of women on the subcontinent who, as in much of the world, were treated as inferior beings. He taught that women should be given full equality with men, not simply thought of as the wives or daughters of men, but as individuals playing a full part in society.

Unfortunately, as we are daily reminded in the news, deep rooted cultural practices often tend to blur or subvert the teachings of religion which challenge unthinking attitudes and behavior. I was vividly reminded of this while working as a young mining engineer in a remote area of Bengal. I had just received news that my wife had given birth to our first child, a daughter. I was over the moon and excitedly rushed to the house next door, that of a Sikh, and told him the wonderful news. Contrary to clear Sikh teachings, his culturally conditioned response was, 'Never mind, it will be a boy next time!' I was not then the gentle, easy-going soul that I like to think I am today, and it took great restraint not to punch him!

The reluctance of the owners to put necessary funds back into the mine finally proved too much for me and I handed in my notice and we parted on friendly terms.

Chapter Eight
Back to the UK

Rather than look for another job in the area, we decided to go back to England. While some people would be happy with the life of being the wife of a mine manager, waited on hand and foot by servants, Kawal wanted something more challenging and we also felt it was not the best place to bring up our little daughter. So, we decided to take the boat back to the UK.

It was still impossible to get a job in mine management and I finally decided to join the Coal Board's West Midlands Planning Department. My wife also took a job in teaching, a career that took her to headship before eventually becoming an Ofsted Inspector.

At lunchtime in the planning office we would try to do the daily *Telegraph* crossword. One of the clues was four letters for a Punjabi Hindu. Next day we saw the answer, 'Sikh'. I protested to *The Telegraph*, Sikhs were not Hindus, but belonged to a different religion. The editor responded that he had taken the definition from the highly respected *Chambers Dictionary*!

Within the office there was a lot of good-natured banter about religion and different cultures. One person asked me what are little Singhs called? I ignored the ignorance behind the question and retorted "singlets". Another chap would say, "We civilised the Indians," and I would retort that Indians were civilised when people in Britain were living in caves. One day, someone pointed out of the window to a large rat running in the car park. I responded with my usual one-upmanship, "In Punjab, we would call that a mouse."

In the office, discussion on race and religion was always good humoured, but on the streets, it was increasingly concerning, with Enoch Powell making his famous 'rivers of blood' speech. He was playing to an underlying culture that saw racial superiority as a fact, as some otherwise decent people have done throughout history. Isaac Watts, who wrote beautiful hymns, including the moving 'O God our help in ages past', also wrote:

Lord, I ascribe it not to chance but to your grace That I was born a Christian and not a heathen Or a member of the Jewish race.

Notices for 'accommodation to let' frequently included, 'No blacks, coloured or dogs'. Irish too were also included in the list of undesirables. Today when we talk about our different national values, we often forget that what we see as acceptable behaviour changes with time. I discussed this in a subsequent TFTD broadcast.

38

But, as a well-known hymn reminds us, "New occasions teach new duties; time makes ancient good uncouth." Laws that are socially acceptable at one time are often seen later as unjust, or even barbaric. In this country, we no longer have a death penalty, or flogging, or other forms of cruel and degrading punishment, and the boundaries of law are frequently moved inwards as society develops greater social responsibility, or as Sikhs would say, moves in a godlier direction.

The talk on a proposal to legalise brothels, continued. What worries me about this week's call for the legalisation of brothels is that the proposal seeks to move us to less responsible behaviour. Of course, legalisation of brothels would move many prostitutes off the streets, but in the process, it would seem to me, to be giving a mark of social approval to an activity that demeans women, panders to baser male passions and encourages infidelity as an acceptable way of life.

Perhaps the most usual, and therefore the most dangerous, argument for legalising activities that diminish us as human beings is that the activity prostitution, use of soft drugs or whatever – is so common that we can't do much about it. So, we might as well move the boundaries of the law to accommodate it and give it respectability.

It's a weak and negative argument that gives a cloak of normality to otherwise unacceptable social behaviour. It's an argument that panders to the very passions that our scriptures warn us against, and one that pushes norms of behaviour in a decidedly ungodly direction.

In 1965, war between India and Pakistan briefly erupted and there was concern that this could lead to clashes between Indians and Pakistanis in this country. I was very touched by a report that Pakistani POWs captured in Punjab were embraced like long-lost brothers by Sikhs and Hindus, who were colleagues and comrades in the former British Indian Army, and I was moved to write a letter to the papers about the essential commonalities of cultures, and how people from Pakistan and India should work to unite the partitioned countries into a common federation. To my surprise, my letter was widely welcomed by all communities and I was invited to the House of Commons and different parts of the country. Unfortunately, I then had neither the money nor the time to follow this up. The episode increased my growing interest in the interface between religion, culture and politics.

My work in the planning department was both interesting and depressing. The Coal Board had just begun using rudimentary computers and I wrote computer programmes for planning, but it was mostly the planning of mine closures in a fast-declining industry. I applied for and got a planning post with Whessoe Engineering in Darlington. The work involved planning the construction of gas reformer plants and atomic energy structures and my experience of what was called 'critical path planning' proved very useful. The technique itself is very simple and involves breaking a job down into its component parts and doing as many parts of the job as possible in parallel, rather than sequentially. I referred to this discipline in a subsequent BBC 'Thought for the Day':

The words 'thought for the day', are frequently used as a panic time-check; a reminder that we need to rush off to work, or bundle children out of the house for school.

To help us cope with the morning rush, we generally try to do several things at the same time, rather than one after the other – such as putting on the kettle, popping a slice of bread in the toaster and ironing a shirt while we wait for the toaster.

This approach to saving time by doing as many things as possible in parallel, rather than in unnecessary sequence, is the basis of an important planning technique with the impressive sounding name of critical path analysis that's widely used in the construction industry to minimise delay. It's years since I had anything to do with the construction industry, but I was suddenly reminded of this discipline while listening to the Home Secretary, Douglas Hurd's, remarks on 'Today', a week or so ago, in which he said 'that now we've got the economy under control, we should turn to other areas of concern'.

He was, of course, referring to the increasing violence among the young – even away from deprived inner-city areas. But I wonder about the apparent suggestion that concern on social issues should follow that on the economy, or whether there should be a sequence at all.

It's so easy to think of life as a series of mutually exclusive activities. We do it all the time. For much of the year we work and then we have holidays and we enjoy. And we condition ourselves into thinking of life as discrete phases of enjoyment and work.

It's very much the same with religion. By having a set day or set times of the day for prayer, we divorce religion and the richness of religious influence from our daily lives. It was even worse in the India of Guru Nanak's day, when life itself was divided into a learning stage, an earning stage and a final religious stage.

The Guru was critical of this fractured approach to living and taught the necessity of living life to the full: that is, looking to our material needs and our social obligations as one and the same time while being immersed in, and guided by, religious teaching.

The Guru responded to the usual criticism of how to find time for religion in our busy lives with a beautiful verse contained in our holy book, the Guru Granth Sahib:

> *Young girls bring pitchers to fill them at them at the city well*
> *but keep their minds on the pitchers.*
> *When the child is asleep in the cradle,*
> *the mother is busy inside and outside the house*
> *But she keeps her mind on the child.*

Life is too short and precious to put spiritual direction, care and compassion on some backburner, when we can so easily make these integral to our daily lives.

I never considered my job at Whessoe as anything more than a move towards the building and civil engineering industry, which shared some of the disciplines and challenges inherent in mining. I started to apply for other posts. In more than one interview, I was told to my face that "We would love to have you, but our workforce would object."

A New Career and the Move to a New Home

I finally managed to secure a post with Costain Construction and Civil Engineering, and after a short time in rented accommodation, put down a deposit for a house near Wimbledon. I was keen to carry my wife across the threshold into our new house but was too embarrassed to do this in front of an over-helpful neighbour who just wouldn't go away. It was, however, nice to have friendly neighbours.

Undisguised racist attitudes to anyone that looked different, their food and their supposed differences were all too common, and we were worried that neighbours might complain if we cooked Indian food. Instead, my wife was complimented on the wonderful, mouth-watering aroma that would sometimes waft through the kitchen window.

Sikhs today are among the foremost house owners in Britain, but in those days, the popular image was of newly-arrived communities living in grossly overcrowded rented accommodation. One of my favourite stories is about a political pollster knocking on the door of such a house which was opened by a turbaned and bearded gentleman, who responded to a question on probable voting intentions by saying: "We have fourteen Labour, eight Conservatives, and four Liberals. Mind you," he continued, "I can't speak for the people upstairs!"

It was then also said, probably with a degree of truth, that if a foreigner bought a house in a street, the value of adjacent properties would diminish. I often used this in office banter if anyone annoyed me: "Behave yourself, or I'll buy the house next door to you"; a guarantee that the value of his property would tumble. It was not only indigenous people who sometimes showed hostility to new arrivals. Immigrants already here were sometimes even more vociferous in their opposition.

I've often thought of this negative and faintly amusing aspect of human behaviour and used it as the subject of my first ever 'Thought for the Day' (see section on Broadcasting).

My work in the productivity services department at Costain was all about improving the efficiency of construction operations. We were given stopwatches and were asked to observe different tasks and work out what were called 'standard' and 'normal' times and devise appropriate bonus schemes. The work itself was straightforward and my short time in the method study department in the NCB proved extremely useful. The real difficulty was the attitudes of those being observed. No one likes their work being watched, and it is even more irritating if the person doing the watching is a foreigner. But, somehow or other, I survived and even struck up some friendships.

I had other concerns. Timings to a tenth of a second may have some relevance in a workshop in a closed environment. Most construction work, however, is in the open with progress affected by weather and the nature of the soil, and precise recording of times for different operations can become meaningless. I explained my concerns during a training course about a year into my job and to my surprise, everyone agreed, and I was put in charge of the collection and presentation of planning data that took such variables into account.

My job entailed visiting different projects around the country and spending considerable time away from home. On one occasion, I was asked to visit an opencast mine owned by Costain about thirty miles from Glasgow. I had been asked to look at ways of improving productivity and I expected to be away for about a week. Speaking to the manager of the site, I found the problems were very similar to those I had encountered in the Nemuria mine in India. The manager agreed with my suggestions, which he successfully implemented, and I was back with my family, which now included our second daughter Rema, within a couple of days.

It was while at Costain that I made my first venture into television. London Weekend Television had invited me to advise on a programme about the Sikh religion. Sikhism is essentially straightforward guidance on ethical living. The producer wanted to show Sikhs and Sikhism as something quaint and exotic.

I suggested, as politely as I could, that there should be a change in emphasis. The producer, who later became a good friend, felt affronted and refused to make any change. I wished them well and returned to the office, but after a couple of hours received a phone call saying they had reflected on what I had said and would go along with my advice.

The construction industry in the UK in the early 1970s was going through a difficult time and Costain decided to call in leading American management consultants. I was asked to assist and was not impressed by what they did. There were lots of meetings with different managers in the organisation. Finally, there was a bulky report on the changes needed, which were little more than a splitting of management responsibility to separate home and overseas operations with a chief executive in charge. It might be a coincidence, but the person specification for the chief executive neatly matched that of the lead management consultant, and he was duly appointed.

I have since seen this 'let's change the structure' approach adopted in many different fields, and it is not new. I'd like to illustrate this with a quote, not from some disgruntled civil servant, but from a Roman soldier called Petronius who lived in the first century AD. He wrote:

We trained very hard, but it seemed to me that every time we began to form into teams, we were reorganised! ... We tend to meet every new situation by reorganising – and a wonderful method it can be for creating the illusion of progress while producing inefficiency and demoralisation!

This Roman soldier's misgivings would clearly strike a responsive chord in many who have suffered some of the reorganizations of recent years! While it is sometimes genuinely helpful, structural change is all too often used to ward off criticism and buy time by suggesting a new way forward. This occurs frequently in government departments, with a change in government or even a minister. It is particularly evident in the field of education.

Chapter Nine
Studying for an MBA

A growing interest in management techniques got me thinking of studying for a formal qualification in management and a one year course for an MBA and MCom, run by Birmingham University, seemed attractive, but it would be difficult without financial support.

I discussed this with the director of the personnel department; I was running some training courses for him and he knew me well. He said that the company would pay fees and the cost of accommodation. He then went further and said, "I don't think we should let your wife and children starve while you are away," and generously agreed that the company would continue to pay my full salary for the duration of the course.

Study proved both interesting and intensive. On one occasion, I stayed up all night to complete a finance assignment. It was also harder because I would go home to my family every weekend, continuing my study on the train.

Some of the students from Commonwealth countries had been through similar courses before and responded to questions more frequently. I began to answer a question on industrial relations, when the lecturer stopped me and said, "Can we have a view from a British student?" Everyone collapsed with laughter when I protested, "I am British." I learnt a lot both from the professors and from discussions with fellow students and successfully graduated, receiving my MBA from the Queen Mother.

Back at Costain, I found that the construction industry was facing new challenges. I found myself in a new department giving planning assistance to engineers constructing an airport in newly developing Dubai, where I also spent a little time. Liaising with Dubai from London involved the use of a then new device called a modem, now in common use with computers.

There was little new work on the horizon and people were looking for other opportunities. I felt a little guilty as the company had been good to me, paying for my MBA studies, so I went to see the director of personnel to seek his view. He was frank with his advice saying that the industry should pick up again, but it could take years, and I should look to the future of my family.

After some time, I got a job in local government in the London Borough of Hackney. I agreed to do some consultancy work for Costain for some time, we parted on good terms and I was allowed to keep my company car.

The 'People's Republic' of Hackney

My initial post in Hackney was deputy head of research and intelligence in the chief executive's office department, dealing with the use of statistical data in the planning of council services. A well-meaning former social worker, slightly left of Karl Marx, was a part of our team and we would have many interesting discussions and became good friends.

A local government boundary review took place soon after I joined. The review initially proposed that the number of council wards should be reduced from sixty to fifty. This was vehemently opposed by councillors and I was asked to produce a statistical case to show that deprivation in the borough required the retention of the present number of councillors.

I was invited to present my research findings to a joint meeting of councillors with the Boundary Commission and I answered detailed questions on my findings. A few weeks later, they issued a report which paid tribute to the 'clear and convincing presentation of the statistician who presented Hackney's case', and unanimously agreed that the borough should be allowed to retain the present number of wards. The chief executive, Gren Huddy, was delighted. He had lived in India for some years and came to see me and said in Hindi, "Jith ho gia," 'we have achieved victory.'

Three years later, my much-lauded report suddenly became a banned document and every copy was shredded. Local government elections were due, and it was feared that opposition parties might use the figures on deprivation to suggest that the Labour Party that had governed the council for the last fifteen years might be blamed for allowing such neglect to occur.

At about this time, I was invited to speak at a function at a gurdwara in Croydon. I had for some years been speaking and writing about Sikhism and the gurdwara management invited me to give a talk on the teachings of Guru Nanak, the founder of the Sikh faith. I was followed by the local MP Bernard Weatherill, who was then deputy chief whip of the Conservative Party. Despite my fears that he might have taken offence at some of my comments on social justice, he met my wife and me warmly, and spoke of his close ties with a Sikh regiment he had served with during the Second World War. Bernard, or Jack Weatherill as he was affectionately known, went on to become Speaker of the House of Commons, eventually retiring as Lord Weatherill. The friendship between our families deepened and he and his wife Lyn attended the weddings of both our daughters and we were invited to his daughter's wedding and similar occasions.

Jack was keen that I join the Conservative Party, but I refused saying that I didn't agree with some of the policies, particularly on race relations. Instead, I agreed to write a tract from a Sikh perspective on race relations, entitled 'Strangers in our Midst', which was critical of what I saw as racist attitudes in both main parties.

Willie Whitelaw, the Deputy Prime Minister, was asked to write the foreword by some liberally minded well-wishers. He called me to his office, flicked through the small booklet and said: "You seem to be getting at a certain lady." He was referring to the Prime Minister, Margaret Thatcher, who had made a speech referring to immigrants in derogatory terms and with talk of "stemming the flow", "prevention of ghettos" and threats to "racial balance". He said my criticism was a "bit harsh", before adding with a twinkle in his eye, "Mind you, I don't necessarily disagree with you." Some brief excerpts from the pamphlet are included as Appendix One, to show how little we've moved in our understanding since 1978.

With Lord Weatherill and wife Kawal, 2002

Chapter Ten
Racism in Schools

Despite the passing of the Race Relations Act in 1976, openly racist attitudes, then widely prevalent, are still all too common. In the early 1980s, there were real concerns over attitudes to Sikh school children in Birmingham schools. In one school, when a Sikh boy wore a turban to school for the first time, his teacher commented, "It's gross, like something out of a pantomime." As an 'expert witness' in the case, I drew attention to the harm to self-esteem that must have resulted from the boy hearing an article of his faith being described in such terms. The matter was eventually resolved with a formal apology to the boy.

Solicitors Bindman and Partners acting for the then CRE came to see me about another disturbing case that has become part of case law and is referred to as the 'Mandla Case'.

It concerned a young boy, Gurinder Singh Mandla, being refused admission to another Birmingham school while wearing a turban, because it was not part of the school uniform. The headteacher agreed that it was discrimination but argued that religious discrimination was not against the law of the land.

The CRE wanted me to help them prove that the Sikh community constituted a race and would therefore be protected under the 1976 Act. I replied that this was not possible as Sikh teachings argue against artificial distinctions of race or caste, emphasising that we are all equal members of our one human family.

I did, however, suggest that we could perhaps be considered a separate 'ethnic group', a common ethnic origin then being a protected category under the Act. Ethnicity relates to certain characteristics in common, such as geographic origin, diet and culture, as well as susceptibility or comparative immunity to certain ailments relating to heredity. I suggested that religion could be considered a sub-set of culture, and that we should fight the case based on Sikhs having a common ethnicity as most Sikhs in the UK at that time were first-generation Sikhs born in Punjab. The definition of an ethnic group does not require all people in the group to share the same characteristics, but for most to do so. It was agreed to fight the case on this basis.

The case was heard in the Birmingham County Court, lasting several days. It was closely contested, and as the leading 'expert witness', I was cross-examined for a day and a half.

The transcript of questions and answers below, illustrates the very different climate of attitudes to minorities that then existed.

Excerpts from Personal Evidence of the Editor of the Sikh Messenger given at the Mandla Case to the Birmingham Crown Court, February 1980

The case was heard by Judge Gosling, the late S. Harjit Singh was barrister for prosecution, Indarjit Singh, main witness for the Sikh community, and Mr Chapman, barrister for defence.

Harjit Singh: What is the significance of the turban to a Sikh today?

Indarjit Singh: To a practising Sikh who realises his history and why the symbols are chosen, there can be no greater insult than to ask him to remove his turban. It is something that our forefathers who followed the tenth Guru gave their lives for.

Judge Gosling: It is an insult that puzzles me rather. I can see that if I said to you, "Take your turban off," or if I knocked it off, that could in the one case be a threat and, in the other, an insult. But if I say to you, "I respect your religion, but if you wish to come into this room you have to make a choice, either of not coming in or taking your turban off," how is that an insult?

Indarjit Singh: If you respect my religion, unless there is some fundamental reason that my coming in with a turban would create difficult consequences, it would not be respectful to ask me to take it off. It would be a mark of disrespect.

Judge Gosling: Would you not be insulted?

Indarjit Singh: If it is a public place that is open to all, and if, because of my religion, I am told that I cannot go in, I would certainly feel hurt and aggrieved.

Judge Gosling: Would you be equally offended if you were told you could not enter a church or a school?

Indarjit Singh: No, because for a Sikh it is not necessary to go to a church. For a Sikh it is necessary, absolutely necessary, to be educated. A Sikh child would be placed at a severe disadvantage, especially when, to add to the hurt, he is told, "We are doing this in the interest of racial harmony."

Judge Gosling: Which I should have thought you would accept. Why would you, therefore, feel insulted, because it is nothing personal? Nobody is saying that you are a wicked man and somebody we despise or anything of that kind. It is important because that is what the plaintiff says. He said, "I felt hurt and insulted," and I am just wondering why?

Indarjit Singh: I think I would feel the same. I would feel hurt. Perhaps more so having lived here and seen society change. At one time, it was an automatic assumption that the turban would be respected. I went to school and my brothers went to school here with turbans. Now, when people from different communities, different parts of the globe, have come together, we should be far more enlightened than they were in those days. It is said that we wish to promote equality, but we should promote religious tolerance and teach each other about different people.

Judge Gosling: In a sense, it could be said that you are seeking to impose upon schools your idea of tolerance?

Indarjit Singh: In a sense, your honour, that is right. A Sikh believes certain things. One must be true to one's belief, and our belief in religious tolerance is that people should be free to worship in the way that they like and to dress in the way they like without hindrance.

Judge Gosling: What is it in the Sikh's mental make-up that the turban becomes such an important factor in his life?

Indarjit Singh: It is a mark of identity, self-respect and history.

Judge Gosling: Would you regard a suggestion that you should cut your hair as being on the same level, in terms of causing offence, as removing your turban? "You can come and join us if you cut your hair short"?

Indarjit Singh: I would certainly see it in the same way, and I would consider it a mark of extreme intolerance. To give a personal example, if I may, having been educated entirely in this country it would have been very much easier for me, in employment, if I had discarded my turban and changed my name. It would have helped considerably because I had been told several times, "We would like to have you, but other employees might object." This was very common. In employment, it meant you may end up at a lower level than you should have been.

Judge Gosling: I understand employers taking the view, "What will the other employees say?" but what were your feelings at that precise time when this suggestion was made to you, "Come back minus your turban and your hair"?

Indarjit Singh: Extreme sadness. In Guru Nanak's time 500 years ago, intolerance was deplorable. It is even sadder that 500 years on, there is still such intolerance.

Judge Gosling: Would you feel humiliated if the suggestion was made, in the first instance?

Indarjit Singh: I would feel humiliated. I think I would feel it less so than somebody who meets it for the first time.

Judge Gosling: You have lived with the system and you have got used to it?

Indarjit Singh: Yes.

Judge Gosling: What about someone who has not lived with the system?

Indarjit Singh: It must be quite a shock.

Judge Gosling: A shattering effect?

Indarjit Singh: Yes, an extremely shattering effect.
[Evidence continued.]

Judge Gosling: Mr Indarjit Singh, may I remind you that you are still on oath. When this matter was adjourned last time, you had elaborated on the history of the Sikhs, and of the factors which, in your view, contributed to the evolution and development of Sikh society?

Indarjit Singh: That is correct.

Harjit Singh: So, you have dealt with the history, and also with the Sikh symbols and the importance the British attached to the Sikh symbols. Can you go on now to look at the Sikh social customs in so far as they are different from all the other communities in India?

Indarjit Singh: Yes, in talking about the history and development of Sikhism, I did briefly mention the threat that Sikhs felt at a very early stage of their formation, the absorption by the Hindu majority, a fate earlier experienced by Buddhism. And being alert to this, the Sikh Gurus did develop protection within the religion, by developing separate social customs at the time of birth, marriage, death and other important occasions. Previously, all these ceremonies were performed by the Hindu Brahmins.

Harjit Singh: How is a Sikh baptised in India?

Indarjit Singh: The ceremony itself has some similarities with the Christian ceremony. There is the baptismal water. It is sweetened water and the sweet additive is stirred with a sword. There is a significance there that self-defence is an inherent part of Sikhism; that is the sword. The sweetness in the water represents the requirement for Sikhs to have something similar in their nature, a sweeter outlook on life.

Harjit Singh: Is there any similarity between this ceremony and, for example, the Hindu baptismal ceremony?

Indarjit Singh: No, they are quite different. The Hindu ceremonies, baptism and marriage, as I understand, are done around fire. This is not done in Sikhism at all. The centre of the Sikh ceremony is the Sikh holy book, the *Guru Granth Sahib*.

Harjit Singh: Are there any other customs?

Indarjit Singh: Right throughout, from the birth of a child right up to the death of the person, every occasion, every major occasion in a person's life, when they are first putting on their turban and all other important stages, they are all celebrated and commemorated with the readings from the holy book, and again that is in contradistinction to other faiths.

Harjit Singh: Can we go on now to look at the Sikh social attitudes? In what way do they differ from either the Hindus or the Muslims or, for that matter, the Christians in India?

Indarjit Singh: Again, there is the religious/non-religious aspect to this. The social attitudes were taught by the Sikh Gurus, particularly Guru Nanak, and they have become part of a Sikh society, whether the people or person concerned are religious or not religious. The attitude to women is of prime importance – that at a time when women were being discriminated against right across the globe, Sikhism very clearly stated that women and men are equals, and to emphasise this, at the time of giving Sikh males the common name of Singh, which is to denote the ideal of courage – it literally means lion – they gave Sikh women the suffix Kaur – which literally means princess – and this was to show the elevated status of women. That is, and was, quite different to the society around, both Hindus and Muslims.

Judge Gosling: When Sikhs marry, does a woman change her name or not?

Indarjit Singh: Strictly, no. If someone is called 'Something Kaur' she retains that name after marriage. She does not strictly become Mrs. Singh.

Judge Gosling: I am wondering what the practice is?

Indarjit Singh: In practice, my wife would be called Mrs. Singh, but really, she should be Kanwaljit Kaur.

Judge Gosling: While we are on that, you can call yourself Indarjit Singh?

Indarjit Singh: That is correct.

Judge Gosling: Of course, you have a family name as well, or don't you? Or a clan name if you like.

Indarjit Singh: Yes. Sikhs originated mostly from the Hindu community. They would, at that time, have had a caste name. Strictly we are asked to drop that name and take this name Singh, and Singh only. Some people still retain their old caste name. My father never used his and I see no reason why I should use mine.

Judge Gosling: Are there difficulties at this end, if Sikhs do not use their caste names?

Indarjit Singh: I can envisage difficulties, but they are sometimes overplayed, your honour. The number of Singhs in the telephone directory is still considerably less than the number of Smiths.

Judge Gosling: The plaintiff is called Sewa Singh Mandla. Is Mandla a caste name?
Indarjit Singh: Yes.

Harjit Singh: You have told us how Sikhs, at the time when women were discriminated against in India, regarded women as equals.

Indarjit Singh: That is correct.

Harjit Singh: Was that equality of status reflected in other spheres of an Indian woman's social life?

Indarjit Singh: Certainly, your honour, Sikh women do, and have always, played a very prominent part in the life of the society. For example, a Sikh woman can lead and conduct religious services, whereas in some other religions, women are excluded from entering the prayer hall.

Harjit Singh: Is there anything else you would like to mention about Sikh social attitudes, which are distinct from other religions?

Indarjit Singh: One important one, which I should not omit, is the emphasis on equality of human beings. Whereas this is said quite often these days, at the time of the formation of the Sikh community it was quite revolutionary. Sikhs were very strongly opposed to the whole principle of caste, that is the superiority by birth of any individual. All people should be allowed equal opportunities. This is something that is stressed again and again in the religion and not only in the teaching but in practice.

Harjit Singh: A Sikh may have originated from a Hindu family but once he becomes a Sikh there is no longer any caste?

Indarjit Singh: That is correct.

Harjit Singh: Going on to language, you told us last time that the Sikh national language is Gurmukhi. I think you explained to us last time that it is called Gurmukhi because it is the language of the Gurus?

Indarjit Singh: That is correct.

Harjit Singh: Is Gurmukhi Punjabi?

Indarjit Singh: Punjabi is the name given to the language of an area of the Punjab. That is the language. There is more than one script in which it can be written. Gurmukhi is, in fact, strictly a script for Punjabi.

Harjit Singh: Does any other group in India write Gurmukhi apart from the Sikhs?

Indarjit Singh: No. Can I just elaborate? That can't be 100% true. It is predominantly written by Sikhs and developed to propagate Sikh teachings.

Harjit Singh: On that basis, which language do you identify with the Sikhs?

Indarjit Singh: Punjabi and Gurmukhi script.

Harjit Singh: In which language is Sikh literature written?

Indarjit Singh: Again, in Punjabi and Gurmukhi script.

Harjit Singh: That is the language of the Sikh bible, the *Guru Granth Sahib*?
Indarjit Singh: That is correct.

Harjit Singh: Apart from the Sikh bible, what other Sikh literature is there?

Indarjit Singh: There is considerable literature, novels, plays, poems, all developed around the history and aspirations of the Sikh people.

Harjit Singh: We come now to the final factor in your definition of the ethnic pattern of Sikhs: Sikh aspirations. How do they differ from the aspirations of the Hindus and Muslims?

Indarjit Singh: Sikh aspirations are to see a society in which birth, caste or occupation do not affect an individual for life, where women are treated equally;

a society where there is, above all, tolerance of another person's view, and that tolerance must, in the Sikh view, be a very positive tolerance, not, "I don't mind what you do." That is not tolerance. Tolerance is the willingness to uphold the next person's right to determine his or her own way of life. Sikh aspirations are that this sort of society should eventually predominate on this earth. It does not mean that everyone should become a Sikh. That should be emphasised. Sikhs should only work to ensure that injustice, evil and bigotry – bigotry in wishing to change another person's view by force or undue pressure – these things are resisted in every way.

Judge Gosling: I am sure that most people would commend that, but it cannot quite mean what you say. I do not imagine that the Sikhs would encourage Gobbels to follow his way of life?

Indarjit Singh: Certainly not. If any so-called religion or belief system was preaching bigotry, Sikhs would be obliged to oppose it as they did, to a very great extent, oppose Goebbels and Nazis in the last war. Hundreds of thousands of Sikhs died fighting the evil of fascism.

Judge Gosling: Real toleration in the sense that everybody should be allowed to do his own thing simply does not exist. It must be his own thing in accordance with certain accepted principles?

Indarjit Singh: I absolutely accept that, your honour. Those principles are those I have outlined. If someone wants to follow the Christian way, or the Hindu way, Sikhs should support them. If, on the other hand, any people belonging to any other religion or no religion wish to persecute or harm the weaker segments of society, or weaker nations, Sikhs are certainly not supposed to be tolerant of those things.

Harjit Singh: Since the independence of India, has there been a demand for a Sikh homeland?

Indarjit Singh: Yes, a very strong demand, and perhaps a part of that demand has been met. There is in India a state of Punjab where Punjabi is given the status of the state language. India could quite easily develop a federal system where states have more independence.

Judge Gosling: Are the Welsh considered a nation or not?

Indarjit Singh: Your honour, this is subjective. Many Welsh people would consider themselves a nation.

Harjit Singh: Would you regard the Sikhs as a separate community even if they were not a nation?

Indarjit Singh: They are certainly a separate community. This is where the dividing line between community, nation or ethnic group is so difficult. They are certainly a community because they have all these distinctive features: language, customs, religion, practices, aspirations, origin.

Judge Gosling: You did, at the very beginning of your evidence, define what you meant by, let me have a look. An ethnic group: "A group of people who live together and see themselves as distinct and others as different." That is an ethnic group?

Indarjit Singh: Yes, your honour. I think I agree with Dr Ballard there. The word does stem from the Greek word 'ethnos' which means a group of people who see themselves alike and others as different. A group of people living together. That is an ethnic group. I think where it becomes important is that the 1976 Act talks about race, but race is an imprecise term that has lost most of its meaning.

Judge Gosling: It is scientifically meaningless?

Indarjit Singh: It is scientifically meaningless because it was based on biological suppositions, which have since been proved false. Race assumes permanence. A person belongs to a fixed race and, therefore, his children will belong to that race and so on. Ethnicity does not automatically assume permanence. As long as people living together see themselves as a group and, importantly, are identified as a distinct group, they are an ethnic group.
I have two girls but supposing they were boys wearing turbans and they go to school or they go, later on, to work, to employment, people will not say, "Well, you're all right because you are English." It is what people, the beholder, sees that is important.

Judge Gosling: They will say, "You are a Sikh." They will say, "You are Indian"?
Indarjit Singh: Possibly, yes. And it could be a person of a fourth generation and they could still say that.

Judge Gosling: And what would be the population of Sikhs in the United Kingdom?

Indarjit Singh: It is estimated in different ways, but the range would be between 150,000 to 250,000.

Judge Gosling: Amongst those 150,000 to 250,000 what would be the percentage of the orthodox element compared to the unorthodox element?

Indarjit Singh: The percentage today would be between two-thirds and three-quarters who would be orthodox.

Judge Gosling: Two-thirds and three-quarters?

Indarjit Singh: It may be three-quarters. It may be a little less.

Judge Gosling: Amongst the unorthodox, what is the present social trend? Do they tend to continue as unorthodox Sikhs or is there a movement back to fold?

Indarjit Singh: Historically, when people came directly from the Punjab in the 1950s, many cut their hair in the belief that they would have no chance otherwise of securing employment.

Judge Gosling: We have had this evidence. You were telling us about the pattern.

Indarjit Singh: So that trend is now back towards Sikhism.

Judge Gosling: Is it going back towards orthodox?

Indarjit Singh: Yes.
Cross-examined by Mr Chapman

Mr Chapman: Just dealing with the last point first, I take it you go to a temple regularly?

Indarjit Singh: I go to various gurdwaras, yes.

Mr Chapman: So that your experience is drawn from a number of different temples, is it?

Indarjit Singh: That is correct.
Mr Chapman: And it is in that experience that you say it would be two-thirds to three-quarters that would be orthodox.

Indarjit Singh: It is an experience from a number of different temples. It is an experience of meeting Sikh social groups. It is an experience of working with the Sikh community, writing a magazine for the Sikh community, not solely on observance of a few temples.

Mr Chapman: When you speak of them being orthodox, do you mean that they do not cut their hair and wear a turban?

Indarjit Singh: That is correct.

Mr Chapman: Would it surprise you to find that a census taken at a temple in Birmingham showed that almost 60% of the men going inside had shaved and were not wearing turbans?

Indarjit Singh: It wouldn't surprise me if that census had been taken in the 1950s.

Mr Chapman: Last week. To be precise, the 8th June?

Indarjit Singh: It would surprise me, and I would say that that was not a representative sample of Sikhs.

Judge Gosling: So nearly 60% had short hair and no turbans?

Mr Chapman: Yes, your honour. Let me give you the times so that you can comment further. nine-thirty in the morning until twelve-thirty on the morning of Sunday, 8th June. Of those who went in, 271 wore no turbans and had cut hair and a handkerchief over their heads as they went in. Would that be the practice of those who were generally unorthodox?

Indarjit Singh: I think you have to be very careful here, we have to remember that not everyone who frequents a Sikh temple is a Sikh; that very many Hindus do go to Sikh temples. It's not at all uncommon and Sikhs and Hindus don't think twice about it.

Mr Chapman: So really there is no way in which one can test the attendance at a temple and say whether it is in the main Sikh or in the main Hindu?

Indarjit Singh: There are special occasions where Hindus feel they have to go to a place of worship and they are, like all people, welcomed in a Sikh temple.

Judge Gosling: Are there no Hindu temples in Birmingham?

Indarjit Singh: I don't know if there are or not, your honour, but I do know that in the development and organisation of temples, Sikhs are very much ahead of the field. There are more Sikh temples, and a Sikh temple is more accessible. On the question of samples and census – I speak as a qualified statistician – I would be loath to take much cognisance of any sample taken at one place on one day because of the wide variation of different groupings.

Mr Chapman: When you go into a temple and see a number of people worshipping, some of whom wear their turbans and do not cut their hair and some of whom have no turbans and have shaved, how can you tell which of those others are patit Sikhs and which are Hindus?

Indarjit Singh: One cannot tell. One can tell who is a Keshdhari Sikh. That is by observance. One cannot tell whether the next person is a patit Sikh or is a Hindu or whether he is a Muslim or a Christian.

Mr Chapman: I do not know whether you can answer this, but if you can I would like your help. Do you think that of those living in East Africa, more wore turbans than those remaining in the Punjab?

Judge Gosling: You mean by percentage?

Mr Chapman: Yes.

Indarjit Singh: No, I couldn't give a precise answer, but I can give an indication, and that does depend on influences. When any community is under pressure they tend to unite and keep together, if a group are isolated somewhere they tend to keep together, so it would be possible that slightly more in East Africa wore turbans than in the Punjab, but there wouldn't be that much in it.

Mr Chapman: Of those who immigrated to this country in the 1950s and 1960s directly from Punjab, I think that from what you have said you would concede that most of them did abandon the turban and cut their hair?

Indarjit Singh: Your honour, in the 1950s I wouldn't say most, but the majority. That is more than 50%.

Mr Chapman: Is one of the reasons that they have changed radically that in the 1960s and 1970s, particularly in the 1970s, perhaps because we had an influx of immigrants from East Africa who had been used to wearing turbans? They had not had to abandon the turban in East Africa and brought turban wearing with them back into this country?

Indarjit Singh: Yes, your honour, those in East Africa had grown up from childhood in a country foreign to the Punjab and had, in that country, survived with a turban and, therefore, came here on assumption that it would be possible to do so. And often the fear is worse than the actuality. When they came and found they could survive, the percentage would have increased just by the process alone. It would also increase by the confidence that gave to others already here.

Judge Gosling: Example rather than preaching?

Indarjit Singh: Very much so, your honour. Exactly.

Judge Gosling: Perhaps the two things do not strictly tie together, but if there have always been temples here for Sikhs to attend, perhaps it is fair to say this: in the 1950s and 1960s it must have been the case, from what you say, that many of the Sikhs attending those temples would have been shaving and without a turban?

Indarjit Singh: That is correct, your honour.

Judge Gosling: More than 50%, but now, according to you, it is falling, down to 25% or thereabouts?

Indarjit Singh: Well, that is my estimation. At one stage in the 1950s, your honour, one of the earliest, not purpose-built but purposely- procured, temples in this area was the one in Smethwick. And at one stage, the vast majority there were clean-shaven. Even some of the office bearers.

Judge Gosling: It may be that that is what Parliament was intending to prevent, and that is what I am suggesting is the case. Let us turn to race. As I understand it you agree with Dr Ballard that it is now impossible, with the advantages we have of modern science, to define Sikhs by reference to race?

Indarjit Singh: Your honour, it is impossible to define anyone by reference to race.

Judge Gosling: To define any group, I suppose?

Indarjit Singh: To define any group.

Judge Gosling: We should have this Act amended.

Mr Chapman: It may be after this case. Would it not be possible to define, for instance, a Red Indian by his race?

Indarjit Singh: No more, your honour, than an inhabitant of central Europe or anyone else. A Red Indian is someone that we have grown up with through cowboy films as an inhabitant of North America who chases people called cowboys. But any person who was born on that continent before the arrival of people from Europe would be termed Red Indian.

Mr Chapman: Yes, that may well be, but can he not be identified by reference to his race?

Indarjit Singh: That is impossible because Red Indians can, and do, marry other people and what do they become? There is no pure race.

Mr Chapman: I fully accept that there is no purity anywhere and there never could be, but what troubles me is that you say this word race is meaningless and yet Parliament in 1976 put it into the Act.

Judge Gosling: We have to put a meaning to it.

Indarjit Singh: Yes, of course, your honour, and Parliament put it into the Act because although it is meaningless, it is a word of common parlance.

Mr Chapman: Let me just dwell on that a little longer. Would you not agree that in very broad terms it is possible to make some definition of certain groups of people by reference to race?

Indarjit Singh: Your honour, I just cannot agree with that statement unless an example is given me. What people and in what broad terms?

Mr Chapman: A Maori?

Indarjit Singh: A Maori is a person who is an inhabitant of New Zealand, and that is all.

Mr Chapman: And if one were to refer to Negroes, as a group there are certain, again, characteristics which are common to them, and is that not what is normally meant by race?

Indarjit Singh: Yes.

Mr Chapman: In common parlance?

Indarjit Singh: There is common parlance and there is scientific parlance. In common parlance one can talk about Negroes as a race. One can talk about Mongoloids as a race. Those were the original races when these words were coined in Victorian times. Since that time, we have Aryan and Caucasoid and then there is the Australoid. These were the basic types that were considered races, and various measurements were taken of brain capacity and so on of these different groups and they assumed that these measurements would show clear differences. One of the major differences that was shown was that the Mongoloids appeared to have bigger brains than the white races, which dampened the enthusiasm of white people.

Judge Gosling: They ceased to study the subject?

Indarjit Singh: But also, it was shown to be statistically meaningless. An average has no meaning unless it is accompanied by some measure of spread, a deviation from the norm, and the deviation from the norm was so great that these terms, these artificial divisions, were clearly meaningless.

Judge Gosling: And if the expert witness comes along and says this word – and they are all saying that about race – is meaningless then we shall have to disregard their evidence, right as it may be, because it is a word, and see what the dictionary says about it.

Indarjit Singh: Your honour, the Oxford Dictionary definition of Sikh is totally incorrect.

Judge Gosling: It is incorrect?

Indarjit Singh: It is incorrect, because in one dictionary a Sikh is defined as a Punjabi Hindu, and in the other dictionary, Sikhs are called a military sect. These dictionaries and definitions are not foolproof.

Judge Gosling: Let me turn now to the next group, and I think that is nationality. Do you claim to have Sikh nationality, or would you say you had Indian nationality or British nationality or what?

Indarjit Singh: If I were asked, your honour, I would claim, and hope, that I have the nationality of human race. That is what I consider of prime importance.

Judge Gosling: The human race is not a nation.

Indarjit Singh: It is the human race to which I owe allegiance. It is all humanity, and I hope I would not take the side of an Indian against an Englishman where it is morally wrong. I have great loyalties to this country. I have British nationality. I have an affinity with, and sympathy for, the Indian nation and, of course, for Sikh community. These could all, Britain, India and Sikhs, be considered nations.

Mr Chapman: No, I do not think that will do, I am sorry. I daresay you can have loyalty to many different countries. It may be possible to have more than one nationality, but in the main – well, exclusively, I think, you are saying your nationality is British?

Indarjit Singh: By legal definition, at the moment I hold a British passport. Someone else could hold a British passport and a Pakistani passport.

Judge Gosling: Yes, that has been conceded, but what about you?

Indarjit Singh: No, myself as an individual, I have British nationality.

Judge Gosling: A person cannot change the physical characteristics that he has. If I would like to be a foot taller I cannot make myself a foot taller?

Indarjit Singh: No, but if I wanted a shorter nose I could have one.

Judge Gosling: Within limits. With modern surgery really you are right, but broadly speaking, one cannot change one's appearance?

Indarjit Singh: Broadly speaking, that is correct.

Judge Gosling: One cannot change one's place of birth?

Indarjit Singh: Even on such an obvious point it is still very difficult. I was born in British India, in that part of British India, which is now Pakistan.

Mr Chapman: You cannot actually, by some act of your own, change the place at which you were born?

Indarjit Singh: I was, your honour, born in India. My birthplace is now Pakistan.

Judge Gosling: But it is still the same place?

Indarjit Singh: It is still the same place, yes.

Judge Gosling: You cannot change that?

Indarjit Singh: I can't change it, but history has changed it.

Mr Chapman: What do you say about Punjab now? It is divided up, of course?

Indarjit Singh: The original Punjab, at independence, went half to Pakistan and half to India. Sikhs became very concerned about their language; the Hindu community disowned the Punjabi language, which was spoken by many Hindus, and Sikhs began agitating for a separate state. A very truncated Punjab has been allocated to Sikhs as a separate Punjabi speaking state, and agitation is still on for complete independence.

Mr Chapman: I have not asked you this before, perhaps I should: would you regard the Muslims in the old boundaries of the Punjab as being a racial group, an ethnic group?

Indarjit Singh: Your honour, I can speak for the Sikhs because I have some knowledge of the Sikh community and about Sikh history, Sikh aspirations and language and so on. I don't think I can really answer for the Muslims. They have certainly some of the aspects of an ethnic group, but in other cases they don't.

Mr Chapman: It is what I recall you saying last time. You want integration, but you do not want to be absorbed so that you draw your own boundaries and say, "This is what we preserve. This identifies us as Sikhs"?

Indarjit Singh: Yes. I do believe that the Sikh religion has something to offer the people of this country and the religion and the society of this country has something to offer the Sikhs. Integration is learning from one another. It is not just drawing boundaries and saying, "This is where we stand and that is where you stand," it is understanding one another.

The case was lost in the County Court and in the Court of Appeal. It then went to the Supreme Court sitting in the House of Lords. The transcript of the Supreme Court Judge's findings was published just before it was formally announced, and I was invited to the Lords to hear that we had won, and Sikhs were entitled to protection under the 1976 Race Relations Act. The judgment also helped secure similar protection for Jews.

A Word about the Sikh Religion

Sikh teachings are advisory, rather than rigidly prescriptive. 'Should' or 'should not', replaces the more prescriptive 'thou shalt not' of Abrahamic religions. Sikhism is a simple guide to positive and meaningful living that advises us what to do and what to avoid to get the best in our journey through life. It is widely appreciated by many non-Sikhs, while some Sikhs see it only as cultural background to their lives.

Religious literacy has now become a buzz phrase with everyone agreeing it is necessary in today's multicultural society. I am a member of a Parliamentary Committee on Religious Education that recently ran a series of lectures on the theme. Unfortunately, the academics invited spent forever talking about the difficulties in defining what we mean by religious literacy. I believe that all we need to know is a brief outline of different beliefs and practices that can be written on one side of A4, so that we can recognise and rejoice in commonalities, and respect or even challenge differences which appear to cut across today's norms. Such discussion can even lead to us looking more critically at some of today's attitudes and behaviour that we take for granted. Challenged to summarise Sikh teachings in this way, I wrote the following note.

A Brief Outline of Sikh Teachings

The Sikh religion was founded by Guru Nanak who was born in Punjab in 1469. It was a time of hostility between the weak, majority Hindu community and Muslim invaders from the North, bent on forced conversion. Each claimed that theirs was the one true religion. Against this background, Guru Nanak, in his very first sermon taught, "The one God of us all isn't in the least bit interested in our different religious labels like Hindu or Muslim," or by today's extension, Christian, Sikh or Jew. "God," the Guru taught, "is only concerned with what we do in life, particularly to help the disadvantaged and oppressed."

Sikhism teaches that different religions are simply different paths to our understanding of God and our responsibilities in life. The Sikh teaching that we are all equal members of the one human family naturally follows from this, as does the emphasis on the full equality of women. Sikh women often lead congregational worship and are encouraged to fully participate in all walks of life.

Guru Nanak instituted a system of successor Gurus who showed by the example of their own lives that the principles of Sikhism remained relevant in different political and social circumstances. It wasn't easy, and two of the Gurus were cruelly martyred for teaching tolerance and the right to freedom of belief. The first of these martyrs was Guru Arjan, the fifth Guru and main author of the Sikh scriptures, the *Guru Granth Sahib*, in which, in addition to compositions of the Sikh Gurus, he also included verses of Hindu and Muslim saints to emphasise that no one religion has a monopoly on truth.

The ninth Guru, Tegh Bahadhur, though disagreeing with some aspects of Hindu worship, was publicly beheaded for defending their right to freedom of worship against attempts of forced conversion by the Mughal rulers. At the time, Sikhs had no distinguishing symbols and were too cowed to be identified as Sikhs and claim their Guru's body, which was eventually removed by stealth.

The tenth Guru, Gobind Singh, son of the martyred Guru, thought long and hard about this lapse of courage, and how to ensure Sikhs always stood up for their beliefs. On the Spring festival of Baisakhi 1699, he challenged Sikhs to come forward if they were ready to stand up for their beliefs, even at the cost of their lives. Sikhs readily came forward. The delighted Guru knew that Sikhism could now flourish without the guidance of further living Gurus. He gave Sikhs a distinct identity as a constant reminder of a commitment to live true to Sikh values. The most noticeable of Sikh symbols is uncut hair covered with a turban. Others are a small comb as a reminder of the need for cleanliness, a steel bracelet, a kirpan or short sword, and shorts or trousers to replace the cumbersome Indian dhoti. The Guru then added verses of Guru Tegh Bahadhur to the holy *Granth* and asked Sikhs to follow the teachings of the *Guru Granth Sahib* as they would a living Guru.

A Sikh place of worship is called a gurdwara, and essentially consists of a prayer hall and an area for communal eating, the langar hall. All people, regardless of race, religion or social standing are always welcome to join Sikhs for langar, which, in larger gurdwaras, is served from dawn to dusk.

Sikhism is not a religion of renunciation, but one of a commitment to positive action for self-improvement and improvement of society as a whole. Sikhs are expected to follow the threefold path of *naam japna, kirt karna* and *wand chakhna*, that is: reflecting on spiritual guidance, earning by honest effort and using talents, wealth and experience to help others. Sikh teachings see people in three categories: 'manmukhs' who care only about themselves, then there are those who, while doing little harm to others, do little to make the world a better place, and at the positive end of the spectrum, there are the 'gurmukhs', those committed to working for the wellbeing of others who leave the world better for having lived. The whole thrust of Sikh teachings is to move us to the gurmukh end of the spectrum.

Chapter Eleven
Work in the Community

Widening Horizons

I found myself spending more and more of my free time writing and broadcasting about religion, race relations and issues of social and political justice. In the latter part of the 20th century, religious communities used to work together more than they do today, and on one occasion I gave evidence at an industrial tribunal in support of a Muslim nurse who wanted to wear trousers at work rather than the regulation dress.

I was also invited to become a Justice of the Peace and attended court half a day a fortnight. It was an enjoyable and interesting experience sitting on the bench, listening to sometimes complex cases and coming to a rational verdict. I was less keen on sitting on traffic offences as police always seemed to give evidence in practised, ponderous and sonorous tones. It was then I learnt the art of yawning with mouth almost totally closed; it is a skill which I find useful when listening to discussions on the minutiae of legal arguments in the Lords.

Board of Visitors, Brixton Prison

While at Hackney, I was also invited to join what was then called the Board of Visitors (now the Independent Monitoring Board) of Brixton Remand Prison. In my monthly visits, I was given free access to all prisoners to ensure their fair treatment. During my visits, I met many who had made headline news. These included Neilson, who was responsible for multiple murders in North London, and Lyons, who used to persuade elderly ladies to commit suicide by placing plastic bags over their heads and would get upset if they tried to change their minds. On one visit, I wondered what a pleasantly smiling Chinese person with immaculate manners was doing there, only to learn that he had gone berserk with an axe. I realised more than ever before that appearances can at times be quite deceptive. I also met one of those involved in the Iranian Embassy siege which led to the death of a young policewoman, WPC Fletcher. He was a lad of 18 who said he just happened to be in the embassy at the time and was desperate to get hold of a physics book to further his studies.

No one covered my work when I was doing my half day a fortnight JP duty or for my monthly visit to Brixton, and I had to work harder to keep up with things. Nor was work time involved when I did my occasional BBC Radio 4 'Thought for the Day' broadcasts. They were written the evening before and broadcast live from the BBC studio early the following morning. This allowed me to be early for work. Despite this, I encountered considerable jealousy from some colleagues. I had publicly criticised some of the racial and social policies of Margaret Thatcher in writings and on the radio. However, I also felt unable to pledge loyalty to the extreme left-wing politics of the Borough of Hackney.

My work at Hackney included responsibility for all capital expenditure and grants to community groups. Council policy was to fund social activities and provide support for groups organised around race. When I suggested that religious groups were also doing work that benefitted the wider community and should be considered for funding support, I received a short sharp reply: "We want nothing to do with all that bowing and chanting." I later referred to this reluctance to involve religion in public life in a 'Pause for Thought' broadcast with Terry Wogan on 'consultation fatigue'.

Terry, I'm feeling a bit harassed and stressed by what they call 'consultation'. There was a time, not so long ago, the good old days, when no one took any notice of faith communities. Religion was considered of no relevance to social debate. A local government official once said it all: "We want nothing to do with all that bowing and chanting."

Today, everything has changed. Whole forests are being chopped down in the name of consultation. The morning post brings loads of bulky documents and reports, requiring an early response. And then there is e-mail, with complex questionnaires, more reports and invitations to meetings on such diverse topics as: coroners' services, burial practice, chaplaincy in courts, faith response to bird flu, and, you're not going to believe this, a faith perspective on the depletion of cod reserves in the North Sea! Some of the documents sent by email are more than 50 pages long, and we are given the privilege of printing them off at our own cost.

There's a strong temptation to ignore the lot, but if we do this, there is the fear that we'll be labelled as a community that wants to remain aloof from mainstream life. I'm not even sure that they really expect or want us to read it all. The very act of sending out all this stuff enables the sender to place ticks against boxes labelled, 'Have you consulted with relevant minorities?'

Or perhaps it's all part of a cunning plan to get us to use up all our resources and energies on such exercises, so that we have neither the strength nor stamina for the real role of religion, namely, nudging secular society to more responsible living. Many people are still deeply suspicious of religion and would prefer to keep us occupied by consulting us on everything, other than how we can help make ours a better and more caring society.

My increasing prominence in society didn't help me in Hackney. I found the work there challenging and interesting, but it was becoming difficult to cope with the jealousy and intrigues of colleagues who resented my reluctance to express unthinking loyalty to left-wing political policies. I began to think seriously of leaving local government and pursuing my own interests. Fortunately, I had made some sound investments over the years; we had paid off our mortgage and our two daughters were pursuing their own medical careers. I knew that my wife and I could comfortably manage if I took early retirement. It would allow me to devote more time to writing and broadcasting. An odd, and somewhat unpleasant incident brought matters to a head.

Members of the senior management team were required to get approval on a signed leave card before taking leave to ensure that their work was covered. I did this before going on a short half-term break with the family to Cheddar Gorge. When I returned to work, I found my signed leave card had been removed from a locked drawer in my desk and it was suggested that I had gone on leave without due authorisation. Fortunately, I had kept a photocopy of the signed authorisation at home and produced it in evidence to clear myself, to the embarrassment of my accusers. I asked the Race Relations Unit to investigate what I saw as near criminal activity, but they were too interested in furthering their own careers to do anything. Frankly, this did not come as a surprise to me as they were known for not helping minorities in the workforce. Those needing advice or assistance in matters of discrimination or unfair treatment would, often, come to me. This did not endear me to the political establishment.

The leave card incident helped me make up my mind to go for early retirement and pursue my interests full-time. When word got out that I was leaving, I was moved and embarrassed by the number of people coming to see me or writing to wish me the best for the future. Many thanked me for help, advice or support that I had completely forgotten about. Working at Hackney, although fraught with pantomime political intrigues, also had its rewards in meeting many kind and decent people, some of whom still keep in touch.

The Sikh Messenger

I had been co-editing a magazine called the *Sikh Courier* since 1969. It was a quarterly English language magazine about Sikh religious teachings, history and culture. Its editorial policy did not allow discussion on political concerns about increasing discrimination against Sikhs in India. By the early 1980s, negative attitudes to Sikhs in India had grown to open persecution and my co-editor, Pamela McCormack, and I decided to leave the *Courier* and we began the *Sikh Messenger*. The 1984 attack on the Golden Temple did not come as a surprise to our readers.

1984: A Horrendous Year for Sikhs

At the time, I, like other Sikhs in the UK, was outraged by the killings and suffering of our community in India. The UK media simply accepted the Indian government propaganda that Sikhs were extremists trying to destabilise the country.

I appeared on radio and television and wrote to the papers trying to set the record right. This included articles in the French, Arabic and US media and a full-length article in *The Guardian* (see Part Two). It made little difference.

I was then a member of the Home Secretary's Advisory Council on Race Relations and sought a meeting with him about events in India. The Home Secretary, David Waddington, was a decent and likeable person and agreed to meet at short notice. After listening to me patiently, he responded: "Indarjit, we know exactly what is going on, but we are walking on a tightrope. We have already lost one important contract" (Westland's Helicopter Contract). I was disappointed but not surprised by his answer. In an Editorial in the *Sikh Messenger*, I had written:

Truth is high, but higher still is truthful living – Guru Nanak. Truth is high, but higher still is trade – British government.

Despite overwhelming evidence of the Indian government's complicity in the mass killing of Sikhs throughout India, the British media, conscious of trade, simply echoed the Indian propaganda against Sikhs. This media negativity led me to enlist the financial support of some large gurdwaras to take out expensive quarter-page adverts in *The Times* and *The Guardian*, drawing attention to the silent genocide of Sikhs in India. A journalist, then with Channel 4, visited me for background information before flying out to India to film mob violence against Sikhs. The police seized her film. A JP colleague on the Wimbledon Bench visiting friends in India, went to the local police station with a Sikh family to report the ransacking of their house. At the station, they found the police enjoying their newly-acquired furniture!

It was a dark and difficult time for Sikhs, but also one which saw the best in some predominantly Hindu civil-rights organisations. A group of Delhi academics produced a devastation report called 'Who are the Guilty?', which gave eye-witness accounts of the atrocities against Sikhs, naming ringleaders, including MPs. Another group called Citizens Commission for Democracy, headed by a former Chief Justice of India, produced another detailed report on the clearly planned and systematic killing of Sikhs, the rape of Sikh women and the destruction of homes. I managed to get hold of smuggled copies before both reports were banned in India. These were sent to every MP, many of whom wrote back, expressing sympathy and support for the suffering of Sikhs.

I spent much of my free time in 1984 in rallies and meetings of protest in various gurdwaras throughout the country. There was a real sense of hurt and betrayal, with countries looking the other way rather than risking their trade relationship with India. Minorities without a majority in some other country to speak for them, have few friends.

In all the emotion and sadness there were also some unconscious lighter moments. Representatives of other faiths had been invited to a large remembrance gathering at a gurdwara in Crawley, Sussex and out of courtesy, the speeches were in English rather than Punjabi. But there was a problem with the pronunciation of the word 'which', with words beginning 'w' often pronounced with a 'b' in parts of Punjab. Speaker after speaker referred to suffering 'bitch' Indira Gandhi had caused! I could almost hear guests thinking, 'These Sikhs don't mince their words!'

The Economist saw Sikhs as a bit uppity; the Yorkshiremen of India.

In fairness, they published my response below:

Letters
Sikhs

SIR – Your report on the Sikhs, "Not according to the Book" (June 16th), should have been entitled "According to the Book". Sikhs do not, as you claim, worship the Granth Sahib; *it is its contents that we revere. There is a tremendous difference between reverence and deification.*

You say that Sikhs are a practical people, not mystics; the Yorkshireman of the subcontinent. True. The characteristic features of both Yorkshireman and Sikh are honesty, an aversion to humbug and a practical approach to life. The life of a mystic, totally devoted to abstract self-realisation, is criticised by our Gurus as a selfish abandonment of our social obligations. A Sikh is expected to be both mystic in his pursuit of godly ideals and a practical social being at one and the same time. We are taught that a Sikh should: "Be like a lotus flower, which having its roots in muddy water still flowers beautifully above it." Another Sikh teaching, which should have been mentioned to help explain Sikh bitterness at events in the Punjab, is our strong emphasis on tolerance. Not the negative tolerance of "putting up with", but a willingness to lay down your life for another's beliefs. In today's context it should be remembered that our ninth Guru did precisely this when he was publicly beheaded by the Moguls for defending the right of Hindus to worship in the manner of their choice. Would that there were more Yorkshiremen in the world today!

Indarjit Singh
Editor, Sikh Messenger, *London*

Two curious and rather sinister incidents illustrated how the government of India, perhaps with the help of the UK government, was working to discredit those who dared draw world attention to the government-backed, mass killing of Sikhs in India.

The first concerned an Englishman who would knock on the door of our house and ask if he could help in the killing of Hindus. He eventually stopped after being repeatedly told that Sikhs had no enmity with Hindus and respected people of all religions.

Then there was the occasion when, while attending a meeting of the then Commission for Racial Equality, I was approached by an Indian gentleman who, after confirming that I was the editor of the *Sikh Messenger*, asked me what car

I drove. It was a (not very new) Ford Sierra. Then, to my astonishment, he smiled and said: "Write for me instead of the *Sikh Messenger* and you could be driving a Mercedes!"

Further Background to the Genocide of 1984 Resolution of the UNA, London, July 2004

The Indian Government and the Sikh Community in the Punjab

In accordance with a request previously made by Mr Indarjit Singh to the Chairman, the Committee agreed to hear a statement from Mr Singh on the present dispute. He said it had been impossible to get an effective presentation of the Sikh case from the media. The root of the present trouble lay in promises made to the Sikhs by Gandhi and Nehru at the time of independence, which had not been fulfilled. Later promises of autonomy had also not been honoured.

The attacks on the Golden Temple compound, and on every other Sikh gurdwara in the Punjab, also the unexplained disappearance of many Sikhs, raised human rights issues which he felt should be the concern of this Committee and the UN Human Rights Commission.

After discussion, it was agreed that Mr Singh and Mr Harper should be authorised to draft a resolution on the human rights issues which would be submitted to the next meeting of the UNA Executive, and if passed, would be sent to the UN Human Rights Centre in Geneva. Copies would be sent to members.

The Resolution: The Executive Committee of the United Nations Association:

ANXIOUS to see a strengthening of the observance of human rights standards in keeping with the United Nations Declaration of Human Rights and its associated protocols;

BELIEVING in the right of all people to freedom of religious expression without interference or hindrance;

DEEPLY DISTURBED by the violence especially in the Punjab and in the Golden Temple of Amritsar;

GREATLY CONCERNED that the assault on the Golden Temple was timed to coincide with the anniversary of the martyrdom of the Great Guru, Arjan, founder of the Temple and the main compiler of the holy Granth, when a very large number of visitors and pilgrims would have been at prayer in the Golden Temple and other gurdwaras; and that priceless Sikh treasures and literature were looted, damaged and destroyed, many of them irreplaceable;

NOTING that no warning appears to have been given that a major assault was about to take place and that a military occupation of the Temple would prevent open access for all to it;

URGES the UNA of India to play a full and positive role in promoting good relations between Sikhs and others throughout India;

REQUESTS the UN Human Rights Centre to continue to keep this situation under review and to bring any further breaches of religious freedom to the attention of the Commission;

CALLS UPON HMG TO:

EXPRESS to the Government of India its profound concern at these events; SEEK to promote the lessening of tension through the good offices of the UN Secretary-General, the Commonwealth Secretary-General, and all other possible channels;

CALL UPON the Sikh community and the Government of India urgently to seek positive ways of reconciliation and mutual understanding and respect.

Reported in Sikh Messenger, *Summer 1984*

The UK government completely Ignored this Humanitarian Request.

Thirty Years Later

Release of government documents under the 30-year rule in 2014 showed evidence of UK government support in the planning of the Indian government attack on the Golden Temple in Amritsar. Prime Minister David Cameron, speaking in the House of Commons, sought to minimise the assistance given to the Government of India and asked the cabinet secretary, Sir Jeremy Haywood, to investigate. Sir Jeremy invited me to visit him in his office, and, in view of concerns I had expressed over trade and UK government support given to Indira Gandhi's government, he sought to reassure me by saying his staff had looked through thousands of pages of documents and found no link between minimal support given and trade. I said that I had taken only a cursory look at the documentation released from the office at Kew Gardens, and handed him a document detailing discussion on a £5 billion helicopter contract!

I felt that the embarrassing revelations about the then Thatcher government's support in the action against Sikhs in India might help in getting support for an international inquiry into the events of 1984, and to this end, managed to secure a debate in the Lords.

3 March 2014 9.10pm

*Asked by **Lord Singh of Wimbledon***

To ask Her Majesty's Government what further steps they will take to improve relations with the Sikh community arising from the publication of government documents regarding British involvement in planning the attack on the Golden Temple.

Lord Singh of Wimbledon (CB): *My Lords, the first week of June will mark the 30th anniversary of the Indian government's attack on the Golden Temple – the Vatican of the Sikhs. The attack was deliberately timed to coincide with the martyrdom anniversary of the temple's founder Guru Arjan, when the huge complex would be full to overflowing with* *pilgrims. Tanks and armoured vehicles were used. On conservative estimates, well over 2,000 pilgrims were killed. Eye-witnesses told of how some who surrendered were tied up in their own turbans and shot. Other eyewitnesses outside the temple complex, including my own in-laws, described with horror how they saw groups of pilgrims being herded together and then dispatched with hand grenades. Many of the atrocities were reported in the British and world press.* **The President of India at the time, Zail Singh, a Sikh, who was the nominal head of India's armed services, was not even consulted.**

Every June, Sikhs remember the huge loss of life and the mindless damage to the Golden Temple, the historic centre of the Sikh faith. The question arises: why did Indira Gandhi resort to such brute force against the Sikhs? The Indian government version unquestioningly accepted by our government and I speak as a British Sikh – was that there were 17 wanted separatists "holed-up" – to use the Indian government's jargon – in the Golden Temple. They were a threat to a country of one billion people. The absurdity is obvious. In addition, this version does not explain why 40 other historic gurdwaras in Punjab were attacked at the same time. Sikh gurdwaras are open to all. Why were the so-called separatists not simply arrested by the hundreds of soldiers and police who daily entered the gurdwara for the traditional free food?

What Sikhs were demanding at the time was a fair share of Punjab's river waters to irrigate their fields – and, more importantly, fair treatment for all India's minorities against growing evidence of majority bigotry. Earlier in the same year, hundreds of Muslims in Mumbai were massacred, with the mob carrying banners proclaiming: 'Majorities have their rights.' The true reason for Mrs Gandhi's vindictive attitude to Sikhs stemmed from her prison conviction for electoral fraud in the election of 1975 and her subsequent seizing power and imposing dictatorial rule. Her son Sanjay had married a Sikh and she turned to Sikhs for support. Sikhs, although less than 2% of the population, were at the forefront of the opposition to dictatorial rule, in which the poor – particularly Muslims – were forcibly sterilised and others dumped in the wilderness to make Delhi a tidier place for the Asian Games. Maneka Gandhi, Sanjay's wife, true to Sikh democratic traditions, openly opposed the dictatorship.

Sikhs were never forgiven by Mrs Gandhi. When she returned to office, she cynically decided to play to majority religious bigotry, first against the Muslims and then even more vindictively against Sikhs. The June 1984 carnage in the Golden Temple far exceeded in numbers and barbarity the 1919 massacre led by General Dyer at the nearby Jallianwala Bagh. Even worse was to come.

The widespread killing of thousands of Sikhs following Mrs Gandhi's assassination was blamed on spontaneous mob violence. All the evidence is that it was pre-planned for the anniversary of Guru Nanak's birthday and was simply brought forward, with the government-controlled All India Radio constantly inciting the killers with the words "Khoon ka badla khoon", meaning 'Take blood for blood'. The army was confined to barracks for three full days to allow free rein to organised gangs carrying Sikh voter lists, armed with identical steel rods and an unusually plentiful supply of kerosene, to go around the capital in municipal buses beating and burning male Sikhs and gang-raping women and young girls. Prominent Hindus and Sikhs begged the new Prime Minister, Rajiv Gandhi, to order troops to restore order. His chilling response was: "When a big tree falls, the ground is bound to shake." The same scenes were enacted throughout the country. We know all about the disappearances and killings in General Pinochet's Chile, but a signed report from the American Embassy in India shows that more Sikhs were brutally murdered in just three days in 1984, than those killed in Pinochet's 17-year rule.

I turn to our government's involvement, as revealed in documents that have now come to light. In their initial reaction, the present government said that support for Mrs Gandhi was "minimal". I beg them to think again in the light of the evidence of persecution of Sikhs that was freely known at the time. A Government committed to human rights must question the morality of "minimal" involvement in the persecution of minorities. The released documents praise Mrs Gandhi and cast aspersions on UK Sikhs, with not one word of concern over the murder of thousands.

I was not in the least surprised to read of SAS involvement; I wrote about it at the time in the summer 1984 issue of the Sikh Messenger. *Nor was I surprised by evidence linking British support for Mrs Gandhi to a £5-billion arms contract and the need to "keep Mrs Gandhi happy". In November 1984 I went to see a senior cabinet minister to seek government support to end the pogrom against Sikhs. I received the reply: "Indarjit, we know exactly what is going on but we're walking on a tightrope; we've already lost one important contract."*

At the time I was a member of the United Nations Association (UNA), where we discussed the killings. The director, Malcolm Harper, formally raised evidence-based concerns with the government, asking them to support a UN inquiry into the killings. I made a presentation to the All-Party Parliamentary Group on Human Rights, then chaired by the noble Lord, Lord Avebury. The APPG decided to send two parliamentarians to investigate but the High Commission refused them visas. They appealed, saying that the visit would help to improve Hindu/Sikh relations. They were again refused.

Sikhs accept that today's government are in no way responsible for the mistakes of the past. However, they can and must help to heal wounds. I was in Westminster Abbey this morning and heard Archbishop Desmond

Tutu quote the words: "The time for the healing of the wounds has come." This is true for the wounds in the Sikh community, opened further by the new revelations.

I take this opportunity to thank many in the Hindu community who hid and sheltered Sikhs at the time of the killings. Others risked their lives carefully documenting the names of Congress Party leaders inciting mobs to kill. Sikhs owe them a great debt.

Two of the three main political parties in India have declared their support for an open inquiry. Even Rahul Gandhi, leader of the Congress Party, has admitted that some Congress officials were involved in the killings.

Speaking in the Indian parliament in 2005, Prime Minister Manmohan Singh made the revealing comment: "Twenty-one years have passed ... and yet the feeling persists that somehow the truth has not come out." I urge the government to add their support for an open, independent inquiry into the massacre or genocide of Sikhs in 1984 in the same way that they are backing a UN-led inquiry into the killing of Tamils in Sri Lanka. Against this, all offers of government assistance and offers to talk to Sikhs pale into an unnecessary distraction.

Eighty-three thousand Sikhs gave their lives supporting Britain in the two world wars. In comparison, giving public support for an open, UN inquiry is a small ask. Not to do so will give a clear message to Britain's half a million Sikhs and others concerned with human rights that the UK government is ambivalent and selective on issues of human rights. As director of the Network of Sikh Organisations, the oldest and largest grouping of Sikhs in the UK, and on behalf of the more recently formed Sikh Council UK, I offer my full and unconditional support to the government to help end the 30-year nightmare suffered by Sikhs. We are confident that our government will not let us down.

Sadly, my hopes were not realised, and although many spoke to voice support, the government declined to push for the inquiry.

Earlier, speaking about the mass killing of Sikhs, the Prime Minister, David Cameron, described the genocide as "the darkest stain on the history of post-partition India". However, instead of going on to support a demand for an inquiry, he continued, "What is of importance now is what Sikhs in the UK can now contribute to this country."

I and many other Sikhs found this insensitivity and the total absence of support for an open inquiry into the genocide deeply hurtful. In protest, I and others refused to attend the Baisakhi celebration at No. 10.

Broadcasting and Journalism

The BBC flagship *The Today Programme* of news and current affairs includes a reflective three-minute 'Thought for the Day'. Initially, this was provided almost entirely by Christians with an occasional contribution by a

Jewish Rabbi. In the autumn of 1983, the BBC, to mark the 40th anniversary of One World Week, decided to make it a bit more inclusive with occasional contributions from other faiths. A Hindu, a Muslim and I were invited to make contributions. I have been broadcasting ever since.

My first 'Thought for the Day'

The talk, repeated below, was a light reflection on human prejudice that is still sometimes used for teaching in schools:

I once worked for a large Civil Engineering Company on the seventh floor of an eight-storey building. At the end of the day, we would leave our desks and make our way to the lifts, and as the doors opened, a curious sight would meet our eyes. Those already in the lift, who belonged to the overseas section of the same company and felt themselves superior to us home civil engineers, would stick out their stomachs a little to give the impression that the lift was fuller than it was. Anyway, we would ignore their less than cordial invitation, and pile in. The lift door would close and, in the short space of time it took to reach the floor below, those in before us would step back a little and make genuine efforts to make their fellow civil engineers feel at home.

Now, the floors below ours contained a lower order of society, truly inferior people – civil servants – to be precise. People who did nothing but sit around all day drinking tea and creating mountains of useless paperwork. It's odd how we get these prejudices. Now that I'm in local government and a public servant myself, I know how untrue these can be, anyway, it's not tea, but coffee!

Naturally, we would stick out our stomachs to prevent those lazy bureaucrats getting into our lift. But, crazed with non-stop tea or coffee drinking, they would get in none-the-less. And, by the time the lift reached the ground floor, we had forgotten our, by then, seemingly petty differences, and as fellow workers, we'd leave the lift and make our way home.

I think my little story tells us a lot about human nature. It's rare for anyone getting into a lift, or train, or entering a new country, to be made welcome by those already there. But soon, the newcomer and the original inhabitants assume a near common identity, and perversely, strengthen this in joint hostility to further newcomers, or simply foreigners in general.

These false notions of national or racial superiority were fairly harmless in earlier times. But after the Holocaust against the Jews, and with the social and political changes of recent decades, coupled with our new-found scientific ability to destroy all life on our planet, such behaviour carried to extremes can lead to major conflict.

Guru Gobind Singh, the tenth Guru of the Sikhs, speaking some 300 years ago to an Indian society bitterly divided by caste and religion, stated:

'Recognise the oneness of the whole human race.'

It is a message of even greater relevance today. In this very special anniversary of One World Week, celebrating the 40th anniversary of the founding of the United Nations Organisation, we would do well to reflect on the enlightened teachings of the Gurus, who, in stressing the equality of all human beings – men and women – their emphasis on social and religious tolerance and their brave and forthright attack on all notions of caste, class or racial superiority, gave us, in a sense, the forerunner of the UN ideal, the key not only to sanity and survival in the world today, but also to the positive realisation that different cultures, different ways of life are not barriers between people, but gateways to a fuller understanding and enrichment of life itself.

I continued to do 'Thought for the Day' on *The Today Programme* for more than 35 years. The programme was initially less formal and more relaxed than it is today, with the presenters frequently getting the time wrong! In the mid-1980s, although Sikhs were the victims of state terrorism in India, the media in the UK, copying that in India, would often describe Sikhs as terrorists. In pre-broadcast banter, the celebrated broadcaster, Brian Redhead, asked me where I had put my bomb? I replied I didn't want to bring it into the studio and had left it just outside the office marked 'Director General!' On another occasion, while off air, he joked with me about terrorism, and then went on air to read a news item about two tourists being lost in France. Still thinking about our discussion, he inadvertently spoke on air of 'missing terrorists', instead of tourists.

It is heartening to know that my contributions have been widely appreciated by many listeners. The Prince of Wales, former Prime Ministers Tony Blair and David Cameron and the former US Secretary of State, Madeline Albright and others, have expressed their appreciation of my contributions on issues of everyday concern. Former PM David Cameron, speaking at a Baisakhi function in Downing Street soon after my appointment to the Lords, said he had learnt a lot from my uplifting and inspiring broadcasts. The recognition I most cherish, was from the British Ambassador in Estonia who, when introducing me at a conference, described me as "The man who brought Guru Nanak to the breakfast tables of Britain."

A senior BBC producer however, showed increasing resentment to my talks on the relevance of Sikh teachings to the issues of the day. At one time she tried to dissuade me from speaking about Guru Nanak on the anniversary of the Guru's birth, but matters really came to a head on the important martyrdom anniversary of Guru Teg Bahadur, 9th Guru of the Sikhs who gave his life defending the right of Hindus to freedom of belief at a time of forced conversion by the Mughal ruler.

Late in the afternoon of 27-11-18, after I had prepared my script for next morning, I was told I had to talk about something else! I refused.

My complaint against this attempt to censor important Sikh teachings was picked up by the media and was headline news in the Times. The Editorial condemned the BBC attempt to censor a key and moving moment in Sikh history and suggested the BBC Director General should apologise.

Listeners' Lord

In the first week of a new year, the BBC try to take a break from politics and focus on a more light-hearted topic. In January 2004, Radio 4 listeners were invited to name an individual who they would like to see in the House of Lords.

To my surprise Clare Short MP, the then Secretary of State for International Development, wrote to the BBC to nominate me. She wrote:

I would like to nominate Indarjit Singh. He contributes regularly on Radio 4's 'Thought for the Day', and he gives impressive homilies drawing on the wisdom of Sikh teachings to help us think through the moral issues of the day.

I think, currently, one of the greatest dangers in the world is the fanaticism that is creeping into all the world's great religions and Indarjit Singh stands for a much more generous interpretation of religious teaching.

I was short-listed and ended up coming a close second to pop star and social activist Bob Geldof.

I was at the time part of a group of faith leaders who attended occasional meetings on international development at 11 Downing Street with Clare Short and Gordon Brown. I remember being initially cynical about such meetings, thinking they were probably more concerned with the promotion of trade than with genuine concern for helping development in the poorest parts of the world. To my surprise, I found both Clare Short and Gordon Brown to be totally dedicated to alleviating poverty and promoting development in poorer countries. It was a role they both clearly enjoyed, and I was privileged to hear an impassioned address by Gordon Brown on third-world development outside Lambeth Palace. It was one of the finest speeches I've ever heard from a politician. Sadly, the media, who are more interested in controversy, never picked it up.

'Pause for Thought'

'Thought for the Day' is a wonderful and much appreciated opportunity to comment on issues of the day from a religious perspective, but its high profile as a major news programme inevitably means that it is constrained by the imperatives of political balance and religious and political correctness.

I found doing 'Pause for Thought' on Radio 2 with Terry Wogan much more enjoyable and relaxing. I was broadcasting on this slot for several years before the BBC decided that the same person could not appear on both slots.

'Pause for Thought' always began with light-hearted, on the air banter with Terry. We both shared a similar sense of humour and he would tease me about Sikhs always celebrating something or other. He was far more knowledgeable than I had supposed, and we both shared the same aversion to undue political correctness. My talks were highly appreciated by listeners and one talk about celebrating Christmas got a near record postbag. I was told that HM the Queen was also an avid listener.

Some people at the time were arguing, out of mistaken political correctness, that Christmas should be renamed 'Winterwold' to avoid giving offence to non-Christians. Terry, in his usual way, said, "Sikhs are always celebrating something or other, what do you do at Christmas?" I responded as below:

'Pause for Thought' (with Terry Wogan) BBC Radio 2, 6 December 2007

Terry, your comments yesterday on Christmas meanies remind me of the curious correlation between the switching on of Christmas lights and the speed with which scrooges come out of the town hall woodwork and look for excuses to ban Christmas celebrations of any sort. Climbing a ladder to put up Christmas lights is, in their view, a health and safety hazard! They pompously argue that the power used by the lights is a waste of precious, diminishing resources. They even suggest that the word Christmas might offend people of other faiths, and, after chopping down more trees for inter-departmental memos, come up with absurd alternatives. Where will all this end? I know it sounds a bit over the top, but soon they'll even start suggesting that there is no such person as Father Christmas!

It's all great for the media who, in their love of controversy, suggest that these misguided do-gooders have the support of people of other faiths.

Every year I am asked do I object to the celebration of Christmas? It's an absurd question. For Sikhs, the more excuses for a party, the better.

*It's easy to sum up Sikh attitudes to other faiths. It is **total** respect.*

Because of this, I'm delighted that this year the new Commission for Equality and Human Rights is issuing its own Christmas card which I will be happy to sign, along with people of other faiths.

As ever, my family and I will send out our Christmas cards to our Christian friends and others. In the spirit of Christmas, we in the Singh family will, as usual, force ourselves to have extra turkey, Christmas pudding and mince pies, the lot – all in the cause of inter-faith harmony. No one can say Sikhs don't go the extra mile!

Some of the listeners' responses included:

'As always, Dr Singh's words are that of commonsense and wisdom. Respect and recognition of other faiths' beliefs is surely the way to multi- faith harmony.' Eion 'Thank you to you Terry, and to Dr. Singh, it's nice to have your opinion voiced nationwide, and more importantly, to be echoed by a respected non- Christian such as Dr. Singh.' Alex Boldero 'This chap was amazing. He spoke such sense. He has it spot on. Totally refreshing.' Sue 'What a lovely Christmas message. Should be required listening for all!' Ray

Television

Television brings its own challenges and a little more acting than radio. It also requires make-up. The first time I did any TV, I was pushed straight into the make-up studio to be confronted by a lady, powder puff in hand. She searched for somewhere to apply her make up on my bearded face, and eventually gave my nose a little dab with her powder puff.

An early TV programme was called *From Where I Stand*. It was about life, challenges and priorities for me as a Sikh in the 1980s. The house was quickly taken over by the sound and camera crew and we soon learnt about the perils of takes and retakes as we sat to be filmed having a family meal. As we were about to put some food into our mouths, we heard the word "cut" again and again before we eventually began our now cold meal.

The programme was about a trip organised by our local gurdwara in Southfield to take handicapped people from the local Atheldene Centre to the seaside. I was filmed buying food from a supermarket and loading it into the car, ready to transfer it to a coach. Even this simple operation needed several re-takes. Someone had run into the back of my car a few days earlier and when the cameras were poised to film me loading food into the car, the car boot decided to become temperamental, sometimes refusing to open!

The coach trip itself was lovely. The people from the Centre were delighted by the outing, and there was lots to eat and drink. At the seaside, we bought lots of ice cream for our happy guests. Our daughters made some good friends and one lady commented that "Before today, we were frightened by you people and now, I'm crying because I've had such a lovely time."

The programme was very well received by both Sikhs and non-Sikhs and led to other gurdwaras getting more involved with the local community.

I have often found the fear of difference described by the lady on the coach, colouring attitudes in everyday life. At one time in the 1980s, the small gurdwara at Southfields in London wanted to build an extension. The planning application was resolutely opposed by local residents. I decided to knock on the doors of those in the locality to invite them to a meeting at the gurdwara to discuss their concerns over a shared meal. To our surprise, they all came and enjoyed the hospitality. When the time came for questions, the only question asked was "How do you make such tasty chapattis?" Opposition to planning permission was withdrawn and the extension built. Some local residents still come to the gurdwara to share the traditional end of service meal.

I soon found myself involved in other programmes. In one, called *Gods of War*, the interviewer asked, "Religion is all about peace, so why have the Sikhs got a reputation of being a warrior race?" It is a description I've heard again and again. I responded the description was wrong on two counts. Sikhism is a religion and Sikhs do not believe in different races, but in one race of all humanity. Nor are Sikhs warriors. Sikh teachings state that we should resort to force only as a last resort. Unfortunately, Sikhs have often found themselves facing annihilation and have acquired a reputation as doughty fighters.

300th Anniversary Celebration of the Khalsa

The year 1999 marked the 300th anniversary of the founding of the Khalsa on Baisakhi Day 1699. On that day, Guru Gobind Singh gave Sikhs the distinctive symbols of our faith by which we are recognised today. The symbols are a reminder that we should always be ready to stand up and be counted for our beliefs, however challenging the circumstances. Sikhs in the UK decided to celebrate it in style.

The BBC readily agreed to my suggestion that they mark it with a series of radio and TV programmes. I worked with an independent company making programmes for the BBC to make two half-hour TV programmes and went to India to make five programmes for BBC radio. They were well received by both Sikhs and non-Sikhs.

Getting a visa was not easy. The Indian High Commission had not forgotten that I had spoken up against the persecution of Sikhs in 1984 and I was quizzed by several officers, and after BBC intervention, reluctantly given a visa.

The trip was an eye-opening experience for the BBC reporter Christine Pommert. In a visit to a village in Punjab, she was moved to tears by the harrowing story of an elderly gentleman who had been delivering milk to the Golden Temple at the time of the Indian army attack in June 1984. He and other innocent 'prisoners' were ordered to vacate the area. He was only able to move slowly as he had received a bullet in the leg. When he explained this to the soldiers, they laughed and promptly shot him in the other leg. We were told that the Guru Tegh Bahadhur Memorial Hospital had a large board placed across its front, marked PRISONERS OF WAR. When did a country last make war against its own people? Patients were mostly pilgrims who had come to commemorate the martyrdom anniversary of Guru Arjan, the fifth Guru of the Sikhs. Incredibly, nurses in the hospital were ordered under threat of dismissal, not to give soap or water to the Sikhs, or to help with the cleaning of wounds. Christine Pommert was able to make some excellent programmes for broadcast back home.

Filming with the BBC in India for the 300th anniversary of the Khalsa,
with Christine Pommert in the orange scarf interviewing passersby

At Golden Temple, 1999

Baisakhi 1999 in the Royal Albert Hall

Without any experience, I decided that we should have a large celebration in the Royal Albert Hall. There was one problem: money. A sum of some £8,000 was required to make the booking. I called a meeting of prominent Sikh bankers and businessmen. They said they would help but insisted that they be prominently seated on the stage. I insisted that the stage should be reserved for speakers and performers and eventually the impasse ended with me saying, "OK, then I'll do it myself."

The deposit was more than I could afford, but I was confident that with the programme I had in mind, we would get our money back. My wife Kawal was less confident but helped enormously with ticket sales. We found out that some of the prestigious boxes were privately owned and negotiated prices for their release for the day. We then offered these, appropriately priced, to the more affluent and their friends, while keeping other prices low so that all could attend. There was considerable interest amongst members of the community in attending a celebration of the tercentenary in the Royal Albert Hall and every ticket was soon sold, guaranteeing a capacity audience and a small profit, which we put into the coffers of the Network of Sikh Organisations.

The guest of honour was HRH Prince Charles. He made a lovely speech recognising the uplifting and egalitarian contribution of the Sikh Gurus, and there were representatives of the main political parties. Guest speakers were also invited from India and the USA. The presence of the Chief Rabbi Dr Jonathan Sacks and the Bishop of London, who made truly moving speeches, and representatives of other faiths ensured the function, in line with Sikh tradition, was a truly interfaith occasion.

I had planned to include a play about Baisakhi as the centre point of the celebration but to my dismay, was unable to find either a playwright or suitable actors in this country or in India. I then decided to write the play myself and get children from the Guru Nanak School in Hayes to perform it.

The first problem was how to make a play about Guru Gobind Singh and Baisakhi without showing the Guru, as this would be considered offensive to most Sikhs. Taking my cue from *Doctor Who*, the play was about some Sikh children, with the names of our grandchildren, being assistants to Dr Kaun Singh ('kaun' is the Punjabi word for 'who'), travelling back in time to witness the original Basakhi in 1699. Simran, the eldest, stands on the Doctor's telephone box to describe the scene, while using his automatic translator to relay the words and dialogue of the Guru and others to his co-travellers, and to us. The play was well rehearsed and acted and was enjoyed by Prince Charles and a highly appreciative audience.

The year 2004 was also a special year for Sikhs as it was the 400th anniversary of the formal installation of the Sikh scriptures of the *Guru Granth Sahib* in the Golden Temple, known to Sikhs as Harmandir Sahib.

I again booked the Royal Albert Hall as the venue for the celebration and HRH Prince Charles agreed to be the Guest of Honour in the celebration, which was also graced by leaders of other faiths and the main political parties.

Speech by HRH Prince Charles

In inviting me to join you for this afternoon's celebration, Dr Indarjit Singh was kind enough to let me have a copy of some notes on the holy Granth. And reading through these notes, I was particularly struck by the fact that much of what was being said – for example, on tolerance and respect for others – seemed to be in harmony with the views that I, too, have been trying to express for the last 20 or more years – views, I have to say, which have sometimes landed me in some rather hot, unholy water.

Like the great sages of all time, your tradition places much emphasis on tolerance and respect for others. Indeed, I understand that Guru Nanak had two travelling companions, one a Hindu and the other a Muslim; and that your own Guru Arjan asked a Muslim saint, Mia Mir, to lay the foundation stone of the Golden Temple.

In the notes that he sent to me, Dr Singh referred to the difference, in the Sikh tradition, between manmukh (ungodly) and gurmukh (responsible) living. And, indeed, how jarring it is to hear the incessant clamour of a world obsessed with individual rights but silent, it would seem, on individual responsibilities. And are there not great dangers in this? For in a world in which we are increasingly and irresistibly connected, this irresponsibility takes on global proportions.

Thus, it is that your own Guru Nanak has said that "Without realising it, we have become captivated by materialism and have lost our direction of life."

Leading Prince Charles to his seat in the Royal Albert Hall, 1999

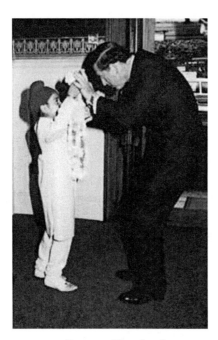

Garland presentation to Prince Charles by my grandson Simran

With Prince Charles

HRH the Prince of Wales being presented with a tapestry of the Golden Temple and the Sikh holy book the Guru Granth Sahib

At 10 Downing Street discussing his participation in the 2004 event at the Royal Albert Hall

Increasing Community Involvement

My work in broadcasting, journalism and as a social commentator began to give me national and international prominence, and my contribution to community understanding was recognised in a joint award of a gold medallion by the BBC and the Council of Christians and Jews for Services to Religious Understanding. In my acceptance speech, I used my experience of a recent family camping holiday in France to illustrate that ignorance and prejudice can have both a hurtful and a comic side.

Indians and Reservations

When our two girls were about five and eleven, we decided it would be fun to go on a camping holiday tour of Europe with a Sikh family who had two daughters nine and 15. Most families would have tried camping for a night or two nearer home before trying anything so adventurous. But we were Sikhs!

We bought a couple of large second-hand tents and bedding and put them onto our roof racks. We put some clothes, a camping stove and cooking utensils in the car boots and some clothes in the cars and got on the ferry to Dunkirk, armed with an *RAC Camping Guide to Europe*. I thought that driving on what I considered the wrong side of the road would be the worst problem, but when we got to the campsite near Abbeville, we found we were barred from the half-full site. Two cars with New Zealand and Australian number plates were allowed in after we were told that the site was full.

The owners of the next, almost abandoned site seemed distinctly dodgy and, fearing for our safety, we decided to go to another, even smaller, site in the now failing light. It was owned by an elderly lady who was vastly amused by what I thought was my faultless French. She welcomed us in.

I felt really bad and irresponsible for not anticipating possible prejudice on our trip and decided to phone the next site on our itinerary, to book accommodation. I explained on the phone in my best Franglaise that we were a party of eight Indians with two cars and our own tents wanting a reservation. The chap on the other end of the line said we would be very welcome.

When we got there, all the staff were lined up to greet us but were a little disappointed to find we were the wrong sort of Indians!

'Pause for Thought' on a Traffic Jam

When returning from our camping and motoring holiday, we got caught up in in a horrendous traffic jam some 15 miles from Paris. The traffic had ground to a complete halt, and I got out of the car to stretch my legs. Almost immediately, a well-dressed American got out of his car, came up to me and began to complain bitterly about the traffic and French incompetence and how he had to be at an important dinner engagement in half an hour. Then another person came running up to us, saying in
the broadest of Birmingham accents, "It's all right, I'm English!"

His 'it's all right' didn't mean that he was a traffic engineer with a magical solution to traffic jams. It meant that he too was English-speaking. So, there we were: an American, a Sikh with turban and beard and an Englishman – all with a sense of common identity based on language and, importantly, strengthened by our common, though totally irrational irritation at French traffic management, and at the French in general!

My story illustrates a law of human behaviour, which I call **'Indarjit's Law'. Simply stated, it is that 'when two or more people find sufficient in common to call themselves 'us', they will immediately look for a 'them' to look down on to strengthen their sense of identity'.**

It is a law that applies over the whole range of human behaviour, from criticism of French traffic jams to more serious racial and national prejudices. This urge to divide ourselves into mutually hostile groups, and to strengthen our sense of identity by looking to the faults in others. It is found everywhere – in politics, religion, even in the arts and in science. We certainly see it a lot at the time of elections.

In Guru Nanak's day, it was religion rather than party politics that separated people into warring factions. Not only were there bitter divisions between Hindus and Muslims, but also between the many factions or holy orders within Hinduism itself. Bitter enmities between rival religious, political and cultural factions around the world today remind us that we are slow to learn.

A couple of years after the receipt of a Broadcasting Gold Medallion, I was awarded the UK Templeton Prize for Promoting Religious Understanding. I received the award at a ceremony in Leicester from the financier and philanthropist, the late Sir John Templeton, better known for setting up the International Templeton Prize, which always carries a cash award greater than that of the Nobel Peace Prize. My prize was for the much smaller sum of £500, which I donated to charity, but it was a great honour for the UK Sikh community.

Setting up the Network of Sikh Organisations UK

As discussed earlier, Sikhs in the diaspora reacted with uniform shock and dismay at the news of widespread killing of Sikhs in 1984. While a few reporters in the UK did draw attention to the injustice against Sikhs, much of the British media simply toed the Indian government line, describing persecuted Sikhs as terrorists, extremists, fundamentalists, etc. The use of such ill-defined catch-all terms, which fog meaning and open debate, is best illustrated by a true story of a visit of two Scotland Yard Officers to our house in 1984.

The front doorbell rang early on a Sunday morning. I opened the door to find two policemen on the doorstep. They explained they were from Scotland Yard and were visiting the homes of prominent Sikhs to discuss dangers from the present unrest in India. Flattered by the word 'prominent', I invited them in and

88

we organised some tea and biscuits. Then came their first question, "Are you an extremist or a moderate?" I replied that I was "extremely moderate". Somewhat confused, they asked me if I was a "fundamentalist". I said, "I believe in the fundamentals of Sikh teachings, such as the equality of all human beings, gender equality, respect for different ways of life, concern for the less fortunate... yes, I suppose I am a fundamentalist." I gave them some literature about Sikh teachings, they finished their tea and left somewhat confused.

It was generally agreed that as Sikhs we had failed miserably in articulating the true extent of the near genocide against Sikhs in India. I attended many meetings across the country where it was said again and again that what Sikhs needed was a central organisation to represent the community. Each of these ended with someone saying, "I'll be president," and to a friend, "You can be secretary." The problem for Sikhs was not the absence of a leader, but too many leaders!

I blame this on our Gurus. Sikhs in India are addressed as Sirdars, literally chiefs; we are a community of chiefs. Sikhism started at a time when the people of Punjab, suffering from repeated invasions, lost the will to stand up to tyranny. The Sikh Gurus taught us never to kow-tow to tyrants. The trouble is that we have taken this a little too far and are reluctant to accept the authority of anyone. Whenever I'm asked by non-Sikhs if I am a leader of the UK Sikh community, I reply, "Yes, along with half a million other Sikhs."

After reflecting deeply on the reluctance of the Sikh community to accept a hierarchical structure of leadership, I felt it would be best to facilitate cooperation between different gurdwaras and organisations on matters of common interest and concern, and this led to the formation of the Network of Sikh Organisations (NSO) in 1995, on the 400th birth anniversary of Guru Hargobind, the sixth Guru of the Sikhs.

I assist as Honorary Director and an elected executive committee, which has ultimate authority, facilitates cooperation in a number of key areas of social and educational provision, and in the interface with government and other communities as described below:

The Sikh Prison Chaplaincy Service (SCS)

This covers all prisons in England and Wales and is responsible for the pastoral care of all Sikhs in prison establishments. Currently, we have more than 60 volunteers working as chaplains. Re-offending is the greatest single cause of a continually rising prison population. The SCS helping prisoners on release with accommodation and work has resulted in reduced re-offending compared to those of other faiths.

Armed Services chaplaincy

After many years, I and colleagues from other faiths helped to persuade the Armed Services to appoint Hindu, Muslim and Sikh chaplains to the Services. In the interview, A Sikh lady, Mandeep Kaur, proved to be the most suitable applicant and she is now, not only the first full-time Sikh chaplain, but also the only female chaplain in the Armed Services.

Education

The NSO is the nominated DfE contact for advice on the teaching of Sikhism and the needs and concerns of Sikh children. We are also responsible for the religious inspection of the Sikh RE curriculum. My wife, Kawaljit (Lady Singh OBE), a qualified and experienced Ofsted Inspector, is the lead NSO volunteer in this area.

Other voluntary social work

The NSO is the first port of call for voluntary agencies seeking the assistance of the Sikh community in a range of voluntary activities to benefit those requiring organ donations, the visually impaired and those with learning difficulties.

Dispute resolution

The NSO has been instrumental in resolving management disputes in major Sikh gurdwaras, including those at Southall (the largest gurdwara outside India), Hounslow, Shepherd's Bush (London) and Tooting (London). All factions in Southall asked the NSO to help resolve a major dispute and our proposals led to subsequent elections accepted by all parties.

International Development

While I dislike volunteering, I feel compelled to jump in if something needs doing and no one wants to do it. Unfortunately, the story of my life is the more you do, the more you are asked to do. It can, however, also be a bit of a privilege as I found out when asked to represent the Sikh community at meetings at 11 Downing Street with the then Chancellor of the Exchequer, Gordon Brown, and International Development Secretary, Clare Short.

In the course of this work I helped to produce a booklet describing the work of Khalsa Aid and others in helping the needy in areas of crisis and conflict. I was also one of the first to buy bonds to help finance a new International Aid Facility. In the course of this work, I was asked to join the then Chief Rabbi, Dr Jonathan Sacks, and senior bishops to head a march to Lambeth Palace to draw attention to the problems of third-world poverty. The march was addressed at Lambeth Palace by Chancellor Gordon Brown who generously acknowledged the support he was receiving from me and others.

Chief Rabbi Sir Jonathan Sacks, with Archbishop of Canterbury Dr Rowan Williams and other faith leaders

Sacks tells Lambeth bishops that all society needs religion

BY SIMON ROCKER

▶ JEWS AND Christians have done more than any religions to "mend their relationship", Chief Rabbi Sir Jonathan Sacks said in the first address by a rabbi to the Anglican Lambeth Conference in its 140-year history.

Speaking in Canterbury on Monday to around 650 bishops from across the globe, the Chief Rabbi recalled the progress made towards reconciliation.

"As I prepared this lecture, within my soul were the tears of my ancestors," he said. "We may have forgotten this but, for 1,000 years, between the First Crusade and the Holocaust, the word 'Christian' struck fear into Jewish hearts.

"Think only of the words the Jewish encounter with Christianity added to the vocabulary of human pain: blood libel, book burnings, disputations,

forced conversions, inquisition, auto da fé, expulsion, ghetto and pogrom."

But since the founding of the Council of Christian and Jews in 1942, the past was "being redeemed", he said. "Jews and Christians have done more to mend their relationship than any other two religions on earth, so that today we meet as beloved friends."

Whereas religion too often presented the face of conflict, he said, Jews and Christians "must show the world another way: honouring humanity as God's image, protecting the environment as God's work, respecting diversity as God's will".

Sir Jonathan had taken part the previous week in the Lambeth Interfaith Walk along with other religious leaders including Reform movement head Rabbi Dr Tony Bayfield and Liberal Judaism chief executive Rabbi Danny Rich. Its purpose was to remind world

leaders of their "Millennium Goals" pledges to tackle poverty and other ills.

Rabbi Bayfield later gave a paper on Christian-Jewish relations to a seminar at the Lambeth Conference.

In his plenary address, Rabbi Sacks focused on the idea of covenant — the shared hopes and ideals that bind a society together. When religion wanes and "there is nothing covenantal to take its place", Dr Sacks warned: "Relationships break down. Marriage grows weak. Families become fragile. Communities atrophy. And the result is that people feel vulnerable and alone.

"If they turn those feelings outward, the result is often anger turning to violence. If they turn them inward, the result is depression, stress, eating disorders, drug and alcohol abuse. Either way, there is spiritual poverty in the midst of material affluence."

Courtesy of Jewish Chronicle photo

With Archbishop of Canterbury, Dr Rowan Williams, and Chief Rabbi,
Dr Jonathan Sacks

Interfaith Activity

The Inter Faith Network UK

In 1987, I was contacted by Brian Pearce, a senior civil servant, to join in starting an initiative to bring different faiths together at a national level. Brian was one of the most genuine people I have ever met. His sincerity and unique diplomatic skills helped to bring leaders of different faiths together to form a national faith body called the Inter Faith Network UK (IFN). Brian Pearce was appointed honorary director and Bishop Jim Thompson and Rabbi Hugo Gryn agreed to serve as co-chairs. I became the first elected co-chair two years later.

Rabbi Hugo Gryn, a survivor of Auschwitz, had a great sense of humour and endless witty stories. He had lived in India for some years after his release from Auschwitz and knew much more about Indian music than I did. He introduced me to the Royal Commonwealth Society and I was invited to represent Sikhs at the Annual Commonwealth Day Service at Westminster Abbey in 1996, something I've been doing every year since.

In those early days, we worked hard to build up strong links between different faiths and, importantly, between faiths and government, resulting in the formation of a minister-chaired Inner Cities Religious Council (ICRC) in 1989.

The task of this group of faith and government representatives was to ensure a faith input into inner city and wider urban development. It wasn't easy, and it had its amusing moments. Governments and representatives of religious communities initially regarded each other with suspicion and distrust, and the minister chairing the meeting would sometimes go into a sulk when asked questions on government policy. Confidence slowly grew, and some excellent initiatives resulted. One in which I was particularly interested was a proposal for the inclusion of a question on religious affiliation in the forthcoming 2001 census. I had become concerned about the different figures being plucked from the air about the size of faith communities to make a particular point or to bid for additional resources.

The then Office for National Statistics called us to a meeting, only to tell us that it was not possible in the short time available. I found myself arguing that it was not only possible but necessary; a line I took in a subsequent 'Thought for the Day' broadcast. The ONS team promised to reconsider the proposal. Then another hurdle. The proposal needed amending legislation and we were told that the parliamentary timetable did not allow for this. I spoke to Lord Weatherill, former Speaker of the Commons and later leader of the crossbenchers in the Lords, for his advice. After further discussion and consultations with members of the Lords, he agreed to sponsor a private member's bill which, unusual for a private bill, was passed by both Houses and a question on religious affiliation was subsequently included in the 2001 census.

Visit to Israel

In December 2000, the Chief Rabbi, Dr Jonathan Sacks, invited me to join him in a visit to Israel with a view to finding ways of reducing suspicion and mistrust between the Muslim and Jewish communities.

It was my first visit to the Holy Land and I was moved by the beauty of the rugged landscape and the splendour of its historic buildings. It was a time of heightened tensions between the two communities and I felt a little nervous, knowing the widespread ignorance about the Sikh community, at the possibility of being mistaken for a Muslim by the Jews, or a Jew by the Muslims. My fears were unfounded, and I was pleasantly surprised when a university professor I spoke to paid an unexpected tribute to the founder of the Sikh faith, Guru Nanak, saying: "If we could all learn to pay respect to all faiths, as he taught,
    there would be no problems of tensions from ignorance and hate."

We spoke to people at all levels of society from both communities who showed a common yearning for peace. I thought about similar tensions between India and Pakistan and left convinced that just as the people of India and Pakistan were one people with a common yearning for peace, divided, not by religion, but by unscrupulous politicians playing on religious sentiment, the people of Israel and Palestine were also one people, with much in common, whose faith differences were being magnified and distorted by those only interested in power for themselves. For me, the best solution to the Israeli-Palestinian problem is not in having two separate states, like India and Pakistan, with a permanent distrust of their neighbour, but a dedication on both sides to reduce tensions and facilitate cooperation as people of one country; a beautiful and historic part of the world in which Jews, Muslims and Christians can work together for mutual prosperity.

Stand-off between India and Pakistan

At a time of increasing tension and a possible Indo-Pakistan nuclear war in the winter of 2001–2002, tensions were rising between different sub-continent communities in the UK. With some initial difficulty, I managed to persuade colleagues on the Inter Faith Network to sign a letter I had drafted addressed to the Presidents of Pakistan and India, saying that a war between the two countries would have disastrous consequences, and it was the fervent wish of faith communities that leaders of both countries look to diplomatic solutions. It is difficult to know what effect our letter had on the leaders of the two countries, but the initiative was useful in reducing tensions in the UK.

Dialogue with French Embassy over ban on turbans in state schools

In 2003, Bernard Stassi, the right-hand man of President Chirac of France, visited the UK and made a presentation to the Inner Cities Religious Advisory Council to explain the proposed banning of religious headgear in state schools in France. He explained that they felt the proposal necessary to prevent extremists from the Muslim community pressuring girls into wearing a hijab, which his government considered unnecessarily magnified religious differences between pupils. He explained that in his government's view, the hijab was a cultural and not a religious requirement.

I explained that the Sikh turban, which was very much a religious requirement, would be caught in the blanket banning of religious headgear. He was visibly moved when I spoke of how Guru Teg Bahadhur gave his life defending the right of Hindus, those of a different faith to his own, to freedom of worship against Mughal attempts at forced conversion. I quoted Voltaire and explained the need to stand to and be counted as inherent in the religious requirement of Sikhs to wear the symbols of their faith.

Then came a surprising admission from Bernard Stassi, "We did not consider Sikhs when we proposed the ban." He gave me his card and invited me to a dinner in the French Embassy where he promised to review the blanket ban after a short while.

Sadly, a fellow Sikh met with French officials and said they could not ban the turban because it was a cultural symbol and not a religious one. This made it easy for the French officials who argued that culture changes with time and that there was therefore no need to provide a religious exemption for Sikhs.

Celebrating the New Millennium

The Lambeth Group

It was once said that *The Times* were left speechless about some legislation or other and took two columns to express their 'speechlessness'. I felt the same when I heard it was proposed to celebrate the millennium by constructing a giant Ferris wheel near Parliament. I expressed my disbelief in a 'Thought for the Day'.

'Thought for the Day', 30 October 1996

*The proposed giant Ferris wheel, to be sited opposite the House of Commons to celebrate the millennium, has had **my** head in a bit of a spin ever since I first heard the idea.*

*My first reaction was what on earth has a Ferris wheel got to do with the celebration of the millennium? But the more I think of it, the more convinced I become that nothing could better encapsulate the values and spirit of our times. Forget the fact that it will be an architectural eyesore. At 500ft, it will be the **biggest** such structure in the world; it will provide **instant** thrills and above all, in the words of the chairman of Lambeth's Planning Committee, it will get tourists and business into the area. What more could we ask?*

And, why stop there, why not turn the House of Commons into a gigantic funfair and make the Lords a plush gambling casino? The money should come rolling in!

*But what has all this to do with the millennium, the 2,000th anniversary of the birth of Jesus Christ, who, in common with Guru Nanak and other leaders of religion, taught many of the values that we have **so** arrogantly ditched and are now scrambling to rediscover through conferences, seminars and party-political rhetoric?*

As a Sikh, I'd be happy if the main focus of millennium celebrations was on the life and teachings of Jesus Christ. Teachings that have powerful echoes in all our different faiths. The Sikh Gurus constantly emphasised this essential unity of religion and the commonality of core values essential for sane, balanced and responsible living in any age.

My talk evoked an appreciative response from many, including Prince Charles, Christian bishops and leaders of other faiths. I was invited to a small meeting at Lambeth Palace to discuss a more appropriate way of celebrating the new millennium. We met on several subsequent occasions and became known as the Lambeth Group. One of the outcomes of the meetings was the construction of the faith zone in the proposed Millennium Dome at Greenwich.

Values for the new millennium

In our discussions, the Lambeth Group reflected on the fact that in the century we were leaving behind, more people had been killed in war and conflict than the total in previous recorded history. I was asked to be a part of a small team to highlight values necessary for a more peaceful twenty-first century. We came up with the following brief statement:

Statement on Values by the Millennium Consultation Group

There is a contemporary saying: "Why not? It doesn't do anyone any harm." The harm is not always apparent, and we believe that the following ethical values are necessary for peace and social justice in the twenty-first century:

- *showing concern for others*
- *putting our responsibilities before our rights*
- *considering the implications of our actions for future generations*
- *putting principles before expediency or mere pragmatism*
- *celebrating diversity*
- *encouraging mutual respect and taking a positive view of tolerance*

Fast forward a few years, another meeting in Lambeth Palace addressed by a charismatic preacher from the States. The gist of his talk, in the very same room as the Lambeth Group meeting that led to the formulation of the above values, was that what the world needed was a list of values! We have admirable values in the UN Declaration of Human Rights; we have no end of lists of values, but simply making lists is not enough. I discussed my own embarrassment in making lists in a 'Thought for the Day':

My long-suffering family have constantly had to listen to me saying that they make too much fuss of packing to go on holiday. "Simply make a list of the things you want to take and throw them into a suitcase, it's easy," I'd boast. Recently, I got my comeuppance.

We'd decided to go on a short break to Cheddar Gorge. As usual, I'd left my packing to the last minute. But I had my list, and soon I had put my things in a case and off we went.

When we got to the hotel, we started unloading the car, and then embarrassment! I'd left my suitcase at home to the intense amusement of the family. And I've never been allowed to forget it since.

I remembered this incident as I packed my case last weekend for a two-day conference on 'Values for the twenty-first century'. I double checked, and this time did remember to take my case with me. But the idea of lists followed me with a vengeance. For two days, representatives of all walks of life worked together to produce list upon list of core values considered desirable for life in the twenty-first century. Eventually, these were narrowed down to a summary list. Looking at it, a colleague from industry said with some frustration that our core values were beginning to look more and more like those common to religious teachings! And they were. Values that we've arrogantly discarded in our obsession with self, personal rights and synthetic supermarket-shelf type happiness.

It's important in our quest for more responsible living that we learn from the failings of organised religion, where those in religious authority rarely lived the values of truth, humility and concern for others taught by religion. For many, religion became a list of good intentions wrapped in dogma, to be recited or chanted to make us certain candidates for paradise.

Guru Nanak, concerned by this subversion of religious teaching, constantly stressed in parables and a memorable verse:

96

Words do not a saint or sinner make
It is deeds alone that are recorded in the book of fate.
My list of things to take on holiday was defective in that it should have had
an additional item: take case and contents with you. In much the same way, a list
of core values is of little use unless we carry these with us into our daily lives.

During our conference, I came across an American expression then new to
me: 'walking the talk', turning words into action. Core values to underpin life in
our rapidly changing times are clearly desirable, but they need a commitment to
'walk the talk'.

Service of celebration and commemoration of the new millennium

My suggestion for a National Service to mark the start of the new millennium
was taken up by the Inter Faith Network UK and supported by the churches and
faith communities. I was asked to plan and compere a National Service in the
Queen's Gallery of the House of Lords.

The service was attended by royalty, the Speaker of the House of Commons,
the Prime Minister and Cherie Blair, and leading religious and civic figures. The
service was broadcast in full on BBC 2. Former Prime Minister Tony Blair
declared it "the most positive and moving celebration of the millennium" that he
had witnessed.

Representing Britain Abroad

In 2005, I was invited to Rome by the British Ambassador, Sir Ivor Roberts,
to give the first of a series of lectures on religious tolerance. I have also had the
good fortune to represent the UK at conferences in the USA, Canada, at
Pontignano in Italy, Graz in Austria, Berlin and Krakow in Poland. In Krakow I
visited the nearby concentration camp at Auschwitz, where I learned about how
innocent children were gassed after being locked in supposed showers. My
distinctive Sikh appearance both inside and outside the conference halls led to
much discussion and enduring friendships and an understanding of the
commonalities shared by people of different nationalities and cultures all over
the world. In 2008, I became the first Sikh to address a major conference at the
Vatican, where I spoke on the urgent need for respect and tolerance between
world faiths to a highly receptive audience.

While involvement in trying to make a small contribution to greater
understanding between people can be demanding and at times disheartening, it
can also be pleasantly rewarding. In September 2006, I was moved to find myself
included in *The Independent* 'Good List' of fifty people who have made a major
contribution to world peace. I have also had the honour of meeting the Pope and
the Dalai Lama.

A reception organised by the Inter Faith Network.
Presenting the Dalai Lama with a token of appreciation for his visit

Pope Benedict XVI's visit to the UK, September 2010

The House of Lords

In September 2011, I was given the honour of a peerage, becoming the first turban-wearing Sikh in Parliament. In the interview following my application, I was told, "Do you know that if appointed, you'll be the first turban-wearing Sikh?" Without thinking, I immediately responded that I did not want to be appointed as a 'token Sikh'. Fortunately, the selection committee took my outburst in the right spirit and after a summer of waiting for the result of the interview, I received a telephone call that the appointment committee had 'unanimously and enthusiastically' recommended my appointment as Baron Singh of Wimbledon.

I have tried to use my appointment as a platform to continue my work with people of all beliefs to increase tolerance, understanding and work for a greater social and political justice in society. Much the same response was given to a Sikh group who asked if I would use my position to advance the interests of Sikhs. I replied that as a Sikh, I would look to the concerns of others as well as Sikhs.

For my introduction ceremony to Parliament's upper chamber, my two 'supporters' were the prominent human rights lawyer, Baroness Helena Kennedy of the Shaws, and Lord Carey of Clifton, the former Archbishop of Canterbury.

Entering for oath

Lord Singh of Wimbledon; the first turbaned Sikh in Parliament

Lord Singh of Wimbledon; the first turbaned Sikh in Parliament

In my maiden speech on 1 December 2011, I reflected on my background and what I hoped to bring to the House of Lords. I spoke of the way in which we form groups based on nationality, religion or even occupation and then project **our** group as being superior by belittling others, making a light-hearted reference to my time in civil engineering consultancy where our absurd attitudes to those we saw as different were all too evident in the behaviour of those in a lift to those trying to get in on different floors, as recounted in my first ever 'Thought for the Day', referred to earlier.

I took the opportunity to stress the relevance of Guru Nanak's teachings to the modern day, and how his unflinching promotion of tolerance and equality for all in the fifteenth century are values that we aspire to adhere to today in our twenty-first century. I said this theme was something central to my own life, from my campaigning against apartheid in South Africa, when it was unfashionable to do so, through to my support for dissidents in the former Soviet Union, and in working for Amnesty International and others for greater social and political justice for all. I also took the opportunity to state my belief that the United Kingdom was light years ahead in its freedoms, and its understanding and respect for other religions and cultures in the UK. There was wide media interest in my appointment, both in the UK and abroad. Various aspects of my life and achievements were highlighted, as well as the work of my colleagues in the Network of Sikh Organisations(NSO), which I founded in 1995. However, to this day, as mentioned earlier, the compliment I value the most was being introduced by the British Ambassador as, 'the man who brought Guru Nanak to the breakfast tables of Britain'.

I've often reflected on the uplifting guidance of Sikh teachings in my 'Thought for the Day' broadcasts, particularly how today's unhealthy obsession with self, rather than the wider needs of society, is creating division and fragmentation. On my appointment in the House of Lords, I said that as Sikhs we see a wider society, where the focus is away from 'me' and 'my', to the wellbeing of all or 'sarbat da bhalla'. I see my appointment to the Upper House in the Lords as an opportunity to work with like-minded people to reverse what I see as a selfish societal trend.

On 16 January 2012, I participated in my first debate in which Baroness Greengross asked the government, "What measures are in place to inform people of the steps they need to take to ensure their wishes regarding medical treatment at the end of life are respected if they lose capacity?" It was the first of many debates in which I found myself stressing the need for society to make greater efforts to assist the elderly and frail. I said:

My Lords, in considering better enhanced provision for end-of-life care for those who have lost capacity, will the minister note that our opinions and attitudes change with the perspective of time? A young boy may consider that after reaching the age of sixty or seventy, life would not be worth living. I think that a sixty-year-old would differ from that opinion. It is important that advance directives – living wills – should be drawn up with care and regularly reviewed.

My contributions have ranged over a number of subjects, such as the government's 'Action Against Hate Strategy', raising issues of human rights abuses overseas, gay marriage, and highlighting the unhelpful terminology used in government circles when tackling terrorism. One of the debates which stands out in my mind was during the proposed visit by the Egyptian president al-Sisi in 2015. Baroness Kennedy asked the government if it was appropriate for him to visit the UK, given Egypt's terrible human rights record and the state of rule of law there. Supporting Baroness Kennedy, I said:

My Lords, we have recently lavished hospitality on the President of China, where, as we heard in the answers to an earlier question, there are gross abuses of human rights and the ruling clique presumes to tell people how many children they can have. We will shortly be lavishing similar hospitality on Narendra Modi, who, until recently, was excluded from this country and the United States for possible genocide against the Muslim community in India. We are rushing around trying to sell arms to Saudi Arabia, which is one of the most barbarous regimes in the Middle East. Would it not be discriminatory even to think of excluding President Al-Sisi from these human rights abusers?

My comments in support of Helena Kennedy raised loud laughter and approving "hear, hears" from across the Chamber.

The year before, my good friend Lord Alton moved a motion, 'To take note on the Universal Declaration on Human Rights'. We are both office holders in the All Party Parliamentary Group on International Freedom of Religion and Belief. Lord Alton said, "Not only is Article 18 a universal human right; it is a human right that is violated universally." I couldn't have agreed more, and made a further observation, which many are reluctant to discuss, and that is, religions themselves do not help human rights with claims of exclusivity and superiority. This can often be reflected upon with the use of words such as 'heathen', 'gentile' or 'infidel'. During the debate, I elaborated:

Such language simply demeans other members of our one human race and suggests that others are lesser beings. We all know what happens in the school playground when one boy boasts – it is usually boys – that, "My dad is bigger or stronger or cleverer than your dad." The result is fisticuffs. My appeal to our different religions and the leaders of religion is to stop playing children's games. Guru Nanak witnessed the suffering caused by this children's game of "my religion is better than yours", in conflict between Hindus and Muslims in the sub-continent in the fifteenth century. In his very first sermon, he declared that the one God of us all is not in the least bit interested in our different religious labels, but in our contribution to a fairer and more peaceful world.

As with many of my contributions both in the Lords and as a 'Thought for the Day' contributor, I invariably find myself going back to the ethical teachings of Guru Nanak.

I've often spoken out against human rights violations across the world. The behaviour of the rulers of Saudi Arabia has been a particular concern, and I have spoken on a number of debates on this subject. It concerns me that we constantly refer to Saudi Arabia as our ally in the Middle East, while ignoring their terrible human rights record. During a debate in 2016 on the execution of political dissidents in Saudi Arabia, I took the minister to task by saying, "I cannot understand why we make only private representations to Saudi Arabia. Is not public condemnation much more effective?" The somewhat unhelpful response from the minister was that this would be "counterproductive" and that Britain should make best use of its diplomatic voice in private. Of course, one of the concerns closest to my heart is seeking justice for the victims of the Sikh genocide in 1984 mentioned in earlier chapters. I've been working for justice for the survivors and the victims' families since that time and was one of the few voices in Britain challenging the then Indira Gandhi government for the persecution of Sikhs by writing columns in the UK broadsheets. I was blacklisted for years from travelling to India and the subject of a complaint to the BBC.

A new development involving Britain's diplomatic ties with India during 1984, which arose from the release of government documentation in 2014 under the 'thirty-year rule', provided me with an opportunity to seek UK government support for an international inquiry into the killings.

The then acting Foreign Secretary at the time, William Hague, smugly dismissed the UK's involvement in 1984 as "minimal". The Minister in the Lords, Baroness Warsi, totally ignored compelling evidence of what constituted genocide again India's Sikhs, saying that the British government could not intervene. She later resigned her government post in protest against the reluctance of the British government to condemn the treatment of fellow Muslims in Palestine.

In 2012 I gave a Sikh perspective on the same-sex marriage debate; the coalition government at the time was pushing for such legislation and there was opposition amongst the Church and Jewish leaders. I made it clear that Sikhs respect the right for homosexual couples to have a civil partnership, but marriage was in effect being redefined with the proposed legislation. In an interview with the *Sunday Telegraph* I said, "The plans would 'dilute' the meaning of marriage in religious scriptures," and went on, "it's being changed for no real gain because the law rightly gives every respect to a civil partnership. It is more of a sideways assault on religion, that 'we can dilute your beliefs and values', and I find that concerning." Sikhs would of course extend a welcome to same-sex couples wishing to have a blessing in a gurdwara, but the Anand Karaj ceremony would remain the spiritual union of heterosexual couples. It was a view understood but not supported by the House.

In July 2016, I challenged the government's use of vague terms in tackling terrorism. Over the years I realised that the government's prevent agenda wasn't really that clear on what it was in fact trying to prevent. I asked the government minister, Lord Ahmed of Wimbledon, what assessment had been made on whether action against terrorism could be helped by clearer language, in explaining what they meant by words such as 'extremism', 'radicalisation' or 'fundamentalism'. I said, "Does the minister agree that what we are really trying to prevent is the out-of-context use of religious texts that advocate the killing or ill-treatment of people of other faiths? Furthermore, does the minister agree that to suggest that such behaviour is sanctioned by the one God of us all is the ultimate blasphemy? Finally, will the government help Muslim leaders to present Islam in the context of today's society?"

One of the surprising responses to my intervention in this debate didn't come from the minister on this occasion, but from Lord Tebbit. It is one of the moments I remember fondly, so much so that I subsequently included a quote from this response on the front cover of an edition of the *Sikh Messenger* in the same year. The former chairman of the Conservative Party said, "My Lords, nobody in this House is better equipped than the noble Lord to get people to understand that the present version of the Muslim religion arises largely from a dispute within that religion and that it is a gross perversion of the Muslim religion practised in the thirteenth and fourteenth centuries, for example."

He went on: "We should all remember that there are very few places where one can feel safer in the face of extremism in this country than in the company of a large number of Sikhs, who have always shown by their great loyalty and understanding of this society that they have their place here."

I've consistently fought for equality for all faiths and none more so, when it comes to public policy, than the government's biased hate crime policy called *Action Against Hate*, published in July 2016. Remarkably the government's four-year plan made no provision whatsoever for non-Abrahamic faiths. The focus was largely on Jews and Muslims. I raised my concerns about the flawed approach with ministers in both debates and correspondence.

The Network of Sikh Organisations(NSO) also gave a written submission to the Home Affairs Select Committee on hate crime and its violent consequences. Our concerns were the subject of significant media interest. The NSO examined 'Islamophobic hate crime' figures from the MET police for 2015. These showed that 28% of victims in this category were in fact against non-Muslims. In September 2016, I tabled a question to ask the government why their report, *Action Against Hate*, ignored the incidents of hate crimes against non-Abrahamic faith communities.

The minister evaded the concern raised, and I responded:

I thank the minister for her response but it does not address my concerns over the narrow and biased thinking in a report that details forty-five examples of hate crime against Abrahamic faiths but not a single example of the many, well-documented mistaken-identity hate crimes suffered by Sikhs and others – and this in a report emanating from a department with specifically designated officers to consider hate crime against the Jewish and Muslim communities but not anyone else. Would the minister agree that that omission is more due to ignorance than deliberate discrimination? Would she further agree that those who preach the need for religious literacy should first themselves acquire some basic religious literacy, and apologise to those they have offended in such a way?

The Minister, Baroness Williams of Trafford, responded accepting the need for more engagement with non-Abrahamic faith communities, but appeared to suggest it was the media who needed to improve on religious literacy rather than the government and society in general. We later met to discuss some of my concerns.

Closing Reflections on 'Desert Island Discs'

Edited interview with Kirsty Young on BBC Radio 4, 8 November 2015

KY: My guest today is Lord Singh of Wimbledon, creator of the *Sikh Messenger*, co-founder of the Inter Faith Network, first turban-wearing Sikh in Parliament. Family arrived in 1933, Asian community in Birmingham less than 1,000; dad found it hard to get work as a doctor. Twenty-five years later he found it hard to get a job with a first-class degree in engineering.

Once, when interviewed on the subject: 'What God thinks of us', you famously replied: "If God had human emotions, I believe the dominant one would be total exasperation at the antics of our human tribe coupled with a renewed determination to keep us light years away from truly intelligent life in the infinity of His Creation."

Indarjit, in doing 'Thought for the Day', are you representing Sikhs or a wider spiritual perspective?

Indarjit: I don't think there's much difference because the Sikh perspective is looking broader at commonalities between religions.

KY: What is the temperature within Asian communities now?

Indarjit: It is pretty high, there is a lot of concern about the rise of extremism, in all communities, all feel that they are being targeted.

KY: How much do you feel you have the right to speak for a community?

Indarjit: Sikhs are all chiefs! Sikhs all consider themselves leaders. This results in people sometimes coming up to me and saying, "You're our leader, now this is what you have to do!" There is a huge responsibility, particularly in the Lords, to articulate a Sikh view, a Sikh perspective, on a whole range of subjects, under close scrutiny from a Sikh community in the UK, India and the wider world.

KY: Your first record?

Indarjit: After all the misery of the war years and a rotten summer in 1946, we suddenly had a glorious summer in 1947. My brother had recovered from pneumonia, my mother had been ill and was better, everything was sunny and wonderful, and we did nothing but play cricket in the park – actually on the golf course, to the annoyance of the golfers, all day long. It was a wonderful world, and this song shows the spirit and optimism of the times, not only in the Singh family, but also in the wider community.
Song: Oh What a Beautiful Mornin', from Oklahoma!

KY: Tell me a bit about your father ...

Indarjit: He was a strong supporter of the freedom movement in India, and he'd just qualified as a doctor in Amritsar in India when there was an agitation to free the gurdwaras, the Sikh temples, from domination by people who were not Sikhs. The Sikhs would go up to these places in a non-violent way, stand there to protest, they would be violently beaten, and it was my father's job to bandage them up. He wasn't caught up physically, but he incurred the wrath of the government. Friends, concerned for his future, persuaded him to move to East Africa. He followed their advice but even there he continued to speak up for Indian independence. He was called by the British authorities who said in friendly terms, "What do we do with you?" He said, "Well, I could do with British qualifications, let me go to England." And that's how we ended up here.

I think my parents were pretty realistic, and knew it wouldn't be easy, but I think it was a little tougher than they thought. He couldn't get a job in a hospital, he never got an interview, and there was no chance, and he realised it. So, he had this bright idea of just setting up in his rented house and putting a board outside saying 'doctor', and waiting for the first patient, who took some time in coming. At one time, it got so difficult that my mother pawned her jewellery to make ends meet.

The first patients were local people, but the word got round quickly that he was a pretty good doctor, and very good and considerate with children.

KT: Your second choice?

Indarjit: My brothers were all pretty mad on cricket. I used to remember the years by which touring team came, for example, 1948 Australia. When the West Indies toured in 1950, their tour was a bit of a shock to the cricketing system, because it was all England and Australia, and suddenly you got this West Indian team with the three Ws: Weekes, Worrall and Walcott, and two wonderful spin bowlers, Ramadin and Valentine. The tour boosted the popularity of the game, particularly in the West Indies, and it showed a resurgence of cricket itself, and a resurgence of cricket in the West Indies shown in the calypso.

Song: Victory Test Match (Cricket, Lovely Cricket)

KY: Did you have to get good at boxing?

Indarjit: I think that's the way it came about. There was a lot of teasing and bullying, and one day I found that I had a very strong left hand. The bullying certainly stopped after that.

KY: In the 1980s you were involved in a test case, the Mandla case, about wearing a turban. When you were at school, did you wear a turban?

Indarjit: My brothers and I did wear turbans at school and, although there was some teasing by children, there was a great deal of respect for Sikhs and the turban, because of the links with the British Army. The discrimination came really in the 1950s and 1960s.

KY: The test case was more than a curiosity?

Indarjit: It was a great victory, because there had been discrimination in all sorts of areas before – a Sikh graduate could not get a job on a bus if he was wearing a turban, it was that bad, everywhere. I was in the witness box for a day and a half giving evidence about the religion, and it was a victory that had repercussions throughout Sikh society.

KY: Is it a surprise that this is still a hot topic, religious people wearing their signs/clothes? Many other European nations decide to keep religion out of schools and the work place, because that is much better.

Indarjit: That's an argument that I cannot agree with at all, because what's the effect of that in France, or in the US? People pretend to be one thing at school, and then show their prejudices outside. There is total ignorance about different religions in France, and even more so in the US.

KY: Tell us about this next song.

Indarjit: This is an American mining song, 'Sixteen Tonnes'. I thought that my father practising as a doctor from his own house was all a bit boring, and I wanted to do something much more exciting. At that time the mining industry, which had been run down during the war, was now being revived. There were a lot of adverts, 'mining is the career for you', 'it's a man's job'. Foolishly, I succumbed to the hype and went down my first mine – it was hard, but being stubborn I thought, 'I'm going to carry on with this,' and so that became my career.

Song: Sixteen Tons

KY: Expectation to become a doctor?

Indarjit: I think that was the expectation, but I think my parents were very liberal in their views, very forward thinking. Many parents would correct someone who is left-handed and say they have to use their right, but they didn't. Whatever it was, they were convinced I would make something of myself, probably more convinced than I was!

KY: You went to study engineering. How much did you socialise?

Indarjit: I was living at home, but had friends from different communities.

KY: No drinking, no smoking, etc. Did you experiment?

Indarjit: No. Not having alcohol seemed good common sense to me. It wasn't drummed into us, in any way, religion was never drummed into us. In fact, I used to be in charge of the budget when fellow mining students would go drinking, because they wouldn't trust anyone else!

KY: Graduate with a first-class degree in engineering. At that point you might feel the whole world is ahead of you. 1959, you apply to NCB as a mine manager.

Indarjit: Yes, I wanted to be a mine manager, and I had this first-class mine manager certificate, it had been a tough course, going sometimes into the most difficult areas of the mine – I think they used to try to test me a bit – and after all of that I got the qualification, and then was called for an interview by the Coal Board. They told me to my face that the miners wouldn't like a Sikh mine manager, what about the scientific department? Surprisingly, I didn't feel devastated; open discrimination was then the norm and you get used to these ups and downs and challenges. At that time I was also thinking of having a look at India, the country of my birth. There was a mining industry there as well, which was supposed to be good and well paid, and I thought I could give that a try, so said no to the scientific job and went off to India.

KY: Your next song?

Indarjit: This is 'On the Street Were You Live' from *My Fair Lady*, a very romantic song, and we hadn't been married that long when we first heard it. My wife loved it, I loved it, and we went on using that song in the family when we went on holiday, singing it in the car.
Song: On the Street Where You Live

KY: Been married for fifty-three years, how did you meet?

Indarjit: I was on a visit from the mining area to my parents' home in Delhi, and my wife came along with her parents, and they were talking about something totally different, and then they mentioned about the girl wanting to get married, and I was on a balcony above, peering at the girl, and felt that she was very pretty. She had been talking to my parents in a very free open manner about the political situation in India. I thought she had some spirit.

KY: Were they hoping you would be a good match – this non-engineered engineered meeting?

Indarjit: That puts it perfectly. We got on well.

KY: Returned to UK with your wife. Might seem surprising given the hostility in the UK to you being a manager. Why did you decide to come back?

Indarjit: My wife had given birth to our first child, my daughter, and we realised that the isolated wilderness of mining was no place to bring anyone up, so we thought 'let's go back to England', where we had gone after our marriage and enjoyed a honeymoon there, so my wife was quite keen too.

KY: Bringing up two daughters in 1960s Britain. Did you have a sense, both you and your wife, that you were bringing them into a more enlightened Britain than the one you had experienced?

Indarjit: They found it certainly more enlightening – they didn't experience the difficulties we found at school. There was still some prejudice, but they had some lovely friends, whom they would invite home – whereas we rarely invited anyone, because it was a different world.

KY: The Race Relations Act in mid 1960s, effective and robust in 1970s. From your perspective, which is better: attitudes making us change laws, or laws first to change attitudes?

Indarjit: I think both are necessary. Attitudes have changed a lot in this country, and laws tend to keep up with these. But there are some laws which should be passed anyway. Anything that promotes the equality of people.

KY: Were you ambitious for your daughters?

Indarjit: I wanted them to be doctors. And so, knowing how people like me rebel against what their parents want, I used to tell them they should be mining engineers or go into engineering of some sort, they said forget it, we're going to be doctors … and it worked!

KT: Your next song?

Indarjit: This is the 'Awal Allah Noor Upaya', a verse taken from the *Guru Granth Sahib*, our holy scripture. The verse was written by a Muslim and is incorporated into the *Guru Granth Sahib* to emphasise the Sikh teaching that no one religion has a monopoly of truth, so our holy book includes writings of Hindu and Muslim saints, as well as the Sikh Gurus. It was written by a potter by trade, and he says in this song that the one divine potter created all humanity into vessels of different shapes. How can you say one is better than the other, when all are created by the one divine potter?
Song: Awal Allah Noor Upaya

KY: Been a contributor to 'Thought for the Day' for thirty-five-odd years. It includes people of all faiths … what about people of no faith?

Indarjit: I personally wouldn't mind, but it's difficult, because an agnostic could talk about anything, and it's an ethical programme. Even with humanists, I have some very good humanist friends, but I can never get out of them exactly what humanism is – they have referred me to different books, which I have looked at, but they all criticise religions without suggesting something better.

KY: People without religion have ethics too … Religion doesn't have the monopoly on ethics.

Indarjit: Yes. You don't have to be religious to be a good person and to have standards. But the point about religion is that it is a sat nav that gives you directions and reminds you to come back to those directions if you go astray. I have a very flexible conscience, and I can talk to it and persuade it to see things my way, and it often does, but it's not always the right way.

KY: Your next song?

Indarjit: This is 'Walk Tall' by Val Doonican. On a Saturday evening the family would always watch *The Val Doonican Show* on TV. He would always be relaxed with his colourful jumpers, and the song itself, walking tall, walking straight, looking the world in the eyes, is the only way to go – never look down on people, never get over-awed by people.
Song: Walk Tall

KY: You were the first Sikh to be appointed to the House of Lords, in 2011. At the time that you were told of the appointments, did you yourself have worries about tokenism?

Indarjit: I did at the actual interview, they said, "Do you realise that if we appoint you, you will be the first turbaned Sikh?" I said, "If you want a token Sikh, don't do it, because I want to be there on merit."

KY: How did they reassure you of that?

Indarjit: They seemed OK with what I said, but there was total silence for three months.

KY: In a recent debate on Islamaphobia, you said that ever since 9/11 there has been a huge increase in attacks on Sikhs and Sikh places of worship, in cases of mistaken identity. What has been done to confront that problem?

Indarjit: Nothing by the authorities at all. Hate crime is deplorable, and we should not just look at one community, whether it is large or small, it still remains hate crime and should be tackled.

KY: Is there any evidence that Sikhs in Britain are beginning to feel more self-conscious about obvious displays of faith, about wearing turbans?

Indarjit: I think that is right, right through society. At one time in this country, even Muslim people would not wear the hijab. Young Sikhs have now

111

taken sometimes to wearing bigger turbans to assert themselves, but it's not a good thing, it's juvenile. Even some Sikh women have taken to wearing turbans. The symbols are important as a mark of identity, but the religion and the teachings go much beyond that, and I would like to see more attention being paid by Sikhs to make their teaching known to others, because they are a healing balm to society.

KY: The House of Lords is over-stuffed … how do you find that?

Indarjit: You literally have to pray to get a seat, because they start with prayers. People who are quite antagonistic to religion still come in for prayers – it's the only way to get a seat!

KY: Your next song?

Indarjit: This is 'Big Yellow Taxi' by Joni Mitchell – I first heard it through my daughters, and it became a family favourite. It reminds us that there are many things around us that we should value, and, all too often, we tend to value them only after they have disappeared – people, things, ways of life – and we should look at and cherish what we have.

Song: Big Yellow Taxi

KY: You are a father to two daughters and a grandfather to five. What is their connection to their heritage and their connection with their Britishness?

Indarjit: I think they see themselves as British, but with the Sikh religion.

KY: Is it important that the religion is central to life, or is it natural that it will become diluted?

Indarjit: So far it is not diluted, but I think there is always that danger or possibility that it may. I would like them to understand and keep to the ethics of Sikhism – the other things are not as important as the ethics. If they want to change, they should have a good reason for changing, as you shouldn't lose something (as we have just heard in the song) that you might later cherish.

KY: So many people will know your voice and beliefs from 'Thought for the Day'. In your own family, are you known as someone who has wisdom, the person people will come to?

Indarjit: No, because that's why I went out to speak! When we go out shopping for clothes, they do value my advice. When they've narrowed it down to a choice between two dresses, they come to me. I point to one, they smile at each other and take the other one! Seriously though, we all get on pretty well together, and my grandchildren constantly put me right.

KY: Not considered the font of all wisdom within your family?

Indarjit: No far from it.

KY: Still working in your eighties. Your wife works part-time too. Any plans to retire?

Indarjit: I thought I was going to retire when I was appointed to the House of Lords! I thought it might be a sort of retirement home. But I keep being given jobs and things to do, it's not retiring – it is interesting and worth doing. I'll retire when I fall to bits.

KY: Quite a practical man, background in engineering. How will you cope on this island?

Indarjit: I have often been in some near-impossible situations in my life, and don't know how I got out of them. I have no doubt I will survive, or in my way, muddle through and find perhaps a way of escaping the island or making something of it.

KY: What's your final song?

Indarjit: 'Island in the Sun' by Harry Belafonte in the film of the same name is a song that resonates with me, because it is not only a song in which he speaks of his love for his island, but the film and the song come from a story where a white politician is defeated and a black one comes in – a changing order of things, with West Indians finding that they are masters of their own destiny for the first time, a new experience for them, which also has implications for the demise of the worst aspects of colonialism.

Song: Island in the Sun

KY: Books – Shakespeare and the Sikh holy book. What other book?

Indarjit: The *Bible*.

KY: Luxury?

Indarjit: I spend hours and hours writing and get infuriated when I see cartoonists with a few flicks of the pen saying something much better than I say it. I'm really envious of cartoonists. The problem is I can't draw. I would like to be able to draw and show my skills as a cartoonist. So, I would like the paper

113

and pens to help me get the skills to do this. Eventually, if I get back to civilisation, I can lobby for 'Cartoon of the Day', alongside 'Thought for the Day'.

KY: Which of your discs means most to you?

Indarjit: I would choose the one which stresses the equality of all human beings, because we are so far from accepting the reality. We say yes, we believe in equality, as long as giving others equality doesn't affect me; we need to go much wider to the automatic acceptance of equality between people; respect between religions; no one should say mine is the only way. That one Sikh hymn which was sung says it all, *Awal Allah Noor Upaya.*

Translation

God created the one Light from which all Creation sprang. If we are all from the same one Divine Light,
How can we call some high and some low?
The Creation is in the Creator, and the Creator is in the Creation The Clay is the same, designed by the One Divine potter
The One True Lord Abides in All.

PART TWO:
Thoughts and Talks

Some 'Thoughts for The Day' From the BBC The Today Programme

Thinking for Ourselves

When I was a little boy, the greatest delight of my life was the weekly comic. I'd readily identify with an athlete called Wilson – reputedly hundreds of years old – who could run a mile in three minutes! There were other heroes too, particularly detectives.

The important thing about these comics was that it was easy to recognise both hero and villain. The anarchist trying to blow up the world carried a round black object conveniently labelled 'bomb'. The burglar inevitably wore a black-and-white striped jersey and carried a bag marked 'swag'. Heroes would chuckle; villains sneered.

The more I look at newspapers today, the more I am reminded of those comics. Word pictures, like 'Iron Lady' or 'Mad Dog of the Middle East', are used to convey images designed to channel our thoughts and mould our attitudes and, worst of all, destroy our capacity for independent moral judgment.

It is a situation made worse by a reluctance to listen to true religious guidance. For it is religion that gives, or should give, moral guidance and perspective to society – as well as to individuals.

The events of the past week have underlined for many of us that not only are we now living in a complex and violent world, but also, in a dangerous moral vacuum.

The situation is very similar to that found by Guru Nanak in India 500 years ago. Hindus and Muslims were then locked in violent conflict, with each claiming to be the one true faith. Guru Nanak courageously urged that they look beyond labels. Different religions, he taught, were merely different paths to the same goal, and no one religion had a monopoly of truth.

But, though the problems of conflicting ideologies are similar, the implications of the moral vacuum we find today are far more hazardous. I know it jars a little to talk about cricket after the recent battering in the West Indies, but I can best explain myself with a cricketing analogy.

The pitch – human society – is basically the same. The batsmen and the bowlers – those in positions of power, and those who oppose them are basically the same in their competence – or lack of it. But today, the pace of scientific change has, like overnight rain on an uncovered cricket pitch, made conflict–today's society is virtually unplayable. The slightest error of judgment can lead to world disaster. It is then all the more important that we look carefully beyond the catchy headlines and the attitude-begging word pictures to the reality of the world today especially to the social and political injustice on which violence so easily thrives.

Manifestos

With all the media discussion and the publication later this morning of the remaining manifestos, I'm sure you'll all agree the election campaign is well and truly on. Each manifesto offers its own mix of enticements – jobs, homes and consumer goods. References to freedom, justice and equality are also thrown in, like decorations on a political cake, and the choice before us is to decide which cake seems the most promising.

At the time of Guru Nanak, religions too, forgetting the teachings of their founders, also behaved like rival political parties, each with its own manifesto, a total contempt for the manifestos of others, and a politician-like faith that salvation was just around the corner. The only difference was that the rewards promised were not of this world but the next – with the slogan, now inverted, of pay now have later.

Religious leaders taught that those who gave them food and money were, in effect, giving it to their ancestors in heaven. And, unbelievably, they got away with it. The Guru found that religion had been reduced to pilgrimages, penances and rituals – all aimed at collecting bonus points for the next world, to the utter neglect of present responsibilities. No wonder people turned away from religion, or what passed for religion, to the pursuit of the equally false mirage of happiness through material possessions.

Somewhere along the road, we seem to have missed out on the possibility of finding true contentment in a balance between the material and the spiritual. Perhaps, we can find this if we go back to the actual teachings of the great religious leaders rather than the campaigning zeal of their followers. Jesus Christ, for example, taught that man shall not live by bread alone. He taught the importance of that material, but emphasised there was more, much more to life than mere material existence. Similarly, Guru Nanak taught three dimensions of life: prayer – the spiritual dimension, earning by own effort – the material dimension, and sharing our good fortune with others – social responsibility.

Perhaps, their manifestos, blurred by time and discarded by many, contain something still of relevance to society today.

Guru Arjan's Martyrdom:
Looking Beyond Personal Grief to the Needs of Others

In the first week of June, nearly 400 years ago, Guru Arjan Dev, the fifth Guru of the Sikhs and founder of the famous Golden Temple at Amritsar, was cruelly tortured to death in the searing heat of an Indian June. His crime, grave in the India of his day, was that he taught tolerance and respect in a climate of religious intolerance, and that no one religion had a monopoly of truth. For this he was cruelly tortured to death in the searing heat of an Indian summer, and his followers persecuted.

In keeping with the Guru's teachings, Sikhs mark the anniversary of his suffering, not by any demonstration of bitterness, but simply by setting up roadside stalls wherever practisable to serve cool refreshing drinks to passers-by. Sikhs remember the thirst and suffering of Guru Arjan Dev by looking to the thirst and suffering of others, whatever their creed.

As a Sikh brought up in Britain, I was very impressed and moved on my first visit to India by the sight of these stalls and the free distribution of chilled lime water and soft drinks. It seemed so positive.

I was therefore delighted when a few days ago, a Sikh philanthropist in this country phoned me to say that he wanted to do something similar in London and give away 20,000 soft drinks in one of London's major parks to mark the anniversary of the Guru's martyrdom.

He asked if I would help him get the necessary permission. I felt his gesture would give a positive lead to young Sikhs, whose bitterness over the Indian Army invasion of the Golden Temple and the resultant loss of many innocent lives has sometimes led to un-Sikh-like behaviour.

I readily agreed to my friend's request and contacted the Department of the Environment for permission to give away the free drinks in Hyde Park. The response was cold and negative. "Hyde Park is a Royal Park. We cannot allow such things in a Royal Park." Undaunted, I tried a non-Royal Park, Battersea Park. It seemed hopeful at first. A diary was consulted. "We have a major event on Saturday." I said that this was for Sunday. "No, we can't have two major events in the same weekend." I tried to stand my ground. "This is not an event that has to be organised; simply the giving of cool drinks to whoever happens to be passing." The voice at the other end of the phone became more suspicious and firm. "I'm sorry we cannot give permission – how do we know that others won't try to do the same thing?"

I had no answer to that. I had never contemplated the likely effect of copycat attempts to demonstrate love and concern for others. It could lead to destabilisation, perhaps to the end of society as we know it.

In memory of the martyrdom of Guru Arjan, 30 May 1606, Lahore, Pakistan. Sikhs present passers-by with cold drinks in his memory, Trafalgar Square, 2006

Fortieth Anniversary of Partition of India: The Fallacy of Irreconcilable Difference

The weekend saw the fortieth anniversary of the ending of the Raj and the transfer of power to the new governments of India, Pakistan and Sri Lanka. The British departure from India marked the end of two centuries of an extraordinary era of colourful pageantry and splendour, of genuine social reform and brazen economic exploitation.

Forty years ago, there were two views of Indian independence. One, fashionable in Britain, was that it was all a sell-out to agitators and extremists, like Nehru and Gandhi, and that Indians were incapable of ruling themselves. A second view, widely prevalent in the sub-continent, was that, now the people controlled their own destiny, all would be unity, peace and prosperity.

We have, in the ensuing years, seen the partial break-up of Pakistan and the birth of Bangladesh – with even these smaller nations experiencing tension and dissent. Severe ethnic conflict has almost torn Sri Lanka apart, and India has restless Sikh, Muslim and Gurkha minorities. The search for unity based on common identity has, as in many other areas of the globe, proved all too elusive.

Many blame religion for these divisions in our human family. And, in a sense they are right in that religions or, more accurately, people who claim allegiance to different religions all too often emphasise differences and blur our common humanity. Guru Nanak drew attention to this when he taught: *'Na koi Hindu, Na koi Mussalman'* – that in God's eyes there are neither Hindus nor Muslims – only human beings. That God is not interested in labels but in truly religious behaviour.

The difference between religion and the misuse of religion is important. One can take hold of a *Bible*, or other holy book, and hit someone hard enough on the head with it to kill them, but are the contents of that holy book in any way to blame?

Today there is an urgent need for both those who aspire to lead and those who use religious books as offensive weapons to pause, open and look at the contents of those books. They may well find pointers to that all too elusive unity between different segments of our human family.

Two Hundredth Anniversary of the Founding of the MCC

The 200th anniversary of the founding of the MCC is an appropriate time to reflect on the impact of a game that many regard almost as a religion.

The phrase, 'it's not cricket' has become a part of the English language to mean 'it's not fair or just'! 'To play a straight bat' is 'to be cautiously correct and unwavering'!

I don't know if it's this ethical dimension to cricket or what, but the game does have the rare ability to bring out the best in human beings. I remember an ogre of an arts teacher at school, who, not recognising my latent – sadly, still latent – Picasso-like genius, used to revel in sarcasm with remarks such as "Which way up?" or "What is it?" when viewing my efforts at art. But even he used to turn miraculously human on the cricket field. Cricket, he said, was his religion.

I wouldn't go quite that far, but I must admit to constantly finding similarities between cricket and the game of life. The length of our life-innings is quite unpredictable, and it is for each to make the best of it, both for ourselves and our team – our family, friends and others with whom we share common aspirations. While we come and go and make our mark, or lose our chances, as individuals, it is in the team, in sharing our life with others, that we begin to lose some of our selfishness and look beyond ourselves to others.

The idea of team, or putting others before self, is an essential aspect of Sikhism. Guru Nanak, while emphasising the need for personal improvement, stressed that this was counter-productive and negative, if pursued in isolation and selfishness – as was common among so-called holy people in the India of his day. A truly religious person, he taught, was not one who merely crossed the peril-filled ocean of life himself or herself, but one who also helped others to do so.

The Guru continually stressed the importance of '*sadh sangat*' or team effort in helping others and working for the betterment of society.

The description of something as 'my religion' is surely used to indicate a degree of commitment, a degree of commitment that ironically is so missing in the practice of religion. Today religious influence in peace-making and building a better social order is conspicuous by its absence. It's almost as if the leaders of religions, finding the modern world too complex, the wicket too difficult, have retreated from the field, when true religion is so badly needed.

If religion is to have real meaning in the world of today, it must show cricket-like commitment, return to the field of ordinary human activity and help us face what Shakespeare might have termed 'the bumpers and bouncers of everyday life'.

Travel Explodes the Myth of Difference

We learnt in this programme last week that tourism is the fastest growing industry in the world. I'm not a bit surprised. An industry with the wit and genius to make capital out of natural disasters like the Grand Canyon, civil engineering fiascos like the leaning Tower of Pisa, or monuments to man's vanity and folly, like the Pyramids of Egypt, is bound to be successful.

I fell into this tourist trap while attending a conference in the United States last year. It was a particularly gruelling timetable with endless late-night seminars and, at the end of it, totally exhausted, I found myself with some five hours to see Washington before flying home.

Guidebook in hand and camera on shoulder, I boarded the tourist bus that took us on a three-hour tour of the city. Eyes half-closed through lack of sleep, I dutifully clicked away on my camera, not realising at the time that the film wasn't properly loaded and that not one of my shots could see the light of day. Determined to get my $9 worth and report back to the family on all the wonders I had seen, I fought an almost losing battle with sleep.

The young guide had all the facts at his fingertips. The relative alignment of the White House, the Pentagon and the Washington Memorial, the number of steps on the Memorial, its floor area, in hectares, square metres, square feet, and the geometric properties of the Obelisk.

Starved of sleep, I grumpily began to ask myself what did those things matter? How important was it to know the exact number of steps to the top, or that there was a delay between commencement and completion? Then, in my half-awake state, I saw more clearly than I had ever seen before that what the guide, like all guides, was trying to do, was establish the uniqueness of the sites we were visiting, whereas the reality of foreign travel is the discovery, that despite differences in language, or culture, or false pride in shape or size of building, we are all much the same.

Restructuring and the Need to Build From the Bottom Up

Reorganisation or restructuring are very much vogue words in the Britain of today, and rightly so, for it is all too easy for those who provide goods and services to become set in their ways and insensitive to the changing patterns of demand.

Unfortunately, reorganisation frequently becomes a panic measure, a tinkering with the management structure to give the reassurance of 'under new management', while, in reality, changing little.

I'd like to illustrate this with a quote, not from some disgruntled civil servant, but from a Roman soldier called Petronius who lived in the first century AD. He wrote:

"We trained very hard, but it seemed to me that every time we began to form into teams, we were reorganised!"

Petronius continues:

"We tend to meet every new situation by reorganising – and a wonderful method it can be for creating the illusion of progress while producing inefficiency and demoralisation!"

This Roman soldier's misgivings would clearly strike a responsive chord in many who have suffered some of the reorganisations of recent years!

Guru Nanak also had problems with restructuring. The trouble, as he saw it, was that society was structured from the top down! At the top were the Brahmins, those born into the priestly class who were supposed to be in direct communion with God, and were to be fed, clothed and revered by the others! At the bottom of the pile were the lower castes who had to serve those above. Religion for the majority consisted of accepting this hierarchy of injustice as God's will!

Guru Nanak was critical of this supposedly religious society – rooted, as he saw it, in inequality, suffering and injustice. Perversely, he took the heretical view that we should build from the bottom upwards, with particular emphasis on sound foundations. To this end, he taught the oneness of the human race; the absurdity of distinctions of birth, caste or race; the equality of women; and the need for tolerance and respect for other ways of life – all, in his view, essential aspects of religion.

I think Guru Nanak's teaching – that we define and adhere to basic core values of ethics and morality in our attempt to restructure society also provides guidance in other fields. Take, for example, those engaged in the mammoth task of sorting out problems in the Health Service. They can start at the top and improve the efficiency of the management structure – or they can, like Guru Nanak, start at the bottom, and define minimum socially-acceptable standards of care and provision! In the same way, we can all use the richness of our religious teachings to guard us and guide us from the shallow and superficial to the positive and lasting!

Multi-tasking

The words 'thought for the day' are frequently used as a panic time-check, a reminder that we need to rush off to work, or bundle children out of the house for school.

To help us cope with the morning rush, we generally try to do several things at the same time, rather than one after the other – such as putting on the kettle, popping a slice of bread in the toaster and pressing a shirt while we wait.

This approach to saving time by doing as many things as possible in parallel, rather than in unnecessary sequence, is the basis of an important planning technique with the impressive sounding name of critical path analysis that's widely used in the construction industry to minimise delay.

It's years since I had anything to do with the construction industry, but I was reminded of this discipline while listening to the Home Secretary, Douglas Hurd's, remarks on *Today*, a week or so ago, in which he said, "Now we've got the economy under control, we should turn to other areas of concern."

He was referring to the increasing violence among the young – even away from deprived inner-city areas. But I wonder about the apparent suggestion that concern on social issues should follow that on the economy, or whether there should be a sequence at all.

It's so easy to think of life as a series of mutually exclusive activities. We do it all the time. For much of the year we work and then we have holidays and we enjoy. And we condition ourselves into thinking of life as discrete phases of enjoyment and work.

It's very much the same with religion. By having a set day or set times of the day for prayer, we divorce religion and the richness of religious influence from our daily lives. It was even worse in the India of Guru Nanak's day, when life itself was divided into a learning stage, an earning stage and a final religious stage.

The Guru was critical of this fractured approach to living and taught the necessity of living life to the full: that is, looking to our material needs and our social obligations at one and the same time while being immersed in, and guided by, religious teaching.

The Guru responded to the usual criticism of how can we find time for religion in our busy lives with a beautiful verse contained in our holy book, the *Guru Granth Sahib*:

Young girls bring pitchers To fill them at the city well
And talk and laugh as they carry them
But keep their minds on the pitchers When the child is asleep in the cradle
The mother is busy inside and outside the house But she keeps her mind on the child.

Life is too short and precious to put spiritual direction, care and compassion on some backburner, when we can so easily make these integral to our daily lives.

Papa with grandchildren

The Environment: A Deafening Warning

There is a saying in Sikhism that, 'We love the gift but forget the giver'. The words are used in a spiritual context, but they are also true of everyday life.

I've long forgotten who it was that gave us a present of a re-chargeable electric toothbrush, some ten or twelve years ago. It was never really suited to the sturdy demands of the Singh family – but it did give rise to a most unusual dream.

The dream started with isolated reports about a strange and deeply upsetting noise. Doctors blamed stress and prescribed tranquilisers, but without success.

The complaint became more widespread not only in this country but also abroad, and soon became the subject of major world concern.

An international conference of scientists was called to consider the situation, and, after days of intensive deliberation, came up with a solution – specially designed earmuffs to filter out the offending noise: it worked at first, but soon people complained that the earmuffs were beginning to lose their protection and that the noise was becoming even more distressing.

In despair, a conference of religious leaders gathered and, after much discussion, concluded that the noise was in some inexplicable way nature's reaction to the way in which human beings were treating each other and destroying the environment in the process. I'll never know what happened next. At that moment, I woke up to the noise of the toothbrush holder on charge in the bedroom.

This strange dream occurred many years before the current concern over the environment. Today it's not nature that's making a noise of protest, but people all over the world, alarmed by the potentially lethal gap in the ozone layer, the hazards from excess carbon dioxide and other known forms of pollution too numerous to mention, as well as others still unknown, undoubtedly lurking around the corner waiting to be discovered. It all adds up to the inescapable fact that the human race is proving far too clever and short-sighted for its own good.

No doubt scientists will come up with their own earmuff-like solutions, but is there any real alternative to major change in attitudes and priorities?

A verse from Sikh scriptures reminds us of an important need for a sense of perspective in considering our role and responsibility in God's creation:

There are many universes And hundreds and thousands of worlds How many vex their hearts to know His limits But seeking to explore infinity can find no bounds.

We puny humans need to lose a little of our arrogance and certainty, in just such reflection. Only then can we acquire the humility and wisdom necessary to see the full extent of our lack of vision, an essential first step in preserving the precious gift of our environment for ourselves and our children.

President Gorbachev Heralds in Democracy and Opposition

The news that President Gorbachev is already having trouble with the Soviet Union's first official opposition for 70 years leaves me with decidedly mixed feelings. While any move towards greater democracy must be a good thing, my sympathies are very much with the Soviet President struggling to achieve genuine reform.

Mr. Gorbachev will also have to face the added paradox present in all democracies as to what extent should leaders lead, or are they there simply to reflect the views of those who put them in power?

It's not a problem for Sikhs. A leader in the Sikh community is unique in being the one person who does what he or she is told. The reason for our robust lack of deference to those in authority lies in both Sikhism, with its rejection of all notions of caste or social hierarchy, and in Sikh history, with the community's constant opposition to all forms of autocratic rule.

Sikhs like to claim the dubious distinction of being the world's first true democrats. Our gurdwaras are run by democratically elected management committees – naturally, there's an opposition – normally, everyone not on the management committee! More seriously, Sikhs, throughout their 500-year history, have constantly been involved in the fight to secure democratic rights and fundamental freedoms for people of all communities; a struggle that led to the martyrdom of two of our ten Gurus. Naturally then, we find it a little difficult to accept the suggestion contained in recent commentaries on the French Revolution that democracy and human rights are peculiarly Western institutions.

There is, however, a more fundamental reason why religion is viewed in negative terms and democracy seen as a panacea for all ills in society. Just as people in Guru Nanak's day believed that ritual immersion in water would lead to spiritual purity, today it is often naively assumed that the ritual placing of pieces of paper in a ballot box is itself a guarantee of human rights and democratic purity.

It's a fallacy that arises out of the constant blurring of the difference between democracy and majority rule, which can be every bit as cruel as the tyranny of the minority. The truth is that the ballot box is only a first small step in the direction of fundamental human rights. The larger step lies in looking to the needs, fears and aspirations of those outside the majority.

It is this wider view of democracy that can move us nearer to Guru Nanak's concept of as just a society as one that recognises both the worth of an individual and the oneness of our human family.

Fall of Romanian Dictator Nicolae Ceauşescu

Shelley's poem 'Ozymandias' describes a traveller in a forgotten land discovering two vast and trunkless legs standing in the desert in a scene of total desolation. He draws our attention to the irony of the words on the pedestal which read:

My name is Ozymandias, King of Kings Look on my works ye mighty and despair

It was similar Ozymandias-like arrogance that inspired the Romanian dictator Nicolae Ceauşescu to construct a palace of gold and marble opulence, so vast that its rooms have never been properly counted. Today it stands silent and deserted; the province of stray dogs and would-be looters; a monument to extraordinary vanity, and the labyrinth of tunnels and torture rooms beneath a continuing reminder of man's inhumanity to man.

We pride ourselves as human beings on our ability to learn from the past, on cumulative wisdom. And yet, in this respect, we seem to have learnt nothing. Similar inhumanity amid vulgar opulence in India led Guru Nanak to declare:

126

The age is a knife Kings are butchers
In this dark night of falsehood No moon of truth is seen to rise

The Guru realised that for evil to succeed, it only requires the good to remain silent and he was very critical of so-called holy people who, instead of speaking out against injustice, retreated into the wilderness to meditate and seek personal salvation.

The parallel with modern times continues with the tenth Guru, Guru Gobind Singh, being forced to take up arms to defend the weak and oppressed against cruel mercenaries bent on exploitation of the masses. It was a struggle that was to cost him the martyrdom of his four sons.

Today in the West, there is a feeling of smugness. It could never happen here. Not to the same extent perhaps. We do have the benefit of the press, media and other democratic institutions to act as safety valves against arbitrary rule. While few now seek escape from social responsibility in the physical wilderness, we still have the widespread philosophy of looking after number one, of not getting involved in the troubles of others, of escape in an inner wilderness.

Guru Gobind Singh taught that such abandonment of social responsibility invites cruelty and oppression. His prayer: 'May I never be deterred in the fight for truth and justice', a sentiment paralleled in the courageous struggle of the East European dissidents, points the way for all people struggling to secure and preserve the sort of freedom we in the West have long since taken for granted.

Russian Dissident, Aleksandr Solzhenitsyn, on Religion

Aleksandr Solzhenitsyn, the famous Russian dissident, was an early recipient of the Templeton prize for religion. The award was presented to him in 1983, and it recognised a wider view of religion. It is a view that accords with Sikh teaching that religion lies not in rituals or ceremonies, but in the way we conduct ourselves.

In his Guildhall acceptance speech, Solzhenitsyn recalled his childhood, when people, appalled by the suffering in the early years of the revolution, would remark: "It's all because we've forgotten God." He continued:

Today, having witnessed suffering and horror that totally dwarfs that of earlier years, if I am asked to explain why the excesses, I can do no better than repeat those pithy words – it's all because we've forgotten God.

It's useful to look at the suffering in the Middle East in the context of Solzhenitsyn's remarks. The immediate cause of the war is, as we all know, Saddam Hussein's naked aggression against the people of Kuwait. But it was the Soviet Union and the West that supplied him his vast arsenal of sophisticated weaponry, including gas, chemical and, as we've heard this morning, possible nuclear capability.

When we consider, what seems to me, the utter immorality of the arms trade, and the proven futility of trying to build long-term peace on the shifting sands of political expediency, I cannot but echo Solzhenitsyn's remark – it's all because we've forgotten God.

It's not so much forgotten God, as having pushed God out of the equation with the modern mantra 'keep religion out of politics'.

Sikh teaching, in common with those of other faiths, insists that the only true peace is God's peace, rooted in justice. Guru Ram Dass, the fourth Guru, warned against factional politics when he said:

Some make a pact with Brother, son and friend,
Others join factions with warlords For selfish ends.
I have a pact with God. I rely on Him alone.
All other pacts are for worldly power That divides man into warring groups. I am of God's faction.

A just peace does not necessarily follow a just war. Nor can it come from new permutations of old factional alliances. A truly just and lasting peace can only be secured by unreserved allegiance to Godly ideals, such as those so clearly enshrined in the United Nations Charter; dedicated allegiance that ensures security of abode and religious and cultural freedom for all the people of the Middle East. Never again should we have to say, "It's all because we've forgotten God."

The Collapse of the Soviet Union

I find there's nothing like time and distance to help me see things in perspective. In our normal domestic life, we're often too close to family and friends to appreciate their true worth. We often focus only on faults and petty irritations. But go to any airport or railway station and see in the hugs and embraces how time and distance reduce petty imperfections to their true proportions.

One man, who has probably acquired not only a clearer perspective of family and friends, but also of world events, is Colonel Sergei Krikalev. Now, virtually marooned on the space station *Mir*, this cosmonaut was a hero of the Soviet Union when he left for space last May. Today, he is almost a forgotten figure, and the Soviet Union is no more.

Orbiting the Earth sixteen times a day, patiently waiting for some unknown bureaucrats to organise his return, he must by now have gained a near god-like perspective to put into focus some of the extraordinary goings-on in his former country: a failed coup; Gorbachev's exits and entrances; the collapse of the Communist Party and of the Soviet Union itself; the rise of ethnic unrest.

From his enforced detachment, and reflections on where, or to whom, his loyalty lies, his thoughts might well echo those in a verse in the Sikh holy *Granth*, on the impermanence of any man-made order:

The Guru taught:
All warring factions Are subject to decay
All such pacts are for worldly power I am of God's faction

It is to God that I give my ultimate loyalty.

The Guru recognised that while ethnic and religious difference can bring colour and variety to life, we should never allow superficial or transient differences to divide our one human family, and our ultimate loyalty to godly truth.

From his vantage point on *Mir*, Sergei Krikalev will no doubt be aware of the rising tide of ethnic and religious conflict – not only in the former Soviet Union, but also in Northern Ireland, the Middle East, India and many other parts of the globe – and its potential for turning men into 'warring factions'.

While praying for the good colonel's safe and speedy return to the embrace of family and friends, the thought occurs – why waste a still functioning space station?

As the Guru reminded us, there are those who, for their own ends, enmesh others in conflict. Such people would clearly benefit from a period of an enforced sense of perspective – and their distance would probably benefit us all.

Dangers of Pride Obscuring a Wider Vision

Sikhism talks of five deadly sins. One of them is pride. In our daily prayer, the Ardas, which has a similar position in Sikhism to the Lord's Prayer in Christianity, we ask for God's blessings to help us to be low in pride and high-minded in our ideals.

I was reminded of the dangers of pride on a recent management course where the consultants introduced themselves as a 'zero defects organisation'. Now, the trouble with such boasts is that they are hard to live to. On day one of the course, the overhead projector broke down and a group photo failed to come out.

The essential thrust of the course – with its emphasis on improving procedures – was fine, though in my view, marred by a lack of parallel interest in the needs and concerns of those involved.

I find religion and business management have much in common. One is concerned with managing an enterprise in an efficient and effective way; the other with doing much the same sort of thing with our personal lives. Both share the same danger of obsession with skills of the trade, blurring our vision of the reality of what we are trying to achieve.

In Guru Nanak's day, so-called holy people felt themselves above ordinary mortals and, not wishing to be contaminated by the crowd, moved away from society to perform austerities and penances to bring them nearer to God.

Guru Nanak was not impressed. He pointed out that their pride had blinded them to the fact that an understanding of God could only be reached through humility and service to those they had so selfishly abandoned.

Similar blinkered vision occurred in some management experiments of the 1930s. In one study, engineers proudly announced that improved lighting on a factory assembly line had increased output. A shrewd office employee, however, persuaded the consultants to go back to dim the lights and see what happened. To their surprise, output continued to rise until it was too dark to see. It wasn't the increased lighting that had boosted production so much as the increased feeling of those engaged in dull repetitive work that they too were important.

At the end of my recent course, we were each given a hefty inscribed paperweight to remind us that we were graduates of a unique management discipline. Mine reminds me of the need for a little humility and less brashness in what we do. Partly because of the Sikh teaching against pride, but perhaps more because of its garish appearance, my paperweight lies safely tucked away in the back of an office drawer.

Commercialisation of Sport

For two weeks every year, SW19 becomes the centre of the world, or at least the sporting world. For two weeks, we locals have the luxury of our own weather forecast — and the more dubious privilege of paying twice as much for strawberries as anywhere else.

It's as a native of SW19 that I'd like to wish all visitors to Wimbledon the best of luck – not with the weather and tennis, so much as with the new one-way system. This nightmare of new lights and roundabouts may make sense on a higher plane of traffic management, but leaves many of us lesser mortals practising the language skills of John McEnroe.

The Sikh Gurus encouraged both sport and physical fitness among their followers. They often compared life itself to a game, that we should play to the full in meeting opportunities and obligations, rather than be silent spectators to evil and injustice. Guru Nanak reminds us that a life lived positively in this way isn't always easy. He wrote:

He who would play this game of love of our fellow beings should come forward, prepared to lose all.

Sikh teachings extend this metaphor of life as a game to the outcome. Win or lose, good fortune or disaster upon disaster, we are taught to accept the result of our endeavours with equanimity as the will of God.

A reminder of a similar approach to sport greets Wimbledon players as they enter the All England Club. On the wall in the landing is a verse from Kipling, reminding players meeting with 'triumph or disaster' to treat those two imposters just the same. In practice though, the increasing pressures of commercialisation makes such a relaxed and sporting approach almost impossible.

Kitty Godfrey, whose death was reported over the weekend, was twice winner of the Wimbledon ladies' singles in the 1920s at a time of far greater sportsmanship and courtesy. But then, with a five-guinea gift voucher as prize, there was far less at stake.

Today, the winning lady's prize is £240,000 and the men's an additional £25,000,[1] and it is easy to understand the tensions, grunts and tantrums. Whoever

---

[1] £2.25 million in 2019 for both men and women.

else wins next week, sponsorship and commercialisation will more and more dominate not only sport, but all fields of human activity.

There seems to be no getting away from it. To me, to use my earlier analogy, it's as if we're going down a fast-moving one-way system, with a distinct feeling that we're going in the wrong direction but are unable to do anything about it.

Perhaps I should just accept it as the will of God and concentrate on watching the play.

Yes Minister and the Need for 'Failure Standards'

An industrial tribunal recently criticised a large employer for dismissing two ethnic minority employees for alleged fraud. The tribunal said 'they had done this' without a scintilla of evidence. The company protested its innocence: "We have an Equal Opportunities Policy." They were reminded by the tribunal that simple statements of intent were, in themselves, no guarantees of good behaviour.

To me, much the same danger lies with the Citizen's Charter, now a year old. There is also the Patient's Charter, and many other charters from public bodies, falling on us like autumn leaves. I make it twenty-nine at the last count! Soon, no self-respecting employer or provider of services will be without a charter!

Such charters seem, at best, to be crude indicators of aims or targets, and are no substitute for genuine dedication or concern. At worst, they give rise to complacency. A framed 'Passenger Charter' at the entrance to a London Underground does little to ease the suffering of an elderly lady, hobbling painfully down a broken escalator.

There are also glaring inconsistencies. Last week's Court's Charter, for example, set targets for reducing waiting times for civil and criminal cases. Maps are to be provided to help users get to court. But it's difficult to square these measures with parallel cuts on legal aid and this week's increase in court fees. On reflection, there is a perverse logic. Fewer people using courts will certainly cut down waiting time!

In many ways, all these charters are like religious creeds. There was a bewildering number of these in the India of Guru Nanak's day, some 500 years ago. Guru Nanak didn't quarrel with the contents of these creeds but was concerned that people seemed more interested in reciting their articles of belief than in living by them. He gently reminded:

Truth is high, but higher still is truthful living.

And in another verse:

He alone is a man of God who practises right conduct.

Our charters are at least a step towards 'right conduct'. But I've always felt something was missing – until I remembered an episode from *Yes Minister*. In it, a young efficiency expert wants all civil servants to state in writing, 'What would constitute failure in my job?' Sensing danger, Sir Humphrey skillfully talks the minister out of it. But the idea of 'Failure Standards' is a powerful one that could be used in the real world to concentrate the minds of those behind the charters ... if the real Sir Humphey would allow it!

Economic Well-being

For the last few days, I've been working in the garage. Not on the car, but I'm clearing a space out for the car to get in. I've got rid of lots of junk, but now I've hit a problem: what do I do with the things that are 'not quite junk'.

The biggest offender is a large fridge, slightly the worse for wear, but otherwise in perfect working order. It was relegated to the garage when we decided to get a built-in fridge. That is, one with a door to its door. With food inside the fridge in plastic containers, it's now a Russian-doll-like exercise to get a quick snack.

The new fridge isn't as nice as the old one. But it is new. Its purchase is the Singh family's contribution to reviving the economy. When the green shoots of economic recovery finally show ... this year, next year, or whenever, you'll know where they had their origin!

We are constantly reminded by the economists that spending money we don't necessarily have on things we don't really need is a good thing. It stimulates production, which creates more jobs and, in turn, greater purchasing power. It's a cycle of growth fueled by need and greed.

This idea of a market economy isn't new. It certainly existed in the India of Guru Nanak's day. The Guru's father was a typical businessman who would have fitted well into today's times. He gave the young Nanak some money and told him to invest it in merchandise for sale at a profit. He said to his son, "Put the money to good use."

The young Nanak went off towards town and, on the way, saw some poor people, hungry and shivering in the winter cold. He bought them some food and blankets. Soon, all his money was gone, but the young Guru felt he had put it to good use.

His irate father clearly thought otherwise, and it took all the diplomatic skills of Nanak's sister to restore peace. It's not recorded, but the Guru was probably penalised by a reduction in his money supply.

The Guru wasn't against commerce or the possession of material goods, but warned against this becoming a compulsion that blinds us to our social responsibilities and the very real needs of others. To underline this, he gave Sikhs the injunction:

Earn by your own efforts, and share your good fortune with others.

My fridge, and other discarded items in our homes, are not the only casualties in our sometimes-crazy quest for more and better. Today, the cold and hungry that Guru Nanak saw by the wayside are seen at our railway stations, bus shelters, or huddled and shivering in the doorways of our cities; in the unemployed and other victims of recession. Their needs should be paramount, even at the cost of upsetting the economists!

What's the Harm?

It's always a bit dangerous to question cherished national institutions. The Anglican House of Bishops were almost asking for it last week, when they voiced concerns over the National Lottery. They were accused of bleating and were branded hypocrites and killjoys – and that was by papers like *The Times*. Tabloids were far less restrained!

The gist of criticism against the Bishops, and similar views expressed earlier by the Archbishop of Canterbury, was – what's wrong with an occasional flutter? To me as a Sikh, the answer must be, 'not a lot'. The Sikh Gurus reminded us that life itself was often like a game of chance, and it was our responsibility to make the best of whatever hand was dealt us. Chance and risk are all around us. We make conscious calculations of odds and risk whenever we take out insurance, invest in a bank or building society or consider a service agreement on a washing machine.

The trouble with what is more generally understood as gambling, as the Bishops remind us, is that little flutters can, all too easily, become big flutters with drastic effects on individual and family. But what bothers me more is the way publicity and hype are used to bolster a weak 'what's the harm'-type argument, and turn a mundane activity into a national obsession.

There's that ridiculous huge hand in the sky that dominates our TV screens, billboards and shops. What's it meant to represent? The hand of fate, or God pointing to the chosen one? It's a sure sign that we've got things badly out of proportion when even the government of the day regards the creation of the National Lottery as one of its main achievements in office.

Any suggestion of misplaced emphasis in these things is sure to be met by the 'what's the harm' argument, that seems to govern our thinking. 'What's the harm in an occasional flutter?' 'What's the harm in sex and violence on TV?' – and we can go on. The trouble is that the harm is not always immediately apparent, and that such attitudes combine to dull our senses to real concerns and responsibilities.

Guru Nanak constantly reminded the people of his day of the need for a more positive attitude to life. He asked us to address the question, 'What good will it do?' It would be easier to live with the hype over the lottery and similar obsessions that seem to dominate the public mind, if, in addition to asking 'what's the harm in?', we add balance by asking, 'what good will it do?' But I'm not laying odds on this happening soon.

Spotlight on Human Rights Abuse

I've recently been trying my hand at DIY security lighting. I was given a couple of infrared detector lights as a sort of early Christmas present, and decided to fit one at the front of the house, and the other at the back, but with mixed success. The one at the back refuses to work, other than as a floodlight. The one at the front does work, but with a will all of its own.

It generally goes on as expected, but also lights up at unexplained random intervals. And it absolutely refuses to come on when I put the rubbish out at night, unless I wave to it with outstretched arm. Our neighbour's probably put my waving of arms at an inanimate object down to some strange Singh custom to appease the forces of light! But, however imperfect my system, we all know that better lighting does help reduce crime. Fear of identification is a powerful deterrent to the would-be criminal.

Amnesty International and other human rights organisations have long held that the same principle applies to those responsible for human rights violations. These human rights groups believe that the focussing of media attention and international concern on those who torture, maim or kill innocent people in distant lands can in itself act as a powerful deterrent.

Tomorrow is International Human Rights Day, and the day will see a renewal of concern for hundreds of thousands of innocent human beings, including the elderly and infirm, and the very young, suffering for their beliefs, or the beliefs of those close to them. In our different places of worship, we will reflect on how such abuse can take place in half the nations of the world.

There are many who argue that the focussing of attention on international wrongdoing is itself flawed and biased, with a common tendency to keep the spotlight away from trading partners and 'friendly nations', and that instead of subjective blacklists and whitelists, we should be looking at and quantifying various shades of grey. These things, like my own security lighting, can be improved.

What is important is that we do not let doubt and cynicism stand in the way of our continuing support to organisations, groups and individuals, who by their relentless focusing on human rights violations give light to those in darkness, and serve as the voice of the voiceless.

Effigies of Hate

John Harington, who lived at the time of the Gunpowder Plot, wrote:

Treason doth never prosper: what's the reason? For if it prospers, none dare call it treason.

Guy Fawkes's treason certainly didn't prosper and last night, despite the stormy weather, effigies of the poor chap were burnt on bonfires, accompanied by ever bigger, noisier and more spectacular fireworks.

It's also at this time every year that Hindus celebrate the victory of Lord Ram over Ravan, the demon king of Sri Lanka who had kidnapped Sita, the wife of Ram. Huge effigies of Ravan are burnt, and celebrations finally conclude with the all-important festival of Diwali, the festival of lights. This marks the triumphant return to India of Ram with his wife Sita; an occasion for more celebrations, and more firecrackers.

Sikhs also celebrate Diwali, but for quite a different reason. It was on Diwali day, nearly 400 years ago, that Guru Hargobind, in his concern for freedom of belief, secured the release of fifty-two Hindu princes imprisoned by an intolerant Mughal emperor. And yes, Sikhs too celebrate with fireworks and lights.

The fact that all these bonfires and displays of pyrotechnics in different cultures and in different parts of the northern hemisphere take place at about the same time is too much of a coincidence. It seems we all feel the need to show a last blaze of defiance against the inevitable onset of winter. All harmless fun, but for the practice of making and burning effigies of those who disagree with our ways of thinking or our beliefs.

Poor Guy Fawkes was a member of a persecuted minority which frequently endured torture and death for simply being Catholic. There was no democratic means of protest and discovery of a 'plot' was itself used as an excuse for further repressive legislation; a formula since used across the world to keep minorities in their proper place.

The burning of effigies of those of different beliefs are all too easily seen as harmless, particularly with the passage of time. But even religious minorities have feelings. Let's have the bonfires and the fireworks, and if we must have effigies, let's have a giant effigy of intolerance: a demon still with us today.

Lessons of History

There is the story of a history professor who was asked by a little girl at a party what he did. He replied that he was a student of Roman history. The little girl, clearly not impressed, answered, "Oh, we finished the Romans last year!"

My reaction was a bit like the little girl's when I first heard of the current BBC documentary on the rise of Nazi Germany. We could be excused for thinking we'd finished with Hitler and racism a couple of years ago, when we celebrated the fiftieth anniversary of the end of the Second World War. But, watching the series, I realised how we continue to ignore major lessons of history.

Five hundred years ago, at a time of ethnic conflict in India, the Sikh Gurus reminded us that Man is of ONE race in all the world, and that nothing but sorrow, misery and suffering results from attempts to divide people into the high and the low, the superior and the inferior.

What this latest documentary does is to show how easy it is to manipulate people to forget such ideals and the lessons of the past, by appeals to baser, but ever powerful, human instincts. There was the harshness of the Treaty of Versailles and resulting suffering. All it needed was a Hitler to articulate and capitalise on the sense of national desolation and identify a convenient scapegoat: the Jews. Importantly, the documentary also reminds us how those who see the evil in such irrational emotion are all too easily cowed to silence and tacit support. More recent events in many parts of the world remind us that there are ever more Hitlers waiting in the wings and no dearth of potential scapegoats.

Could it ever happen here? Frankly, I think any would-be dictator would have a tough and miserable time. What bothers me far more is the growing ability of an ever more powerful media, concentrated in fewer and fewer hands, to tell us what constitutes *normal* behaviour. When to be happy, when, where and how to grieve, and more worryingly, what people want and supposedly think.

My concern is that this can lead to narrowness in thinking and an intolerance towards those who don't share our views, which, in its extreme form, can lead a nation astray. The safeguard, as Guru Nanak taught, is that we base both private and public life not on expediency or fickle public opinion, but on the more abiding values of tolerance, compassion and concern for the rights of others: values common to all our major faiths.

Nearly Expelled on My First Day at School

I nearly got expelled on my first day at school. The building was on a hill, and there were a series of steps leading to the classrooms. To me, the route looked boring, and the moment my mother's head was turned, I began to climb a small mountain of builder's sand to reach the same goal. Knee-deep and sometimes waist-deep in sand, I eventually made it to the top, only to receive a furious telling off from the teacher and, later, from my parents. Other children used the steps; why did I have to be different?

My motive was simply a misplaced sense of adventure, but there are often good reasons for not following the crowd. Guru Nanak once travelled to the banks of the Ganges where people would throw water from the river in the direction of the sun in, what the Guru considered, a superstitious belief that this would somehow reach their ancestors in heaven. The Guru got in the river and began throwing water in the opposite direction. When asked why, he replied that he was throwing water to his fields in Punjab. "How can water thrown from here reach your fields hundreds of miles away?" they argued. To which the Guru replied, "In the same way as it reaches your ancestors in heaven."

The Guru's message was that of the need to distinguish between ritual and superstition, and true religion that gives meaning and direction to life. He taught that we should try to avoid supposedly religious practices that fail to meet the tests of reason and common sense.

I thought of this as I watched the extraordinary crowd scenes on television of half a million uniformly smiling people, in the North Korean capital Pyongyang. Thousands carried identical plastic flowers as they lined up to welcome, until then a figure of hate, President Kim Dae-Jung of South Korea. While fervently hoping that the meeting between the two Presidents would lead to an end of a half century of conflict, in what President Clinton has described as the scariest place on Earth, I find it strangely disturbing that a whole population can be made to alternate between hate and welcome, as if at a turn of a switch. To me, it's a reminder of how easily we can all be manipulated to behave in ways that are either devoid of reason or by calls to love or hate on demand. Our best defence is to keep common sense to the fore and have the courage not to blindly follow the crowd.

136

The Cost of Human Greed

At first sight, there seems little in common between the news earlier this week, of timber from a protected rainforest in Brazil finding its way to Britain, and the shock horror of the death by suffocation of fifty-eight people in a container lorry at Dover. But I believe they are connected by human greed; greed that's prepared to trade the life, limb and well-being of fellow humans for the sake of quick profit.

Of course, greed and the exploitation of the poor have always been with us and the teachings of all the great world religions include it in their lists of deadly sins. A well-known story of Guru Nanak preferring the simple food of a poor carpenter to the lavish hospitality of an unscrupulous businessman is one of many examples in which the Sikh Gurus criticised the exploitation of the poor by the powerful in society.

The rich man in the story made his money by exploiting the poor in a relatively small locality. Today we live in a very different world of shrinking dimensions in communications, trade and travel. It's a world of huge disparities between the haves and have nots in terms of standard of living and political freedoms. Importantly, it's now also a world of greater awareness among the deprived of the extent of their deprivation. Just as national boundaries mean little to global players seeking ever higher profits, poorer people and those fearful of state persecution will increasingly try to better their lot, regardless of national frontiers. It's as inevitable as water flowing from a higher to a lower level. And who can blame members of what Sikhs call our one human family for trying to better themselves?

It's our reaction to these side effects of globalisation that bother me. Perhaps I'm being oversensitive, but I must confess, I was saddened when one politician, talking about the container disaster, went on to express her concern over large 'quantities' of people coming to these shores. We can have quantities of tomatoes or other commodities, but why dehumanise human beings? Unfortunately, it is all too easy to, perhaps unwittingly, create an atmosphere in which victims of inequality are seen as villains. In an era of porous borders and people ready to exploit misery, the only real way to reduce hazardous cross-border movement lies in greater international effort to reduce the gradient of disparity and disadvantage that causes people to risk life and limb in the hope of a decent and fear-free existence.

Torture and Humiliation of Al Qaeda Suspects at Guatemala Bay

News reports of Al Qaeda prisoners being hooded, manacled, sedated and otherwise humiliated are profoundly disturbing, and, if only half true, are to my mind a severe setback in the fight against terrorism.

The September atrocities in New York and Washington, described by President Bush as an assault on civilised society, resulted in worldwide revulsion against those who had shown such callous disregard for human life. In the Sikh view, it is regard for human life and recognition of the worth of others that is the hallmark of civilised society. The Sikh Gurus, who were forced to fight many battles in defence of religious freedom, taught that compassion and concern for others must extend even to foes on the battlefield.

In a particularly fierce battle at the time of Guru Gobind Singh, a Sikh water carrier by the name of Kanhaiya was seen to be serving water to the enemy wounded, as well as to Sikhs. Some Sikh soldiers, incensed at Kanhaiya's behaviour, dragged the water carrier before the Guru, demanding suitable punishment. The Guru asked Kanhaiya to explain himself. Kanhaiya looked at the Guru and replied "You have always taught us to treat others, even our enemies, with compassion and respect. In giving water to the enemy wounded, I was simply doing what you taught us to do." The Guru was delighted by the reply. He embraced Kanhaiya, calling him 'Bhai', or 'brother'. He then gave him ointment and bandages, and told him to look to the needs of the suffering on both sides of the battle line.

Words like 'civilised' are often used far too glibly. When Mahatma Gandhi visited Britain in the 1930s, he was asked in a rather superior way, "What do you think of Western civilisation?" Gandhi paused and then replied, "It would be a good idea." He was suggesting that civilisation meant more than wearing coats and ties and eating with knives and forks. It is in the end, as the Guru observed, all about treating others with decency and humanity.

The war against terrorism is a war for people's minds. It cannot be won by calling Al Qaeda prisoners 'unlawful combatants' to deprive them of rights under the Geneva Convention. Placing manacled prisoners in six feet by eight feet cages, exposed to the elements, is, by any definition, cruel and degrading. Whatever combination of words we use, 'prisoners of war', or 'unlawful combatants', the Al Qaeda captives are humans, and should be treated as such by civilised society.

Limits of a Top-down Approach in Enhancing Community Cohesion

It's common knowledge that people from different backgrounds tend to keep together, and there is generally no harm in this. The danger occurs when this isolation is reinforced by ignorance and fear, which can all too easily lead to hatred and violence. This is what happened in last summer's riots in Bradford, Burnley and Oldham, between mainly deprived Muslim youth and their white counterparts.

Last week, I attended a conference to discuss several government and local government reports on how to prevent such occurrences in the future. The root cause of conflict between communities, prejudice that thrives on ignorance, got little mention at the conference. It was, however, something that was well-recognised by the founders of our different religions.

Jesus Christ pointedly reminded us, in his parable of the Good Samaritan, that good can exist in other communities as well as bad in our own. Guru Nanak, with a Hindu and Muslim companion, visited Mecca and Hindu holy sites to show his respect for other religions. This same message, that no one community has a monopoly of goodness and truth, is underlined by the inclusion of verses of Hindu and Muslim saints in our holy book, the *Guru Granth Sahib*. The thrust of religious teaching is to make tolerance and respect for others a norm of human behaviour, rather than a belated cure.

Today, in our cleverer times, this simple, grassroots approach to higher standards of behaviour is often ignored. Instead, when faced with any social problem, we seem to feel we are not getting our money's worth unless we have lengthy committees of inquiry, producing ponderous reports peppered with numerous acronyms and a host of recommendations. In just one of the reports on community cohesion we discussed last week, there were forty-three recommendations, and references to strategies, and subsets of strategies.

The problem with such undoubtedly well-meaning, top-down approaches is that they virtually ignore the many excellent on-the-ground faith-based initiatives to remove prejudice and enhance respect for other ways of life. My hope is that the new Archbishop of Canterbury, to be announced later today, will make greater support for this valuable work an important priority. It may be my own prejudice, resulting from years in the construction industry, but I believe that, for lasting results, it is always better to build from the bottom-up than from the top-down.

HM the Queen's First Visit to a Sikh Gurdwara

Last Thursday, I had the rare privilege of accompanying Her Majesty the Queen in her visit to a Sikh gurdwara in Leicester, where she was received with typical Sikh warmth and hospitality. It was her first visit to a Sikh place of worship in this country, but you wouldn't have guessed it from her relaxed and confident manner. A police van full of posies of flowers spontaneously presented to her by little children testified to the popularity of her visit.

The previous day, the Queen had gone to a mosque in Scunthorpe. The importance of these visits showing respect for other faiths cannot be sufficiently stressed. It was a clear message from the Queen that showing respect for other ways of life in no way compromises our own religious identity.

In the same way, the Queen has, in these Jubilee celebrations, made clear that she is queen of all her people and believes that our different religions show that God's love extends in equal measure to all humanity. As a verse from Sikh scriptures reminds us:

From the Divine Light all Creation sprang
Why then should we divide human creatures into the high and the Low?

Today, we constantly talk about the globalisation of trade and commerce, but often forget the most important aspect of this irreversible globalisation process; the increasing movement of people, and the greater interaction of different religions and cultures.

Until recently, we could afford to look at the quaint ways and beliefs of those in more distant lands, in a superior academic way that perversely added to a sense of national identity by superficially differentiating between us and them. Now, the same attitudes can lead to disastrous social consequences.

Laws, in themselves, cannot ensure good behaviour. All they can do is define the boundaries of unacceptable behaviour, which is not the same thing. Good, or considerate, behaviour requires a genuine respect for the rights and beliefs of others, as emphasised in our different religious texts. But a mere tacit recognition of fundamental truths is not enough. As Guru Nanak taught:

Truth is high, but higher still is truthful living.

With the Queen, 2002

With the Queen, Leicester, 2002

With the Queen at her Golden Jubilee, 2002

To me, the importance of the Queen's visits to other places of worship is that she translated belief into action, in this very visible demonstration for respect for other faiths. Her initiative is a powerful lead to us all, and will I'm sure, be the most important legacy of this Jubilee year.

Understanding the Causes of Terrorism

Whenever we're confronted with new threats to life, like bird flu, we take urgent steps to understand the nature of the threat and the way it multiplies and spreads, as a way to ultimately defeating it.

In much the same way, terrorism is also a threat to life that can, as we know all too well, also cause the death of thousands. Common sense suggests that to fully eradicate it, we need to consider how and why it manifests itself. We need to know something of the factors that impel often educated people with young families not only to take their own lives, but also to murder wholly blameless innocent men, women and children. Is it a perceived sense of injustice? Outrage at the death or suffering of one's kith and kin, a warped sense of religious duty, or a lethal combination of these factors?

When cholera was first attributed to unhygienic living, no one suggested that such attribution was an irresponsible and insulting comment on a way of life. Instead, active steps were taken to improve sanitation, leading to the dramatic eradication of a killer disease. Yet, when Liberal Democrat MP Dr Jenny Tonge suggested, in a similar way, that harsh refugee camp conditions experienced by many Palestinians might contribute to terrorism, much of the media descended on her like a ton of bricks.

There are two concerns. The first is the right to express genuinely held views. This is considered so important in Sikhism that our Gurus, while stressing the independent path of Sikh belief, constantly underlined their respect for Hindu and Muslim teachings.

The second concern is that our narrow and emotional response to what we term 'global terrorism' makes it difficult for us to see that although terrorism in the Middle East, Chechnya and other parts of the world manifests itself in similar ways, its cause is often quite different. It simply doesn't help the peace process in Israel in this instance to talk of global terrorist conspiracies.

Instead, we should be looking to the real concerns of Israelis fearful of the future, and the Palestinians traumatised by the present, with overreaction by both communities with bombs, bulldozers and suicide bombing. Dr Tonge may have erred in her choice of language, but recognising the strength and depth of genuine concerns is essential for terrorism's eventual defeat.

Creating God in Our Own Image

The philosopher Voltaire was once asked if he believed that man was created in God's image. He thought for a moment and said, "What I am sure of is that man creates God in his own image."

I thought of Voltaire's comment as I read a weekend report that claimed up to fifty young British Muslims were ready to follow the path to martyrdom chosen by Asif Mohammed Hanif, who blew himself up in a bar in Tel Aviv last week, killing three people and injuring more than fifty others. Not only do we create God in our image, but we also distort the teachings of religion to justify the killing of innocent civilians.

The main thrust of our different faiths is to move us to more compassionate and considerate behaviour, but the problem is that such teachings go against the grain of our baser instincts, so we readily bend religion to fit and justify our human weaknesses. It's all done in easy imperceptible stages. First, a belief that our way to God is the only true way. Then, God, in recognition of this, has an exclusive and favoured relationship with us, making others lesser beings. It's an easy move from this to claim that anything done to further the influence of our God must have his blessings and be pleasing to Him. We can see all too easily how this warped logic can descend to the oppression and killing of innocents.

Guru Nanak was very concerned about this arrogance of belief. He taught that God had no favoured relationships. It is the way we behave that counts. He was particularly critical of the hypocrisy of so-called religious leaders who played on the ignorance and prejudices of their followers. He wrote:

They utter God's name but condone injustice Shielding their actions – with religious texts

Words that ring true today. Last year we saw 2,000 Muslims massacred in the Indian state of Gujarat in the name of religion. Today, it is the killing of Jews to protect Islam and Jewish revenge incursions into Palestinian territory. Tomorrow it might be Christians or Sikhs. This grotesque merry-go-round of killing in the name of religion will undoubtedly continue until religious leaders have the courage to point out the real threat to our various religions lies not so much in the behaviour of others, but in our distortion of religious teachings to justify our human failings.

Religion is Not an Exclusive Franchise

I must say that, as a Sikh, I found it a little disconcerting to read a piece in *The Times* a couple of days ago in which Dr Rowan Williams, the Archbishop of Canterbury, firmly declared that no one comes to the Father except through Jesus. When asked about Muslims going to heaven, he did however concede the possibility of "God's spirit crossing boundaries". I'm not sure if that is a yes or a no, but at least Muslims may be in with a chance.

The Sikh scriptures, 400 years old today, take a different view and maintain that there are no rigid boundaries between faiths, and that God is not in the least bit interested in our different religious labels, but in how we serve our fellow beings and how we cherish and value the wonder of Creation.

Guru Arjan Dev, the main compiler of the Sikh holy *Granth*, included in it, not only teachings of the Sikh Gurus, but also verses of Hindu and Muslim saints, to show that no one religion has a monopoly of truth. Earlier, the Guru showed his respect for Islam by asking a Muslim saint, Mia Mir, to lay the foundation stone of the famous Golden Temple, which has doors on four sides to emphasise a welcome to people from different spiritual and geographic directions.

Today, and for the rest of the month, Sikhs throughout the world will be celebrating the first reading of these scriptures in Amritsar 400 years ago; teachings that emphasise respect for other faiths and a balanced and socially responsible attitude to life. An early celebration has already been held in the unlikely venue of the White House in Washington and, later this month, among the many celebrations in this country, there will be a major commemoration in London's Royal Albert Hall.

My problem with all such celebrations is that we easily forget the significance of what we are celebrating. And we Sikhs are no exception here. In our celebrations we can easily forget that Guru Arjan, the compiler of the Sikh scriptures, gave his life in the cause of religious harmony. Today, Sikhs have a clear obligation to work as catalysts for greater interfaith understanding and help show that different religions are not rigid barriers between people, but gateways to a greater understanding and enrichment of life itself. Having said that, the one certainty is that, following this talk, I'll get another letter from a genuinely concerned lady in Devon, reminding me of the terrible fate in store for me for not wearing her religious label.

The Arms Trade

A report in *The Sunday Times* claimed that MPs are to send a delegation to the Prime Minister demanding that he intervenes to save the £10-billion Saudi arms deal threatened by a corruption inquiry. The concern is that the inquiry could put 50,000 British jobs at risk.

Besides the obvious ethical dilemma of possibly condoning corruption to save jobs, other questions also come to mind. Does the supply of billions of pounds of weaponry to Saudi Arabia, by no means a democracy, really extend the cause of world peace? What will it do with its existing weapons? If 50,000 jobs are tied to supplying arms to Saudi Arabia, how many other British jobs are there involved in supplying other countries with sophisticated means of mass killing?

Echoes of the same concerns are found in news that Boeing, one of the largest defence contractors in the United States, is seeking orders from India for the supply of fifteen billion dollars' worth of military hardware. And that India, the land of Mahatma Gandhi, now spends twice as much as China on arms.

If we extend this glimpse at just two participants in major arms deals, and recognise that other exporters of arms include China, India, Russia and France, as well as many less scrupulous nations, we can easily understand why we live in a world awash with arms, which all too easily seep into and fuel horrendous regional conflicts, often in the poorest parts of the world.

What particularly concerns me is that attitudes to defence and the notion of friendly and unfriendly countries have hardly changed in the last fifty years, although the nature of threats to peace and security are now quite different. Today, the threat to security is not so much from nation states as from smaller groups exploiting a real or perceived sense of injustice, and there is now an urgent need to be subtler and focussed in our response.

The Sikh Gurus warned that the way to peace lay not in simply wishing it or even praying for peace with elaborate rituals to please God, but by tackling underlying injustice and standing up to the arrogant pursuit of power, with, as a last resort, the minimal use of force. Tying world economies to the mass production, sale and resale of ever more sophisticated weapons cannot help in this.

Why Ten Gurus?

It's sometimes said that whenever we humans get in real trouble, God sends a prophet or messenger to help sort us out and put us back on an ethical track.

When God looked at the Punjab in the middle of the fifteenth century, He saw people immersed in ritual who had lost all sense of self-esteem; people who looked the other way as their wives and daughters were carried off to captivity in frequent invasions from the north. Rumour has it, God said: "One prophet won't be enough for this lot; I'll send ten!" And so it came to pass that Sikhism had nine spiritual successors to the founder of the faith, Guru Nanak.

A more earth-bound reason for Guru Nanak's nine successors lies in the wisdom and astuteness of Guru Nanak. He realised that it was relatively easy to set out simple principles of ethical and responsible living, but far harder to change human behaviour to challenge injustice, and work for a fairer society. So, the Guru started a system of succession to show that the teachings of Sikhism, with their emphasis on justice and compassion, were a practical way of life in different social and political climates. The task of the successor Gurus was to protect and nurture Sikh teachings until they had taken root in popular psyche. This week, Sikhs throughout the world are celebrating the anniversary of the tenth Guru, Guru Gobind Singh's declaration in 1708 that the mission had succeeded, and the community was now mature enough to stand on its own. He declared that in future the *Guru Granth Sahib*, the book containing the teachings of the Gurus, should be regarded as the eternal Guru of the Sikhs.

Unfortunately, some of us take this too literally and place greater emphasis on looking after and adorning the holy *Granth* with fine coverings than looking to the guidance within it. It's much the same with rituals found in other religions that divert us from focussing on actual teachings.

We live in a world that throws up daily reminders of the damage caused by irresponsible and selfish living; global ones, like damage to the environment and climate change, and more locally, harm to our social environment as seen in family breakdown, rising crime and a culture of greed. Our different religions give excellent guidance to help us to more responsible living, but unless we follow it, ten times ten Gurus, messengers or prophets will never be enough.

Continuing Antics of the Human Race

A few years ago, I was asked to comment on a TV programme on 'what God thinks of us'. I replied that if God had human emotions, he would be angry and bewildered at the continuing antics of the human race, and doubly determined to keep us away from any truly intelligent life in the vastness of his creation.

I was half joking, but continuing widespread disregard for human rights abroad and a sense of despair over self-inflicted social problems here in Britain lend support to my TV suggestion that God is not best pleased about how we on planet Earth conduct ourselves.

We too get upset by human behaviour. The reason for our anger and outrage is that we start from an assumption that decent and responsible living is normal and natural. But Sikh teachings on free will challenge this, recognising a capacity for irresponsible behaviour in all of us. The Sikh Gurus taught we are free to move in either a positive ethical (or what Sikhs call gurmukh) direction, or in a negative manmukh direction. In the Sikh view, the true purpose of religion is to nudge us in a positive direction of respect for others and more responsible living. Does this mean that it's only religion that can get us away from our often-self-inflicted problems? Of course not! But it does mean that a well-ordered responsible society does not come about by itself. We all have to work at it. Government and the rule of law, to which we turn when things go wrong, can do no more than curb our worst excesses. Tougher action against violent crime, harsher penalties for drug or alcohol abuse, government guidance on what we eat and what we wastefully throw away can help alleviate some of the symptoms of unthinking behaviour, but they cannot address underlying human weaknesses.

It's here that the ethical teachings of our different faiths should kick in. My fear is this won't happen unless religions focus on the actual teachings of the founders of our different faiths, rather than on petty internal disputes or aggressive claims about their uniqueness or superiority. Today, there's a lot of talk of interfaith dialogue, but to me as a Sikh, the only dialogue worth having is on how to work together with others, for positive or gurmukh living.

The Shirt of a Happy Man

In the current economic gloom and the risk of one country's woes affecting others, a little bit of good news like the announcement of the royal engagement is doubly cheering. As a Sikh, I also welcome the government's initiative to help us see our economic concerns in a fuller perspective of individual and national wellbeing. The founders of our different religions have long reminded us that there is much more to life than the pursuit of material prosperity. I'm less sure however that the Office for National Statistics will ever be able to come up with a meaningful measure of individual and national wellbeing.

In this search for happiness and wellbeing, I'm reminded about a poem that I used to read our children, called 'The Shirt of a Happy Man'. It tells the story of a king obsessed with his health, who'd fly into a rage when doctors told him there was nothing wrong with him. Eventually, a wise and perceptive doctor told him that he would be restored to full health if he slept for one night in the shirt of a happy man. The king sent messengers throughout the land to find such a man, but all they found were people with *real* concerns. The reports of the suffering of his subjects made the king ashamed of his imagined woes, and, as he began to look to the needs and concerns of his subjects, he experienced true contentment for the first time in his life.

In many ways we've become a bit like the king, a little over-obsessed with our own wellbeing. We are not helped by the media and adverts that constantly pander to our greed and vanity. Guru Nanak urged us to look beyond ourselves when he taught: "Where God exists there is no self, where self exists there is no God." And a Christian theologian put it in even blunter terms when he said, "It's the I in the middle of sin that makes it sin."

Sikh teachings remind us that there is nothing wrong with material comfort, but for a true sense of wellbeing we need to look beyond ourselves to the needs of others, as we will be reminded in this week's Children in Need Appeal. Contentment may be difficult to quantify in an index, but as a Sikh, I believe our own sense of wellbeing is directly proportional to the amount of our life we devote to helping those around us.

Wedding of Prince William and Kate Middleton

The news that Prince William and Kate Middleton are to marry in Westminster Abbey next April is doubly welcome to Sikhs, particularly as it comes at a time when Sikhs are celebrating the birthday of Guru Nanak.

In a refreshing change to the background of his times, Guru Nanak in the India of the fifteenth century taught the complete equality of women. Marriage in Sikhism is seen as the coming together of two equal partners in mutual love and support, and importantly that they should act as one, in common service to the community. The equality is seen in the important positions occupied by women in worship, where women often recite from the scriptures and occupy positions such as secretary or president of the local gurdwara.

Unfortunately, cultures sometimes trump the teachings of the religion and Sikhs still have to work within the community to ensure the equality taught by the Guru trumps culture.

In the past, the roles of men and women in the family were quite distinct with the man being the major breadwinner and the woman the main carer. The welcome move to greater equality in society has resulted in a wider acceptance that both roles are important and there is nothing demeaning in men playing a greater role at home, even though women believe men still don't do enough.

In our family, I am still the hunter, and I frequently brave the charge of supermarket trolleys as I hunt for food. I also put the washing out and chat with the neighbours while I'm doing it. At the moment, my wife is doing school inspections in Abu Dhabi and I find myself in charge of all departments, cooking and washing all the dishes, that is, the plate and the mug.

Of course, in future, Kate and William won't have to bother about such things. They'll have a few people to help them. But they will have even more difficult challenges, particularly a press watching and speculating on their every move, what they wear and where they go. My plea to the media is to allow them some breathing space to get on with their own lives.

It will be particularly hard for Kate coming into what is familiar to Sikhs as an extended family. I'm delighted that they are getting married in Westminster Abbey. The Abbey has been host to the Annual Commonwealth Service, always an interfaith event, since the 1970s. The setting will be an excellent start to what I'm sure will be a happy married life.

Number of Arms of a Hindu Goddess

I spent yesterday morning helping look after a poorly granddaughter. We watched a TV programme on general knowledge on a variety of subjects taught in schools; the idea being to test the knowledge of an adult against that of a schoolchild. RE was one of the subjects chosen and the question was about the number of arms of a certain Hindu goddess.

The question, of course, had nothing to do with the ethical teachings of Hinduism, and, like so much that passes for RE, was about the peripherals of belief found in all religions; about the quaint and exotic; about the form of worship rather than the substance.

Today, Sikhs celebrate the birthday of Guru Nanak, the founder of the Sikh faith who urged the importance of translating rituals of worship, often seen as an end in themselves, to responsible living.

The Guru taught that pilgrimages, penances and ritual acts of giving were, in themselves, not worth a grain of sesame seed in the court of God. He said that such rituals were 'chains of the mind' if they took us away from religious imperatives in leading an honest life in the service of our fellow beings.

Some five and a half centuries ago, the Guru, in a major move towards understanding and cooperation between different faiths, taught that the one God of us all was not interested in our different religious labels, but in our attitude and behaviour to those around us. This required accepting the oneness of all humanity, gender equality and social responsibility. The Guru's popularity, humanity and compassion was welcomed by people in all communities and when he died, he was popularly regarded as a Pir or religious leader of the Muslims, and a Guru of the Hindus.

Today, Sikhs throughout the world will reflect on Guru Nanak's teachings couched in clear uplifting language. Such teachings, like those of the founders of other faiths, give meaning and direction to life but are not always easy to practise. It's much easier to sing or chant religious imperatives than to translate these into responsible living for ourselves and others. But, as Guru Nanak reminded us, unless we live true to such teachings, unless we walk the talk, it all amounts to nothing, reinforcing a growing perception of religion as being irrelevant to the challenges of modern society.

Looking at a Common Problem from Different Perspectives

A favourite poem I used to read to my children begins:

Six wise men from Hindustan to learning much inclined
Went to see an elephant, though all of them were blind

Each touches a different part of the elephant like the trunk, tusk or tail and comes to the instant conclusion that an elephant is like a serpent, spear or rope. The poem reminds us of the dangers of looking at an issue from too narrow a perspective.

I was reminded about this by two reports this week on the widespread use of drugs. One, by a group of parliamentarians, says current criminal sanctions do not combat drug addiction and only marginalise users. They want possession and personal use of all illegal drugs decriminalised and the least harmful sold in licensed shops, with labels detailing the risks.

The second report from the BMA also says that there is too much focussing on criminality and goes on to suggest that drug taking is like an illness and those with serious problems shouldn't be inhibited from seeking urgent treatment.

Both these reports look at different facets of a common problem, but they don't give us an understanding of *why* drug use has become a major problem in recent years. The reports focus on symptoms rather than addressing underlying causes, which, to me, are linked to lifestyles that move us away from responsibility and support from those around us, to a more selfish and isolated pursuit of personal happiness. It's a bit like chasing a mirage; we never quite get there, and drink and drugs are sometimes seen not only as a remedy for disappointment, but as an end in themselves.

Sikh teachings and those of other religions remind us that life has both ups and downs, and of the importance of developing equanimity and a sense of resilience in balanced and responsible living. In a memorable verse, Guru Nanak taught that the lasting sense of contentment in looking outwards to actively helping those around us and working for a fairer society, far exceeds the short-term buzz from drink and drugs.

The parliamentary and BMA reports on drug abuse are useful contributions as far as they go. But the underlying problem lies in lifestyle and expectations. These are far harder to change, but we do need to look at and reflect on the wider picture.

Need for Twenty-First Century Interpretations of Religious Texts

Like many others, I've been trying to get my head around the plight of thousands caught up in the onslaught by soldiers of the so-called Islamic State in Syria and Iraq. Images of cold-blooded killings and terrified and bewildered children haunt the mind. Worse, the killers, some from Britain, say they are doing this in the name of Islam. Their actions have been condemned by Muslim leaders around the world. Over the weekend, some of Britain's leading Muslim clerics issued a statement calling on all Muslims to have nothing to do with what they termed a 'false and poisonous ideology'.

I am sure their views reflect the feelings of a clear majority of Muslims and I can understand the hurt felt by some in the community over the use of language that links them with the actions of a small minority. Some of my Muslim friends find it particularly hurtful to see mindless killers being described as 'Islamists'.

To my mind, neither this tarring of a whole community because of the actions of a few, nor the frequent use of the word 'Asian' to diffuse blame onto an even wider community, help us understand how some in our different faiths justify unspeakable acts in the name of their religion.

In a thoughtful article in *The Times* last weekend, Mathew Syed reminds us that religious texts are often written in the specific context of a very different world of hundreds of years ago. Most people understand this and simply look to underlying ethical guidance within them. Others, however, selectively quote passages out of context to justify clearly unacceptable behaviour. As the saying goes: the devil can quote scriptures for his purpose.

Guru Nanak was aware of the danger from the manipulation of religious sentiment. While he himself put forward key ethical teachings, such as those on equality and responsible living, successor Gurus were charged with the difficult task of keeping these to the fore in changing social and political circumstances.

Today, we are naturally worried about the dangers we may face from returning British religious extremists and the need to safeguard ourselves. But due emphasis should also be given to the urgent need for people *of all faiths* to ensure common underlying imperatives *are couched in today's terms*. In so doing, they will avoid the potential for harmful distortions. It will also help to make religion, what the founders of our different faiths intended, a positive force for good.

Downside of Smart Technology

Media hype over this week's launch of the latest smartphone and the million ways it will help us connect to everyone and everything leaves me a little cold. I'm a bit wary about sophisticated gadgetry telling us what to do with our lives. Admittedly, I'm a bit of a Luddite about mobile phones, the social media and the Internet. I envy those with the speed and dexterity of Madame Defarge, who clicked away on her knitting needles while watching the guillotine in action. I can't cope with lengthy texts demanding instant replies. My granddaughter recently said she would send me an email because "You can't text." Determined to prove her wrong, I slowly and ponderously wrote a text message signed 'master texter' – and then, inadvertently, sent it to her puzzled aunt.

My relationship with the Internet lurches between love and hate. I can't get over the power of the Internet that gives near instant access to detailed information on the vaguest of topics – that is, when it works! At the moment, we have lost our Wi-Fi and have only intermittent Internet access due to a fault on the line. We've all had similar experiences.

My real concern is that it is all too easy to get hooked on such gadgetry in a way that takes us away from due attention to those around us. Guru Nanak too was concerned about the way people often neglected their responsibilities for more selfish pursuits. In his day, some people would leave their families and friends to go to the wilderness in search of God.

Today, there isn't much wilderness left, but it is all too easy to drift into a virtual wilderness in pursuit of virtual friendships to the neglect of real people around us. I am reminded of the poet's words:

We flatter those we scarcely know, and rush to please the fleeting guest, but heap many a thoughtless blow on those who love us best.

Now there's a 'Thought for the Day' – in less than 140 characters!

Need to Demolish Barriers of Dogma or Belief

Last week we were celebrating the twenty-fifth anniversary of the fall of the Berlin Wall; a physical structure designed to keep the people of Eastern Europe isolated from the freedom and democratic values of the West. This week is interfaith week; a week in which we question equally divisive barriers of belief between religions. Barriers built on claims of exclusivity and superiority, seen in the use of language to denigrate those of other beliefs or ways of life. Today, we are all too aware of the way in which words can be used to promote active hatred and the mindless killing of thousands of innocents, as seen in the Middle East and many other parts of our world.

In the past, talking about distant religions in a disparaging way, though wrong, was fairly harmless and gave us a perverse sense of unity based on the superiority of our way of life over that of others. Today, such thinking is food and sustenance for the fanatic. In our smaller and interdependent world, recognising that we are all equal members of the same human family has now become an imperative.

Sikh teachings remind us that our different religions are different paths to responsible living and must all be respected. Religious teachings are not mutually exclusive and frequently merge in shared truths and a heightened understanding of our own faith.

A popular Christian hymn states:

To all life Thou givest; to both great and small
In all life Thou livest the true life of all

The lines have a striking parallel in Sikh scriptures:

There is an inner light in all
And that light is God

The Sikh Gurus frequently used parallel teachings in different faiths to emphasise important commonalities and shared values.

Today, religion finds itself confined to the margin of society as a cause rather than a cure for hatred and violence. We see this in governments focussing huge resources on programmes to combat religious extremism. And yet … if religions work together to live common core teachings of right, wrong and responsibility, who knows? Instead of programmes like 'Prevent', we might even have government programmes called 'Enable', to embed these values in daily living as the founders of our faiths intended. Not easy, but events like interfaith week are at least a step in the right direction.

Plight of Refugees

The weekend news of seventeen bodies being pulled out of the Mediterranean and the rescue of more than 4,000 people in just three days reminds us of the unbelievable suffering in the Middle East. Refugees, from brutal rule in Libya, Syria and Iraq, are continuing to take their chance in leaky boats to escape further persecution. Their plight is mirrored by that of the Rohingya Muslims from Myanmar, starving and adrift in ships for months at an end, because no one will give them sanctuary.

A common feature of such tragedies is the manipulation of religious sentiment to further political power, with selective quotation of religious texts written hundreds of years ago being used to justify brutal behaviour.

Paradoxically, similar selective quotation is used to argue that religions teach only peace.

Most religions suffer this problem of selective quotation to justify different views. Sikhism is a comparatively new religion, with the founder, Guru Nanak, born in 1469. The teachings of the Gurus were couched in lasting ethical principles and were recorded in their lifetime. Sikhs were asked to follow only these recorded teachings. Despite this clarity, we still suffer from selective quotation on emotive issues such as meat eating, and more worryingly, in attempts to introduce new teachings which many Sikhs feel to be of dubious authenticity.

Today, religious leaders now have the additional task of disentangling advice, given to meet the particular social or political climate of several centuries ago, from more lasting and timeless ethical teachings. To move in this direction, it is important that our different religions work together to tackle common concerns. Sikhs believe that true religious commitment goes beyond narrow boundaries of belief and that our religious labels, or membership of different sects, count for nothing in the eyes of the one God of us all. It's what we do to counter poverty and work for peace and justice that really counts. The challenge of putting religious teachings in perspective and working together on common concerns is not easy, but it is essential that we move in this direction to make religion what the founders of our different faiths intended it to be: guidance for responsible living, and the cure rather than the cause of conflict.

Tackling Hate Crime

Last week I attended a meeting jointly called by the Home Office and Department for Communities for faith communities, police and other stakeholders about the alarming rise in hate crime. Many saw the solution in greater vigilance in reporting unacceptable behaviour, and firm action by the police and courts.

To me, as a Sikh, this alone was like applying sticking plasters to surface sores without tackling the underlying malady, namely irrational prejudice that leads us to place negative connotations on superficial differences like colour of skin, dress or foreign accent.

I see this as yet another reminder of what I call Indarjit's law of 'us' and 'them' – that when two or more people find sufficient in common to call themselves us, they will immediately identify someone to look down on to strengthen their sense of unity. We see it in rivalry between football fans, and in its worst form it can lead to the horrors of the Holocaust. Unscrupulous politicians all too often exploit the same irrational prejudices for political gain, particularly at a time of economic or social difficulty.

We all know that in a fog or mist, familiar objects can assume grotesque and frightening forms, and it is the same when we look at fellow humans through a lens of ignorance and prejudice.

Some people suggest that keeping religion in the private sphere well away from politics is one way of addressing prejudice. Nothing could be less helpful.

The Sikh Gurus taught that people of religion and political rulers should work together to build a tolerant and inclusive society.

Living at a time of religious conflict, they were well aware of the dangers of prejudice, and stressed the equal dignity and respect of all members, male and female, of our one human family.

Guru Gobind Singh, tenth Guru of the Sikhs, wrote:

God is in the temple as He is in the mosque
The Shia and the Sunni pray to the same one God
Despite differences in culture and appearance
All men have the same form. All pray to the same one God.

Today, the fog of ignorance and prejudice is still very much evident in attacks on minority communities, including hard-working Poles for speaking their own language. Much of this hate crime is also directed against religious communities, and both religions and secular society have a responsibility to look beyond superficial differences to important commonalities including a shared responsibility for a better future.

Continuing Search for Peace

Yesterday's Commonwealth Day Service in Westminster Abbey was on the theme of peace. But, with the firing of Kim Jong-un's 'look at me' rockets – rockets fueled by the blood and sweat of his impoverished people – Russia muscling in on the chaos and suffering in the Middle East and a record twenty million refugees without food and shelter, a truly peaceful world still seems a distant dream.

I found the service and prayers at the Abbey both moving and uplifting. In the Sikh view, prayers are essentially a charging of spiritual batteries to help us move in a better ethical direction. In this case, to a more active search for peace. And for this we clearly have to look beyond today's policies of deterrence and containment.

Sikh teachings remind us that peace is more than the absence of war; it is a universal respect for the rights of others, and I find it hard to believe that this can be achieved by narrowly focussing on deterrent might, with its inherent dangers of an escalation of rival power. New technologies and new ways of killing make yesterday's lethal weapons obsolete, not to be disposed of, but sold to developing countries, fueling conflict in a world awash with arms.

A moving Christian hymn reminds us that

New occasions teach new duties; time makes ancient good uncouth.
They must upwards still and onwards, who would keep abreast with truth.

Today's strategic alliances, while providing a measure of mutual security for some, do nothing to prevent continuing human rights' abuse for others. Guru Ram Dass, writing of pacts and alliances made in self-interest, taught that the only pact or commitment worth making was to God, in a commitment to an uncompromising pursuit of social and political justice, not only for our side, but for all people; a sentiment that has its echo in the UN Declaration of Human Rights.

Today, while many agree with such sentiments, some political leaders find it expedient to overlook human rights abuse in what are sometimes called friendly countries. The great human rights activist and scientist, Andre Sakharov, made clear his view that there can be no lasting peace in the world unless we are even-handed in tackling the abuse of human rights. Words we must take on board in our search for a more peaceful and fairer world.

Limits of Humanitarian Aid

The weekend post brought its usual appeals for donations to help in alleviating suffering in Syria, Iraq and other areas of the Middle East. The scale of suffering, wrought by internecine political, religious and ethnic conflict, is truly devastating and it is important that we support such appeals and help those risking their lives to help the victims of war and violence.

Next month, representatives of different faiths and secular society will meet at a service at Westminster Abbey for humanitarian aid workers killed in conflict. At the inaugural meeting four years ago, I referred to the extraordinary dedication and concern for others of an American, twenty-sixyear-old Kayla Mueller, captured by ISIS and reportedly killed in a Jordanian air strike. In a letter smuggled to her family, she wrote: 'If I have suffered at all throughout this experience, it is only in knowing how much suffering I have put you through ... The thought of your pain is the source of my own.'

No self-pity; no harsh word about her captors. Only a concern for others. There are many others like Kayla, and they all deserve our prayers and support. The reality however is their dedication and international aid efforts alone cannot cope with the suffering of those caught up in the fighting, and in the huge displacement of people we have witnessed, which just goes on and on.

I believe it is important to look more closely at the causes of such suffering. True, that violence begins with local rivalries, but unfortunately, these are magnified and made more horrific by larger factional rivalry between the great powers, supporting rival factions with ever-more sophisticated means of killing in pursuit of strategic interest. The Sikh Guru, Guru Amar Das, looking at the dubious alliances fracturing the society of his day, wrote:

I am of God's Faction. All other factional alliances are subject to death and decay.

Speaking from a Sikh perspective, if we wish to avoid the continuing man-made suffering of innocents, I believe we must continue to remind all in power to look beyond self-interest, to what Sikhs call '*sarbat ka bhalla*', a single-minded resolve to secure the well-being of all.

Some Talks and Lectures

P ublic life has provided me with many opportunities to talk about religious, ethical and human rights issues in various countries and venues. Some of these are reproduced below.

Gandhi Speak That Cloaks the Murderous Truth

The Guardian, 18 June 1984

During the 1930s and 1940s, Pandit Nehru, first prime minister of post-partition India, learnt from bitter personal experience of the ease with which a repressive government can label someone an extremist and throw him into prison. He was quick to learn the lessons from his British mentors and within months of becoming prime minister in 1947, he in turn incarcerated the more prominent of his political opponents, including the veteran Sikh leader, Master Tara Singh. The latter had dared to remind him of his promise to the Sikh people twelve months earlier, that he saw nothing wrong with an area being set aside in the north of India "where Sikhs could also experience the glow of freedom". Pandit Nehru commented "the situation is different now" when reminded of this promise. The Sikh leader was branded an extremist and duly jailed for demanding a measure of autonomy for Punjab that was in fact considerably less than that enjoyed by individual states in the United States of America.

Mr. Nehru's daughter, Indira Gandhi, with all the cynicism and double-talk of dictatorial governments posing as democracies, has been quick to improve on both the language and methods of repression. First in the 'Emergency', when all pretence of democracy was dropped, and more recently under the guise of democracy a cruel feline viciousness has been unleashed on the people of India. The 'Emergency' saw the disappearance of hundreds of political opponents, the forced sterilisation of the poor and the destruction of their hovels in the name of progress.

In the last two years, thousands of supposed 'terrorists' and 'political agitators' have been shot in Kashmir, Assam and Maharashtra. Now it is the turn of Punjab and the Sikhs. The massacre in Amritsar of perhaps as many as 2,000 mostly unarmed and innocent Sikh men, women and children – 'terrorists' – easily outdoes in barbarity and outrage the 1919 shooting at Jallianwala Bagh, where 379 people were killed by General Dyer.

The killings by General Dyer were in an open park; the slaughter at the Golden Temple was in the highest of holy Sikh shrines. Indira Gandhi's justification was that it was a base for Sikh 'terrorists'. Let us look at the facts. The one requirement for terrorism is secrecy. One could not plan terrorism from, say, the concourse of Waterloo station. Similarly, the Golden Temple with its famous four doors, to emphasise its welcome to pilgrims and visitors from all corners of the globe, irrespective of race, religion or nationality, had, to say the least, serious limitations that would, religious considerations apart, have precluded its use by any group intent on serious terrorism.

A secret telephone number is a useful asset for organising terrorism. The phones into the Golden Temple were known to and tapped by the police. Inside, right up to the time of the government attack, pilgrims and visitors, including the foreign press, were free to go into any part of the temple complex. Outside, a heavy police presence had existed for more than a year around each of the entrances. It is true that as government threats to enter and desecrate the temple increased over the months, parallel attempts to build up defences to deter such a sacrilegious attack also increased. The 'fortifying' of the Golden Temple was nothing but a response to increasing evidence that Mrs. Gandhi was determined to solve the 'Sikh question' by striking at the very heart of Sikhism.

Indira Gandhi is right when she says that terrorism must be rooted out, but who are the 'terrorists'? Those perpetrating organised violence, or those opposed to it? It is not generally known outside Punjab that over the past two years thousands of Sikh homes in Punjab villages have been raided by police and paramilitary forces. Young Sikhs have been dragged away for questioning, never to be seen again. The sight of murdered Sikhs floating in rivers and waterways has become a common occurrence.

The current issue of the *Journal of Amnesty International* cites several harrowing examples of Indian police brutality and torture. More recently, eyewitness accounts of the Amritsar massacre talk of women and children being shot in cold blood and Sikh prisoners being tied with their own turbans and then shot dead. Who then are the terrorists? The myth of 'terrorist base', borrowed from the vocabulary of subtler colonial powers, is not the only way in which this Mrs. Gandhi has allowed truth to be stood on its head. Lack of space forbids a more detailed analysis, but the reader trying to find truth in Mrs. Gandhi's press releases might well find the following glossary helpful:

Sikh extremists. One who believes that he should be allowed to practise his religion unmolested, and that Sikhs and other Punjabis should not be treated less favourably than their brothers and sisters in other Indian states.

Sikh fundamentalists. A Sikh who believes in the fundamentals of the Sikh religion; namely belief in one God, earning by one's own efforts, helping the less fortunate, religious tolerance, the equality of women and universal human brotherhood.

Sikh fanatic*. Alternative for Sikh fundamentalist.*

IG Factor*. A multiplier of 10, used by Indira Gandhi and the Indian government watchers, and based on experience in Kashmir, Assam and elsewhere to convert press release figures to something approaching reality. For example, the initial Indian government figure of 250 deaths in the Golden Temple converts to 2,500; eyewitness reports fear that this may be an understatement.*

Minimum use of force*. 'We went in with prayers on our lips', says an Indian general. It is now being reported that the army was given instructions not to take any prisoners. Cold-blooded slaughter of men women and children.*

No alternative*. The use of any or all of the following clichés to justify excessive use of force: discovery of stockpile of sophisticated weapons, bomb factory, involvement of a foreign power, CIA, etc.*

In the interests of National Security*. In the interests of Indira Gandhi and family.*

Democracy*. The inalienable right of a majority to crush minorities. Rule by Indira Gandhi and family, for Indira Gandhi and family.*

Indarjit Singh is the editor of the Sikh messenger, Member of the Religious Advisory Committee of the United Nations Association.

Ways to World Peace – A Sikh Perspective
Annual Peace Lecture at Coventry Cathedral, 2002

Some years ago, I was invited to make a Sikh contribution to an interfaith service on the theme of 'peace'. I readily agreed and looked at Sikh scriptures to find an appropriate passage, to my increasing dismay, without success. It was then that I realised why a religion that has such positive guidance on the themes of justice and human rights is silent on the concept of 'peace' in its most widelyaccepted sense, namely, 'the absence of war'.

The absence of physical conflict does not itself guarantee or imply political freedom and a respect for basic human rights. All wars, ipso facto, end in an absence of conflict, but this does not necessarily imply justice. All too frequently right does not triumph, and truth and justice are themselves often major casualties of conflict. We all recall how tanks and guns of China's army brought 'peace' to Beijing's Tiananmen Square. It was the peace of the graveyard.

The Roman Empire had its Pax Romana covering much of Europe and the Middle East. It also had its slave markets, torture and death by crucifixion. In more recent years, there was the British Empire with its Pax Britannica. This vast

Empire, one on which, it was said, the sun never set, was more benevolent than some of its predecessors, but Pax Britannica was none-the-less a peace imposed on the unwilling to bring civilisation and supposed Christian-values to natives and heathen. Nor was it without its direct repression, like the infamous Jallianwalla Bagh massacre where, in the spring of 1919, several hundred people in Punjab were massacred in minutes by the soldiers of General Dyer in a brazen display of brute authority. It was an act condemned by the British Parliament and the spark that ignited the freedom torch in India.

It was, incidentally, during the British expansion into India that the British and Sikhs first met face to face in the fiercest conflict seen on the sub-continent. The Sikhs were eventually defeated, but each side recognised the valour and courage of the other. The British, impressed by the tenacity of the Sikhs in battle, described them as a martial race. It was a description that stuck and although intended as a compliment, the term martial race does grave injustice to the peaceful teachings of Sikhism.

Sikhs are duty bound to stand up against tyranny and injustice and did so against the excesses of the earlier Moghul rulers who put a price on the head of every Sikh caught dead or alive. If Sikhs have martial qualities, it is because history and circumstances from Moghul times, through British rule and sadly even to today, have forced us into continued robust opposition to oppression.

The British Empire and Western colonialism had reached its peak by the commencement of the Second World War, which saw the mild racism of the Western world assume grotesque proportions in the horror of Nazism. The war saw the killing of millions in direct combat and this was dwarfed by the horrors of saturation bombing of civilians, including the incineration of thousands in the atomic bombings of Hiroshima and Nagasaki. The war also saw the methodical extermination of hundreds and thousands of, mostly, Jews in gas chambers. About a year ago, I visited Auschwitz in Poland, where the gas chambers have been preserved for all to see. What brought the inhumanity of the human race home to me was a huge mountain of tiny infants' shoes, taken from toddlers before they were herded into the gas chambers.

One of my earliest memories as a child was cinema newsreel footage of the liberation of the Belsen concentration camp at the end of the Second World War. I saw emaciated skeletal bodies of men, women and children, living dead, who had all but given up hope. For many years, I, in common with many others, thought that the genocide was a one-off act of human madness, unique to the Nazis. Sadly, in the years that have followed the ending of the Second World War, we have seen genocide in Cambodia, Bosnia, Kosovo, the horn of Africa and in many other parts of the world. It's a sobering reminder of human brutality that frenzied machete killings of more than a million men, women and children in Rwanda exceeded the killings per hour of the Nazi gas chambers.

For the moment though, I want to take you back to the immediate post-Second World War world, where the discovery of the full horror of the gas chambers and the death camps silenced all talk about superior and inferior races. In the Europe of the '30s, persecution of Jews was not confined to Germany alone. It's often forgotten that the word Jew was a common term of abuse in this country, both before and during the Second World War.

It was this myth of racial superiority that had sustained rulers and cowed the ruled, in Empire and colonies, and its collapse in the ruin of the Third Reich gave a major fillip to independence movements around the world. For the first time in human history there was a brief recognition of the proposition put forward by Guru Gobind Singh, tenth Guru of the Sikhs, some two and a half centuries earlier.

Manas ki jath sab ek he pacharbo.

(Recognise the oneness of the human family.)

The formation of the United Nations Organisation in 1945 echoed this sentiment, although great power rivalry seriously hampered its effectiveness. The UN Charter, and the later Declaration of Human Rights, gave powerful support to the proposition underlined again and again in Sikh teachings, that true and lasting peace is dependent on the recognition of the fundamental human rights of every man, woman and child.

In the words of the preamble to the Declaration of Human Rights on 10 December 1948:

It is essential, if man is not to be compelled to have recourse, as a last resort, to rebellion against tyranny and oppression, that human rights should be respected by the rule of law.

On the adoption of the UN Charter, the Great Powers could have moved in either of two directions: active efforts to ensure basic human rights for all in the spirit of the Charter, or to pay lip service to the Charter with last ditch attempts to preserve the status quo against the tide of human history. Sadly, the Great Powers chose the latter course, with the Soviet Union determined to hold onto its new Empire in the East, and the Western powers equally determined to salvage and hold onto what they could of their colonial possessions and, as these crumbled, to emerge in new power block politics for political and economic gain. The rivalry between the Communist and Capitalist worlds manifested itself in the ensuing 'Cold War' and in recognition of the capacity of either side to destroy the other.

There was peace of sorts between both sides, but it was a peace not based on justice but on the horror of total destruction which continued until the economic and political collapse of Communism in the late '80s and early '90s.

Many in the West have complimented themselves on the long interval of peace, conveniently forgetting more than sixty lesser wars in the Third World, often fought by proxy between the Superpowers, in which more people have been killed than in the whole of the Second World War. The double tragedy is that those living in what is called the developed world have become so inured to such conflicts that we see nothing wrong in the use of Third World nations as pawns in some global game of chess between the Superpowers. We saw it as the natural order of things, and still see it as such today.

We talk of a common brotherhood, of one world, and have ritual celebrations of One World Week, and yet are prepared to accept our brothers and sisters being destroyed by bullets and bombs manufactured by ourselves and other developed and developing countries. Most industrialised nations see the arms industry as an important earner of foreign exchange as well as a means to political leverage on the less 'developed' world.

As our grandchildren and their children look back on today's times, I am sure that they will do so with loathing and revulsion at a generation prepared to countenance and continue the suffering of millions for its own economic prosperity.

Today the talk is about Iraq and the dossier of evil perpetrated by Saddam Hussein on his own people. We recall how in 1988 he used poison gas to massacre thousands of Kurdish men, women and children. Britain publicly condemned Iraq at the time, and yet within weeks it dispatched a trade mission to Iraq to negotiate the sale of additional arms. Some three years earlier, I was told by a Government minister that "we are well aware of the suffering of the Sikhs in the India of Rajiv Gandhi", but, he continued, "it's very difficult, we are walking on a tightrope and have already lost one major contract".

The arms trade is continuing to grow. Third World nations are encouraged to buy arms to match those of their neighbours. The more they spend on arms, the less of their GNP they have to spend on food and industrialisation, and the less competitive they will be in world trade. Poverty inevitably breeds discontent and instability and further opportunities for exploitation.

Sometimes the elements add to this catalogue of human suffering as with recurring famines in the Horn of Africa. When conditions are sufficiently bad to become news and we see Belsen-like emaciation on our TV screens, we salve our consciences with Band Aid type concerts and famine relief collections. And in a very real sense it is a 'band-aid', like putting sticking plasters over deep and festering wounds. The plaster covers or hides some of the suffering but does little to cure it.

In the India of Guru Nanak's day, the rich would often give small donations to the poor, to those they exploited, in the belief that this would earn them merit in the next world. The Guru was critical of such giving which induced a smugness in the giver whilst perpetuating injustice. These ritual acts of charity were, he said, not worth a grain of sesame seeds. Much the same can be said about Western aid which gives with one hand and takes back through protectionist tariffs and low prices for raw materials with the other.

We see then, peace enjoyed by the industrialised world today is one based on politics and alliances, which mask and perpetuate injustice and is far removed from the peace based on a universal acceptance of human rights as envisaged in the UN Charter. It is a fragile peace that will not easily endure. What do we need to do to make it more lasting and based on true justice?

Guru Nanak was an acute observer of the human scene, some 500 years ago where religion had been reduced to ritual and superstition for ordinary people, dominated by a tyrannical priestly class, the Brahmins. The Brahmins taught that they and only they could commune with God and people's ancestors in heaven and extracted money and food from the poor to intercede with God on their behalf. As if this was not bad enough, the country had been conquered by the Moghuls, fierce Islam-professing descendants of Genghis Khan, bent on forced conversion.

The Guru saw common people being exploited in the name of religion. He saw conquerors inflicting untold misery on their subjects. He saw one set of oppressors being replaced by another and realised that we would do well to understand today that there can be no real peace without justice. He therefore set out his blueprint for a just society.

Looking at the world around him, he started with the need for religious tolerance. In his very first sermon he declared:

Ne koi Hindu Na koi Mussalman.

That is, in God's eyes there is neither Hindu nor Muslim and, in today's extension, neither Christian, Sikh nor Jew. God is not interested in religious labels but in the way we conduct ourselves. God, he taught, has neither enemies nor favoured people, and no one religion has a monopoly of truth; an important lesson for the world today, where bigotry of belief so often incites and sustains horrendous conflict. This is particularly true of the three Abrahamic religions where each claim to have an exclusive relationship to God. We are all free to believe what we like, but to parade these beliefs or denigrate the beliefs of others in our smaller inter-dependent world is to invite conflict. For peace in the world today, we must look on other religions with tolerance and respect. Today we need to look beyond the commonly accepted meaning of tolerance, suggesting a reluctant willingness to put up with, and look more towards the Sikh meaning of the word, which is a willingness to defend to the death, if necessary, another's right to belief. This is precisely what our ninth Guru, Guru Teg Bahadur, did when he was cruelly martyred in 1776 for upholding the right of Hindus to worship in the manner of their choice.

Religious fundamentalism is a growing cause of conflict in the world today. The Gurus showed respect to the Hindu and Muslim faiths by incorporating some of their texts in the Sikh holy book, the *Guru Granth Sahib*. It was an important lead which we would do well to remember today in learning to substitute dialogue for fanaticism. There is a further reward in such dialogue. While we learn to respect genuine differences, we also find that different faiths have much in common and our understanding of our own belief is heightened by resonant echoes in other faiths.

The Guru understood that there can be no justice if some people consider themselves inherently superior to others. Today we talk of race. In India the talk was of caste. Very much the same thing.

Guru Nanak taught:

Janan jot, na pucho jath
Agee jath nah koi.
Look to a person's inner light (God)
and forget all ideas of caste or race,
for there is no caste or race in the hereafter.

It was a sentiment echoed by each of the succeeding Gurus. As Guru Gobind Singh, our tenth Guru, put it:

Recognise the oneness of the human race.

Compare this directness with the fuzzy fudging world of today, where we talk of the need for understanding or harmony between the different races. There are no different races. The sciences of genetics and anthropology confirm what common sense tells us: we are all members of one human family.

Most people in the affluent world, however, would balk at the logical extension of this proposition of allowing other members of our human family the right to live and work where they like. There are fears that in our far from just world of today, those fleeing from political tyranny or from adverse economic or climatic conditions would, to coin a phrase, 'swamp' our culture and reduce our standard of living. It would be irresponsible and a recipe for chaos to suggest a sudden abandonment of all immigration controls, but the reality of globalisation is that more and more people will gravitate towards areas of greater economic opportunity and political freedom. A phased and worldwide reduction of such controls should be high on the political agenda. Sikhs feel that beliefs have their own imperatives, and that we have a moral duty as well as a practical one of moving towards a world of freer movement of members of our single human family.

If we truly believe in the ideal of one human family, we cannot support the notion of power blocks and friendly nations and factional alignments. Such factions and alignments are not new and the Guru in a beautiful hymn constantly stressed, 'I am of God's faction'.

Not only do such factional politics divide us into warring camps but they also blur our sense of morality and injustice. In the world of today we turn a blind eye to human rights abuses in a friendly country while criticising those in other lands. Those who oppose governments in rival power blocks, whatever their motives or methods, are proclaimed freedom fighters. Similarly, those who rebel against perceived injustice in a friendly country are automatically dubbed 'terrorists'. There is today a lot of misleading talk of an international terrorist conspiracy. Would people really meet and risk life and limb to harm others without some trigger of real or apparent injustice?

Sikhs would argue that it is right and proper to oppose those that would harm innocent people, whatever the provocation. We would also argue that the best way to fight terrorism is to look to the underlying malady on which it parasitically thrives.

Sikhs heartily endorse the views of the late Andrei Sakharov who said that for real progress in human rights we must be even-handed in our condemnation of human rights abuses no matter where they occur, whether in friendly or less friendly countries. Similarly, we applaud the work of Amnesty International and similar human rights organisations who even-handedly expose what nations and power blocks try to mask: the full extent of human degradation with detailed dossiers which show that torture of suspects or innocent protesters against injustice is now routine practice in more than half the nations of the so-called civilised world.

A 'religious' person in Guru Nanak's day was one who left family and friends and sought spiritual enlightenment in mountains or forests. Guru Nanak was very critical of such a selfish approach to life. Once when on a visit to a group of such holy people, the Guru was asked "How goes the world below?" The Guru angrily replied, "The world is suffering and how can it be otherwise when those with knowledge and understanding selfishly desert society?" He taught the then new concept of social responsibility, both for individuals and religions. How is this relevant to the world of today?

Firstly, on the role of religions. The industrialised world has, since the Industrial Revolution, increasingly seen religions marginalised as a force for good. Keep religion out of politics, is from a Sikh perspective, like saying keep truth, justice and compassion out of politics. These concerns may have little relevance to the cold blinkered world of a free-market economy but are highly relevant to the building of a just, stable and peaceful society.

The fault also lies with leaders of religion who, finding the outside world complex and challenging, all too readily turn inwards to cloistered contemplation of the hereafter. Or worse, pay increasing attention to rituals, customs and divisive practices that have nothing to do with true religion.

Today, one of the most frequently heard boasts is, "I've led a good life, I've never done anyone any harm." Countless sticks, stones, rivers and mountains could boast the same.

Allied to the hollow boasts of doing no harm is the equally smug one of having no enemies. The poet Charles McKay examines this in his poem 'No Enemies':

You have no enemies you say?
Alas! my friend the boast is poor
He who has mingled in the fray
Of duty, that the brave endure
Must have made foes! If you have none,
Small is the work you have done
You've never turned the wrong to right,
You've been a coward in the fight.

Sikhism demands a far more positive commitment, particularly from those who claim to be religious.

Alexander Solzhenitsyn, in a Guildhall lecture to mark his receipt of the 1983 Templeton Award, spoke of his childhood when people, appalled by the suffering in the early years of the Russian Revolution, would remark: "It's all because we've forgotten God." He continued, "Today, having witnessed cruelty and horror that totally dwarfs that of earlier years, having researched libraries of books and documents, if I am asked to explain why the excesses, I can do no better than to repeat those pithy words: it's all because we've forgotten God."

Sikhs wholly endorse these sentiments. In our arrogance, we fail to see that our human vision of justice is blurred, short-sighted and distorted by baser human emotions of greed, envy and pride. As Guru Nanak taught:

The highest vision of justice
Lies not with man, but God.

Despite the arrogance of our all too clever materialistic world, we need the guidance of religion to give us a truer perspective of justice and our responsibilities to our planet and our fellow humans.

We were all thrilled by the dramatic changes in Eastern Europe at the end of the '80s which caused the disintegration of a totalitarian Empire and removed a major threat to world peace. It would be nice to believe that the prime motivation was human rights and the democratic ideal. But I fear that it was more the recognition that the free-market economy was a more effective means of producing consumer goods and a higher Western style standard of living.

The dangers from an obsession with consumerism are twofold. First, the fallacy that happiness and contentment are related to the number of such possessions. Secondly, the instability in society arising from competitive consumerism. On the national level, this is manifested in strikes, inequitable taxation and civil unrest. On the international level, the effects are even more serious.

We have seen how economic greed finds expression in the international arms trade. In a similar way, political and economic pressures have combined to produce a grossly inequitable distribution of wealth, with industrialised powers manipulating the price of raw materials and inflating those of manufactured goods in a way that keeps the poor and makes the rich richer. It is here that we have to remember the Gurus' teaching:

Kirt karo and Wand chakho.
Earn by your own effort, earn fairly and share or distribute your good fortune equitably.

Not to do this is not only wrong in itself but also a sure recipe for social and political instability that threatens not only the poorer nations but, in our shrinking world, threatens the peace and stability of all of us.

The Sikh teachings that I've elaborated are, in my view, foundations for the establishment of a just world order and lasting peace. Sikhism does not believe peace can be obtained by merely wishing it. Peace is the natural corollary of a just worldwide social order. If we wish peace, we should look to eradicate social and political injustice in all its forms.

Compare this approach of building sound foundations for peace and justice with the political approach of trying to perpetuate the status quo of inequality and trying to graft peace onto this by treaties, conferences and rhetoric; a sort of building downwards. Which approach is likely to succeed?

I have spoken at length on Sikh requisites for peace and justice. While it is incumbent on us all to work for such ideals, what do we do about those who selfishly and deliberately tread the path of tyranny and oppression?

Let us again look briefly at the UN Declaration of Human Rights which states:

Whereas it is essential that if man is not compelled as a last recourse to rebellion against tyranny and oppression, that human rights should be protected by the rule of law.

The words are almost an exact echo of Sikh teaching in this respect. In the words of Guru Gobind Singh:

When all other means of overcoming injustice fail
It is rightful to use the sword.

Both statements recognise the right to rebellion or the use of force when all other means fail.

Sikhism lays down clear conditions for a violent response to injustice. Firstly, violence should never be used in response to personal injury. The correct response to personal attack or insult is, as stated in the holy *Granth*, 'To kiss the feet of those that do you wrong'. Secondly, force should never be used for personal gain or to acquire even an inch of territory. The Sikh Gurus had to fight many battles against tyranny but never sought to acquire any area of territory. Some years later, the Sikh General, Bhagel Singh, concerned about the sanctity of the place where the ninth Guru, Guru Teg Bahadur, was martyred, marched to Delhi from Punjab with his army, captured the city and, when satisfied with guarantees that a gurdwara would be built at the place of the Guru's martyrdom, astounded both rulers and later historians by marching all the way back to Punjab in literal interpretation of the Guru's teachings.

Violence can only be justified in the protection of human rights if all other means have been tried and failed. The Sikh Gurus only turned to arms after the fifth Guru, Guru Arjan, was martyred for his support of religious freedom. The Sikhs were among the first to use non-violent protest against the British. The Sikh 'morchas' or non-violent campaigns for the freedom of their shrines from corrupt British-backed priests are chronicled in history with its daily batch of volunteers being beaten senseless by the army. The Sikh victory in freeing their places of worship in this way was hailed by Mahatma Gandhi with a telegram saying: 'Congratulations! First battle for India's independence won.'

It is fundamental to Sikhism that we are duty-bound to oppose tyranny and injustice in all its forms. And in a world where tyranny is all too widespread Sikhs have had to fight for their very survival. Hence, the image of the martial race. Sikhs were taught by the Guru to be Sant Sipahis – Saint Soldiers – saintly in conduct even in battle, as Bhai Kanhaiya was when he gave water to the thirsty and suffering in the enemy ranks and was commended by Guru Gobind Singh for so doing.

Let me now conclude by briefly summarising key points.

Peace without justice is no peace at all. Real and lasting peace can only emanate from social and political justice and it is the duty of all of us to work towards this goal. It is especially the duty of religions to make a more positive input. To religious leaders in both my own and sister faith, I make this plea. What is the use of all our talk of spirituality and higher moral values if not to help our fellow man? We have in the United Nations organisation a framework for a more just world order. What we now need to do is to ensure our politicians stop simply paying lip service to its ideals and work positively to ensure that our children and their children live in peace based on justice.

International Meeting at the Vatican, 27–28 March 2008

Extracts from a talk on Intercultural Education and Religious Pluralism

Friends, I have been described in the Programme as a member of the Sikh community. While this is correct, I need to emphasise that Sikhism is a religion in its own right. A religion that emphasises:

- belief in one God; creator of all that exists
- the oneness of the human race
- respect for different ways of life
- an uplifting moral code
- a welcome to those of any faith or cultural background, while not seeking to actively convert others
- and importantly, how to live positively in peace and harmony with others in our increasingly global society.

I welcome this opportunity to give a Sikh perspective on intercultural dialogue in education and, if I may, I'd like to extend it to the wider role of religion in society, particularly in helping our children become responsible citizens in a fast-changing world. In the Sikh view, education is all about preparing our children to make a positive contribution to the well-being of the world around. While we rightly teach our children the 3 Rs, to be literate and

166

numerate, we seem to place less emphasis on the other, equally important, 3 Rs which are the essence of religion, namely right, wrong and responsibility.

Many believe that this responsibility lies with parents; others assume it lies with the school. In the Sikh view, it's the responsibility of both parents and teachers to help children to grow up to be considerate and responsible members of society. Unfortunately, it sometimes slips between the two, and children are left to develop their own sense of right and wrong, guided by television, with its questionable output including dramas and so-called comedies, in which infidelity is seen as something of a giggle while ignoring the hurt that transient adult relationships can cause to children.

Until very recent times, we could all grow up in the comfort and security of a religion that we shared with those that lived around us. It was common and patriotic (it still is for some) to go into raptures about *our* way of life compared with the inferior ways of foreigners. Many believed that even God acknowledged our natural superiority and was always on our side. Schools, in the teaching of literature and history, often contributed to the promotion of false ideas of superiority and difference.

We see it again and again in literature. Some of you may recall the famous lines of John of Gaunt in Shakespeare's *Richard II*.

This happy breed of men, this little world
This precious stone set in the silver sea,
Which serves it in the office of a wall,
Or a moat defensive to a house
Against the envy of less happier lands
... and more!

We learnt to study the literary style, the use of figurative language. We never thought to criticise the xenophobic insularity of its general sentiment. Nor did the possibility occur to us in Britain, that other nations might have different explanations of God's purpose in isolating the British! Seriously though, it's important to understand that this sort of thinking was common to most nations and cultures. Many in India even argued that to leave the shores of the subcontinent would pollute them forever.

In the past, we could strengthen our sense of cohesion and identity, including religious identity, by misrepresenting the ways and beliefs of others, or describing them in disparaging terms.

There is a law of life that I call Indarjit's law: that when two or more people find sufficient in common to call themselves 'us', they will find a 'them' to look down on, to strengthen their sense of unity. You see it when a person leaves a small group talking together. The odds are that those remaining members of the group will make some negative comment about the person that has just left! We often see this group or mob unity in conflict between rival football supporters. More dangerously, our human tendency to see fault in those we perceive as different can lead to active hatred of whole communities.

I saw a reminder of this descent to evil on a visit to Auschwitz in Poland, where many Jews, blamed for all the ills in Europe, were callously murdered. While going around the former concentration camp, I saw the shower area where new arrivals were asked to wash before receiving promised new clothes and food. Once in, the doors would be closed and deadly gas fed in through vents in the ceiling. I saw the gas canisters, the conveyer to the incinerator and mounds of human hair, but what really got to me was a huge pile of infants' shoes. In my mind's eye, I could see little children skipping and laughing, blissfully unaware of what was to befall them.

A few years ago, I did some work for Amnesty International, looking at genocide and human rights abuse in a number of different countries; abuse which often involved unbelievable depravity. Almost as bad as the abuse was the realisation that those whom we learn to trust are often the perpetrators: police and soldiers, and, even worse, priests and teachers and previously friendly neighbours. Why do people behave in such ways?

The reality of human nature, and the evidence is all around us, is that we humans do not come with preloaded software of right, wrong and responsibility. Decent responsible behaviour has to be taught and learnt. We cannot have a better society without better people. We cannot have better people without responsible

Teaching. The question is, who should do the teaching?

Today, with the increasing movement of people in our global society, there is an instinctive and understandable reaction to hold on to the past and rediscover national norms of behaviour and responsibility. This is seen in calls for formal declarations of allegiance, with emphasis on citizenship training and conforming behaviour.

I think it's important here to differentiate between two types of behaviour. The first is behaviour that keeps us out of trouble. For the small child, it's not throwing food about, or indulging in unruly behaviour; for adults, it's being reasonably polite to those around us, and complying with those in authority and the rules and laws of society.

Is religion necessary for teaching behaviour at this level? Of course not. No more than it's necessary to involve religion in teaching a dog to stand on its hind legs, or a dolphin to perform tricks. Sanction or reward are sufficient motivators. In many ways, the teaching of citizenship to help children understand and appreciate the society in which they live falls into this category. It's important for children to learn about national institutions, democracy, the media and our view of the world about us. These teachings of citizenship, or conforming behaviour, are not however the same as the teachings of religion.

Conforming behaviour, or social norms, are constantly changing. What is acceptable today may seem narrow and bigoted to others and ourselves with the passage of time. For example, the law of the land in France prohibits the wearing of the hijab for Muslim girls and the turban for Sikh boys in state schools. Citizenship education in French schools would support such a policy.

The reality, however, is that the prohibition is bound to harm integration, and hurt self-esteem by forcing children to have one identity at school and another at home. State policy in France is at odds with both common sense and the ethical imperative for all of us in today's world to understand and respect different ways of life. Sikhs are grateful that the French policy of insisting that children grow ignorant of the values of others has been strongly condemned by the Catholic Church in France.

Last year we celebrated the 200th anniversary of the abolition of the slave trade, perfectly respectable at the time. In the UK in the 1960s, accommodation adverts in shop windows often had the words 'no blacks or coloureds', perfectly legal at the time. Citizenship teaching at the time would not have criticised such behaviour.

Religion, on the other hand, bases its teachings on what it sees as fundamental truths that, unlike the law of the land, do not change with time and place. In his very first sermon, Guru Nanak declared *"Na koi Hindu, Na koi Mussalman"* that in God's eyes there is neither Hindu nor Muslim, and by today's extension, neither Christian, Sikh nor Jew. God, he taught, is not interested in our religious labels, but in the way we behave.

It is important, then, that we look beyond labels, customs and dress to the reality behind different ways of life in our increasingly multi-faith and multicultural society. You will all be aware that in a fog or mist, normally familiar objects can assume frightening proportions. In the same way, looking at the customs and practices of others through the fog of ignorance can lead to genuine fear and alarm. What is so important in education today is that in our schools and workplaces we work to remove this fog of ignorance and see and respect others as they really are.

Take, for example, Sikhs and the wearing of a turban. To those who see virtue in dress conformity, the turban may be seen as an obstacle to integration. However, further probing as to why Sikhs feel they should be recognised for what they are will reveal an episode in Sikh history that has strong parallels with a key moment in Christian history, when Jesus Christ's disciples denied their association with him.

The wearing of the Sikh turban is linked to a similar incident in Sikh history. In the mid-seventeenth century, Guru Teg Bahadhur, the ninth Guru of the Sikhs, true to the Sikh teaching of tolerance and respect for other ways of life, was publicly beheaded by the Muslim rulers for defending the right of Hindus, people of a different religion to his own, to worship in the manner of their choice. The Mughal rulers challenged Sikhs, who then had no distinguishing appearance, to come forward and claim their master's body. But, in the event, courage failed them and the body was removed under the cover of darkness.

Guru Gobind Singh, the last of the Sikh Gurus, decreed that in future, Sikhs should never hide under anonymity, but should always be prepared to stand up and be recognisable for their ideals. Our turban reminds us of this, particularly the need to stand up to injustice in all its forms. It enables visible appearance to be measured against actual behaviour and action. It reminds us that we should be true to Sikh teachings twenty-four hours a day, and has much the same purpose as the dress of a priest or other cleric. With knowledge, the turban, far from being a stubborn impediment to integration, becomes a reassuring symbol of a commitment to high ideals.

Let's now look at how can we make ours a more cohesive and caring society. Voluntary effort and, increasingly, government and other statutory effort are becoming more alert to social ills in our society. But in focussing on problems, rather than more holistically on causes, we sometime tend to look through the wrong end of the telescope and seek to treat spots and sores of social maladies, rather than look further to underlying causes.

Let me give some examples. If problems resulting from drug abuse take up too much police time, the call is to legalise use and free police time, rather than question why the use of drugs has risen so dramatically. The huge rise in child and teenage pregnancies is met with a call to issue contraceptives in schools. Surprise, surprise, the rise in teenage pregnancies has increased almost in direct proportion to contraceptive education. Increasing alcohol abuse? Let's extend or abolish licensing hours to spread the incidence of drunken or loutish behaviour. Result: a rise in binge drinking. Too many people ending up in prison? Let's build more prisons. Extend this thinking of looking to the wrong end of a problem to the behaviour of the little boy who greets visitors to the house by kicking them in the shins. Solution: issue visitors with shin pads as they enter the front door!

Today's society that seeks happiness in consumer goods, drink or drugs, or in pampering ourselves 'because we're worth it' or making money through exporting the means of killing to distant lands in the name of a defence industry, clearly needs a bit of ethical uplift. The Catholic Church is doing much to provide this uplift through its courageous stance on combating poverty and working for social justice throughout the world. Much more can and must be done by religion to move drifting society away from an obsession with a futile pursuit of the mirage of material happiness, towards more positive, peaceful and ethical living.

Sikhism sees other religions as different paths to a truer understanding of God; like paths up a mountain. We can start from different points, but still reach the same goal. This is not to say that all religions are the same. There are important differences that should be understood and respected. The paths, however, are not necessarily mutually exclusive. In the Sikh view, they frequently merge in ways that give us a heightened understanding of our own faith.

Take, for example, the Sikh teaching: 'There is an inner-light in all; and that light is God.' Exactly the same sentiment is conveyed in the line of the Christian hymn: 'To all life Thou givest, to both great and small; in all life thou livest the true life of all.' It is important to remember that a major benefit of our study of other religions is that it gives us a wider view of religion and a new and fuller perspective on our own beliefs. We learn that different religions are not barriers between people, but gateways to a greater understanding and enrichment of life.

As I mentioned earlier, the role of religion is to challenge the often-inequitable norms of society and lift society to a more ethical plane. Far from accepting the status quo on social practices, Guru Nanak was boldly critical of divisive practices such as the caste system, or superstitious dietary customs, and taboos on eating with or socialising with those of other faiths. He and his successor Gurus taught the oneness of our human family and, in this, emphasised the dignity and complete equality of women; teachings wholly at odds with the practices of the day.

Religion reminds us of the need for balance in life. Sikhism, for example, requires us to live in three dimensions at one and the same time. *Naam japna, kirt karna* and *wand chakhna*. *Naam japna* is meditating on God or reflecting on our direction in life in a way that allows us to distinguish between the trivial, which so often obsesses us, and the real priorities of life. *Kirt karna* is earning by honest effort, and *wand chakhna* is the sharing of our good fortune with the needy, a common and important teaching of all our great religions.

Let me conclude. Whenever I undertake any sort of do-it-yourself activity, I inevitably get into difficulties. When all else fails, then, and only then, I turn to the book of instructions. Today, having pushed the ethical teachings of religion to the margins of society, we see that our smug do-it-ourselves approach to a fairer and more peaceful society has clearly failed. It's time to turn to the book, or books, of instructions; to our holy scriptures for true guidance on balanced and responsible living.

One of the greatest gains in adopting a wider view of religious education in today's world is that in our study of our different religions we discover common, uplifting, ethical imperatives, lacking in materialistic society. Our different religions are, in essence, overlapping circles of belief and ethical guidance, in which the area of overlap is far greater than the smaller areas of difference.

Sikhs believe that in that area of overlap lies common values of tolerance, justice and compassion. Values that make us more considerate and responsible human beings; values that should be the essence of both national identity and wider human aspiration; values central to our different religions that are the key to both personal happiness and the wellbeing of the wider society.

Talk on Disadvantaged Groups in East London, 2013

I am grateful to Linda Bellos and others for giving me this brief opportunity to talk to you on Sikh teachings on disability.

Two factors influence Sikh attitudes to disadvantage, disability and sickness. First, there are the teachings of Sikhism encapsulated in our holy scriptures, the *Guru Granth Sahib*, which teaches that all members of our human family – men, women and children – should be treated with equal respect, care and compassion.

There are no 'Old Testament' type strictures against marginalised groups like gays and lesbians. The Gurus criticised all notions of caste and the lower status of women found in Indian society. So-called lower castes were welcomed into Sikh society and the writings of some of their saints are included in the *Guru Granth Sahib.*

Guru Nanak and other founding Gurus all lived true to Sikh teachings of care, compassion and concern for the vulnerable and marginalised in society. The eighth Guru, Guru Harkishan, died while aiding smallpox victims in Delhi. Guru Gobind Singh, the last of the ten founding Gurus, embraced Bhai Kanhaiya, a Sikh water carrier accused of comforting the enemy wounded, giving rise to an earlier version of the Red Cross and leprosy suffers, and others with disabilities were welcomed and cared for in Sikh places of worship.

The same Guru, when giving all male Sikhs the name Singh, literally 'lion' to remind us of the importance of courage, also emphasised the individuality and equality of women by giving all Sikh females the name or title Kaur, literally 'princess'. In Sikh society, women do not have to take their husband's name and are considered individuals in their own right. Women have an equal right to manage Sikh places of worship.

The second factor which can influence attitudes to disability and supposed difference is the influence of sub-continent culture which can, at times, be negative and insensitive and can at times lead to some Sikhs forgetting uplifting religious teachings. Fortunately, there are many others in the community who live true to Sikh teachings and are a real inspiration to others.

Let me tell you the story of one man, Puran Singh, who devoted his entire life in pursuit of these Sikh ideals. Puran Singh, affectionately known as Bhagat Puran Singh, was born in the early 1900s and was both a contemporary and a friend of my father, Dr Diwan Singh. Incidentally, my father's own selfless service as a young doctor in bandaging up and looking after demonstrators against British rule, beaten up by the police, led to his exile from Punjab and our family's eventual settlement in Britain, and is the reason why I am here today.

Puran Singh's story began when he was walking down one of Amritsar's busy streets. He saw an emaciated crippled child at the side of the road virtually ignored by the hundreds of passers-by. Puran Singh thought about Sikh teachings about helping those who had no help, as told to him by his mother. A lanky teenager, he bent down and lifted the crippled child onto his shoulders and carried him home. Soon, Puran Singh carrying rejected disabled people on his shoulders to his home became a familiar sight. He worked as hard as he physically and mentally could and resorted to whatever options were available to care and provide for his 'patients', just like a father or mother would care and provide for their children. No barrier or hurdle could stop him in his effort to care for these 'community rejects' who had no one to turn to. His work led to the establishment of a home called Pingalwara for those with physical and mental disabilities.

Puran Singh's wonderful work struck a chord in the Sikh community with collection boxes in gurdwaras and at the roadside marked 'Donations to Pingalwara'. Today, Pingalwara is a thriving, internationally recognised complex.

Others have been inspired by Sikh teachings and the work of people like Bhagat Puran Singh and have set up similar facilities including a home for the handicapped as far afield as Ranchi in Bihar.

The Sikh scriptures, *Guru Granth Sahib*, has been translated into Braille. Blind people in the community are generally well supported and cared for. Some train as musicians and are always welcomed in our gurdwaras. One such person who I value as a friend, Sital Singh Sitara, travels by bus across London to different venues to teach children to play musical instruments and the singing of kirtan.

Many Sikh gurdwaras in the UK organise camps in India where volunteer surgeons perform thousands of cataract operations. Sikhs widely encourage children with physical disabilities, or those with autism and learning difficulties, to come with them to the gurdwara and to social functions. Most gurdwaras have youth wings which organise charity events to provide funds not only for hospital items like scanners, but also vehicles and drivers to ensure disabled people and the elderly always have care and transport facilities. There is, however, no room for complacency, and with a growing elderly population we have much more to do to ensure that we are living true to Sikh teachings of respect and concern for all and the inspiring lives of our Gurus.

Role of International Diplomacy and Education in Promoting Respect for Religion and Belief

Talk at the UN in Geneva, October 2016
There was a dachshund once who hadn't any notion
how long it took to notify his tail of his emotion.
So oft when his countenance was filled with woe and sadness
His little tail went wagging on because of previous gladness.

Society today is a bit like the dachshund in the poem, with the head and tail emotions reversed. We live in a time of rapid advances in technology, communications and ethical understanding that propel us towards a world of growing cooperation and interdependence, while at the same time experiencing the powerful reverse pull of a yearning for the political certainties of the past. Dated political thinking and popular prejudice, including religious prejudice, pull us back to a rose-tinted past where life appeared to be less challenging.

Nineteenth-century political diplomacy, still very much with us, was all about looking to the strengths and weaknesses of foreigners in promoting trade and strategic interest abroad. European countries, and later America and Russia, would play off rulers in the less developed world for short-term gain in power, trade and political influence. Flattery, hospitality, lavish gifts, clever exploitation of religious rivalry and, where necessary, brute force were used to allow, for example, the British to rule over millions in India with an army of a few thousand.

Most European powers were involved in carving up Asia and much of the rest of the world in their thirst for power and influence. Petty dictators were, and still are, backed by the great powers and chosen for readiness to subdue dissent rather than for any concern for human rights and freedom of religion and belief, and then, when no longer useful, the same rulers are toppled and replaced by new despots. A few years ago, I was invited to a reception by the then British PM in which the guests of honour were President Assad of Syria, now downgraded to public enemy number one. Iraq's Saddam Hussein was once also considered a friend of the West. Britain was always a leader in carving out areas of strategic and commercial influence, dividing and partitioning countries in Asia, Africa and even Ireland with reckless abandon, regardless of the reality of religious and ethnic divides. One hundred years ago, Britain and France embarked on the Sykes–Picot agreement to carve up the Middle East into the cauldron of seething religious and ethnic instability we see today. If anyone doubts the utter failure of old-fashioned diplomacy in our much smaller and interdependent world, they should look to the tragedy of the Middle East today, where both Russia and the West, in pursuit of strategic interest, are literally bombing the life out of the long-suffering people of Syria.

I have focussed on the Middle East, but similar abuse of human rights exists in much of the world today and is propped up by nations in the West, who still put trade and so-called strategic interest above human rights. In the genocide against Sikhs in India in 1984, I asked a British minister why they were silent over the killing of Sikhs in India. The response: "Indarjit, we know exactly what is going on, but our hands are tied: we have already lost a major defence contract." More recently, a former Trade Secretary, now Minister of Defence, said: 'When we talk trade with China, we shouldn't raise issues of human rights.'

On Tuesday of this week in a House of Lords questions on Syria, I said that while atrocities by ISIS against Yazidi and Christian women were undoubtedly a war crime, didn't the bombing of innocent civilians by the forces of Russia and the West for so-called strategic interest also amount to a war crime? The Minister's response amounted to 'our bombs were dropped to further democracy'.

Friends, in today's smaller and interdependent world, nineteenth-century pursuit of strategic interest that ignores fundamental human rights is, as we see all around the world, simply a recipe for disaster. Today, in the interests of all of us, and those of succeeding generations, we need a new diplomacy that recognises that our individual wellbeing is inextricably linked to the wellbeing of all. If we do not make the UN Declaration of Human Rights, particularly Article 18 on Freedom of Religion and Belief, central to all we do, we will all be the losers, and those that come after us will look on the present generation of leaders with disbelief and contempt.

Let me now say a few words about freedom of speech and freedom of belief. As a Sikh, I believe we should all be free to believe whatever we wish, so long as it has no adverse effect on the rights of others. To put it light-heartedly, I don't mind someone believing the Earth is flat, so long as they do not try to push me off the end! In the West we quote Voltaire in support of this basic human right. Voltaire said: "I may not believe in what you say, but will defend to the death your right to say it." Years before Voltaire, Guru Teg Bahadhur, one of the founders of the Sikh faith, gave this noble sentiment stark reality when he was publicly beheaded by Muslim rulers for defending the right, not of Sikhs but of Hindus, those of a different religion, against forced conversion.

Freedom of speech is not an absolute freedom. We do not have a right to cause fear and unnecessary hurt to others, or to deliberately give offence. But we have both a right and duty to point out to both the secular and religious, political policies and interpretations of religious teachings which offend basic human rights. Constructive criticism of religious practices is fine, but it must be based on fact, rather than on prejudice arising from ignorance.

We all know that in a fog or mist, familiar objects can assume grotesque and frightening forms, and it is the same when we look at fellow humans through a lens of ignorance and prejudice. It was this ignorance and prejudice that led to a Sikh being killed in a mistaken identity reprisal attack immediately after 9/11, and an attack on a Sikh place of worship with the killing of several people. We all need basic religious literacy to remove dangerous ignorance and prejudice in us all. Nothing complicated, but key facts on religious teachings to help us differentiate between those that clearly support human rights and attitudes and practices that have become embedded in religious belief that should perhaps be challenged. Religion that tells us all how to live, move and have our being should itself be open to question and challenge.

Guru Nanak, the founder of the Sikh religion who championed the right of freedom of belief, was forceful in his criticism of practices that had become embedded in the religion of his day, that flout basic human rights: the unequal treatment of women, the caste system with its rigid hierarchy of social difference, and rituals and superstitions that take us away from the core ethical teachings of religion. We pride ourselves that we have now become more enlightened, but in our politically correct times, I cannot quote some of the Guru's concerns in my talks on the BBC for fear of giving offence, yet in Guru Nanak's less tolerant times, the Guru's concerns were widely appreciated by both Hindus and Muslims.

Let me conclude. Religion can provide an important ethical uplift to society, but those religions that teach that they and they alone have a special relationship with the one God of us all, or those that flout basic human rights in the treatment of women and attitudes to other people, have some basic and urgent reforming to do. Their leaders should stop playing to the prejudices and culturally conditioned attitudes of their flock, and lead in addressing the needs and challenges of the world today. Religion and secular society must work together in building a better and more peaceful future.

Lecture on the Humanity and Spirituality of Medicine

Royal College of General Practitioners, Fiftieth Anniversary

A golden anniversary is very special, and I would like to offer my congratulations on this important celebration of the founding of the Royal College. Today also happens to be Baisakhi, one of the most important days in the Sikh calendar; the day on which Sikhs pledge to be true to the principles of Sikhism. So, I suppose, it's a bit of congratulations all round. Baisakhi is also very much a reminder of our common humanity, and the need to look beyond self, to wider responsibility and the service of others; a theme I'll return to during the course of this talk.

The subject of my talk, 'humanity and spirituality in medicine', seems a bit intimidating, so let me set minds at rest. I'm not going to bore you with deep reflections on spirituality that ignore the real world around us. Having said that, I would like to start with the words of a popular hymn which, to my mind, encapsulate the challenge of ensuring new scientific advances proceed with due regard to ethical values in a rapidly changing world.

New occasions teach new duties
Time makes ancient good uncouth
They must upwards still and onwards
Who would keep abreast with truth.

The verse refers to our need to re-discover truth and moral direction at times of social and cultural change. Nowhere are the words truer than in the changing world of the medical profession, which has had to adapt to new diagnostic techniques and new treatments that, perhaps more than any other profession, interface with major ethical and religious dilemmas. Let me briefly outline the extent of this change from personal experience. At the start of the Health Service in 1948, my father was a GP, practising only a few miles from here. Prescriptions were free, and although, as today, there were waiting lists for hospital beds, and long delays in outpatients, hospitals seemed less crowded and free from the atmosphere of crisis and collapse that is a common feature today. Doctors were regarded with uniform awe and respect, and nurses held in great esteem. Visiting hours were much more restrictive than today. Prolonged exposure to relatives was not considered a good thing, for either patients or hospital staff.

At the time, the new miracle drug was penicillin, used with little thought given to long-term bacterial resistance. Polio, or infantile paralysis as it was then commonly referred to, existed in endemic proportions. A popular brand of cigarette was advertised as 'good for your throat'. Widespread spraying with newly discovered DDT almost helped eliminate malaria, but as we've learnt since, almost is not good enough.

It's important to look to the recent past, to understand and appreciate the massive changes in scientific progress, and the huge advances in clinical

176

techniques which medical practitioners, patients and wider society have had to take in their stride since the start of the NHS: whole families of new drugs, scanners and new imaging techniques, transplants and lasers to name just a few. New aids to our continuing quest for a longer and healthier life.

Speaking from even more personal experience, until about a year or so ago, I served as a lay member of the BMA Medical Ethics Committee. I was amazed at the constant stream of complex, major ethical issues arising out of new discoveries and new procedures. Let me list just *some* of those that exercised our minds, to give an indication of the need for new thinking, new learning, and the constant questioning of ethical boundaries derived from religious or from social morality. They are in no particular order.

1. **Advance directives, or living wills**
2. **Genetic testing** where there is a family history of genetic disorder, implications for insurance, genetic screening of populations.
3. **Making decisions on behalf of mentally incapacitated adults**
4. **The ethics of xenotransplantation**
5. **The meaning of informed consent**
6. **Consent for the collection, storage and use of gametes**
7. **Ethical issues in ITU**
8. **BMA view on abortion**
9. **Physician-assisted suicide**

More recently, we've had news coverage of the dilemma of would-be spouse-assisted suicide of a female patient suffering a major diminution in quality of life.

Alongside major medical advances, there have also been huge changes in society itself, and it is impossible to understand the problems, challenges and opportunities of today's Health Service without looking at and understanding the nature and magnitude of these social changes and building them into the equation of our quest for better health for all.

The start of the Health Service coincided with a post-war baby boom that has now become a generation nearing the end of economically active life. The labour shortage of the early 1950s led to the arrival, by invitation, of then youthful immigrants, now in retirement. These factors, combined with better medical techniques, have resulted in a steady growth in the proportion of the elderly in the population; a growing segment of the population that is not only economically inactive, but also a larger than average consumer of NHS resources. Many of the new advances in treatment and care are enormously expensive, with the effect that the care of the elderly takes up a growing proportion of the Gross Domestic Product.

In the past, the important nursing aspect of the care of the elderly would have been absorbed within the family unit. But here also, there have been major social changes, which impinge directly on national resources.

Cohabiting and extra-marital relationships are nothing new, but the discovery of the contraceptive pill has made such relationships more common and no longer subject to general, social or moral censure. This has had a major effect on the family unit, with more transient and, frequently, less dedicated relationships. It's not a moral judgement but a statement of fact that, both within and outside of marriage, a sense of responsibility to partner, parent, grandparent or even children has shown a marked sense of decline in the last half century. Obsession with personal happiness: my life, my right to do my own thing, has become central to the life of many.

I believe today's misplaced stress on the importance of the individual, or self, has a lot to answer for. I speak partly from a religious perspective. Guru Nanak, the founder of Sikhism, taught that where God exists there is no self; where self exists there is no God. The same sentiment was echoed by a Christian theologian who said it's the 'I' in the middle of sin that makes it sin. We have clearly become more selfish in our attitude to those around us.

It has also become more common today for both parents to go out to work, making it physically impossible to care for an infirm family member. Responsibility then passes to the state – at a monetary cost and reduction in the funding available, and there is a less tangible, but nonetheless important cost arising from a weakening of family ties and responsibility. Family care at minimal cost has now been widely replaced by state or private nursing homes and the trauma of means testing and/or selling one's home to meet the cost of care. For others, particularly the mentally sick, 'care in the community' becomes total social abandonment.

Another area of concern is the growing disparity between the health care available to the wealthier and the poorer extremes of society. Particular concern for the children of the poor is highlighted in the BMJ publication *Growing Up in Britain*. It shows that poor families in Britain have some of the unhealthiest children in the developed world, destined to grow up as illness-prone adults. Infant mortality in Britain is said to be worse than that in Singapore and, in Europe, only Albania has a similar proportion of dangerously underweight babies. In the report, Dr James Appleyard, consultant paediatrician and chairman of the BMA's child health working party, emphasising that prevention is better than cure, estimates that every pound spent on improving a child's health would save eight pounds in later health care. A cash-strapped Health Service cannot afford to ignore such costings.

While Britain may lag behind much of western Europe in certain areas of health provision, no such criticism can be made of our country's pioneering work in many areas of medical research, such as IVF, cloning techniques and much else. To the layman, the advances in medical research have been truly breathtaking, bringing us to a point where we can now play with the very building blocks of life in attempts to eliminate many genetically inherited disorders. We are now on the brink of spare parts farming within animals to provide spare parts for arteries, heart valves, skin grafts and other body parts.

But, to the layman and to many within the medical profession, there is also a growing sense of unease. It's a feeling that we may be being too clever for our own good and that we are moving too fast to understand the moral, ethical, social and even scientific implications of our discoveries. The case of Dolly, the prematurely arthritic cloned sheep is an obvious example of scientific uncertainty. There is a sense of unease that society is being led into uncharted waters by a powerful combination of scientific and market forces, beyond the shoreline and safety of ethical and moral understanding.

Some of the new medical advances now available, or on the horizon, are or will be enormously expensive, and by today's standards, clearly unethical. But at least for the more wealthy, there is the increasing prospect of a considerably longer and disease-free lifespan. But how far do we want to go down this road at the expense of basic health provision for the many? It may seem a bit fanciful, but I must confess that the prospect of the likes of the Bin Ladens of this world, perhaps more spare parts than original, spanning the centuries, doesn't fill me with enthusiasm.

While we would all like a normal healthy life span, and perhaps a little bit more, I feel most people would agree with the Sikh teaching that it's not the number of years we live, but what we do in them that is important. In India, during the Gurus' time, and even today, there were and are ascetics and yogis who devote their entire life trying to live that bit longer, without contributing any added value to the world in which they live. As Sikh teachings remind us, a life lived pandering to our own desires is a life wasted.

On the other hand, let's look at those who have given so much to us all. Jesus Christ, who exerted such a powerful uplifting influence on world society, was in his thirties when he was crucified. Guru Arjan, author of much of the Sikh holy scriptures and founder of the Golden Temple, was martyred in his forties. Alexander the Great had conquered much of Asia and the Middle East by the time of his death at the age of thirty-two. Getting away from age, Stephen Hawking, severely stricken with disability, is nearer than any of us in fathoming the mysteries of time and space.

Clearly, the quality of life is important to us all, which brings me to the question of euthanasia and related living wills or advance directives. While it is, in my view, clearly wrong to artificially prolong the life of a person in a vegetative state with no chance of recovery, the argument that 'it's my life and I should be free to decide when to end it' ignores the reality of no man being an island. We are all part of the mainland. Our actions have a ripple effect on others, particularly those close to us.

It's generally agreed that we should adopt a more holistic approach to individual and community health. Religion and spirituality urge that we go further and adopt a more holistic approach to life. For the sake of clarity, in discussion, let's take God out of religion for a moment. Sikhs, like Christians, believe there is a Creator of all that exists. But for the moment let's take Him or Her out of the equation and think of religion purely as moral and ethical guidance and ask ourselves if religious guidance has anything to offer the world of the

179

twenty-first century. Today, in the developed world, the former Communist block and other areas, we are all lured by the siren call of materialism which says that we can buy happiness, health and contentment by, as I said earlier, pandering to self. We are told that we can do this by having a larger home or a bigger car, or other material goodies, because we're worth it. It doesn't work, and our different religions have long warned us about this. Christianity warns us about greed and half a dozen other deadly sins. Incidentally, Sikhs list only five!

As we all know, rising affluence in the West has been paralleled, with remarkable correlation, by increasing family breakdown, alcoholism, crime (particularly violent crime), drug abuse, record teenage pregnancies and a general fracturing of social structures. There has been a vast increase in suicide rates and in problems of mental health. Today it's common to say we're stressed. It's worth reflecting that the phrase hadn't been invented when the Royal College came into being in the austere and difficult 1950s. It's interesting to read this week that some doctors want to remove what they term 'lifestyle problems', like alcoholism and stress, from the category of medical illness.

The lesson of all this is that while we all want to live comfortably, selfish pursuit of material comforts, or quick-fix solutions through drugs or alcohol abuse, do us no good, and cause society a great deal of harm. I know that a famous lady once belittled the notion of society, saying there was no such thing. In my view, Mrs. Thatcher could not have been more wrong. Society is very much like a ship on which we are all afloat; it's the environment in which we live, and its well-being is inextricably linked to our own.

There is nothing wrong in living comfortably, but religion reminds us that it is balanced living and responsible living that is the key to true contentment and fuller health.

I have spoken at length about many aspects of life seemingly remote from healthcare, that do, in fact, affect both individual health and the health of the community in which we live. To these I'd like to add two more. The first is a growing lack of respect for those in authority and the second is increasing expectations of what may be possible, arising from media obsession with new discoveries; with theory being misinterpreted as treatment which may be many years away.

Let me then summarise some of the intertwined medical, ethical, social, and I believe spiritual factors affecting healthcare today: an ageing population with increasing costs of treatment and care, the availability of highly expensive new drugs, costly new techniques, a reduction in family support (for the reasons outlined earlier), an increase in healthcare needs of the poor and their families . Individually, all these factors increase the cost and complexity of healthcare provision, and in combination make for the continual funding crises that now characterise the National Health Service. The reality of Health Service funding today is that there is nowhere near enough money available to meet the basic costs of healthcare, let alone heightened public expectations.

Today we live in socially more enlightened times. While we must educate ourselves against unreasonable expectations, we must, at the same time, look to minimum standards of treatment and care for all, and be prepared to pay for these. Painful though it may be, the way to meet current shortfalls is through higher taxation, increasing efficiency, and where necessary, a system of rationing based on priorities.

A system of priorities, or priority categories or age groups, in some ways appears to cut across the ethos of healthcare being equally available to all. But it already exists, and I believe it has become a necessity. What is important is that provision is equal throughout the country and that the poor are not disadvantaged. Rather, provision, particularly of public health measures, must be weighted in their favour to reduce an intolerable level of sickness and poor health. Of course, it is also important that national policies work to reduce the extremes of wealth all too visible today.

At the same time, we need to set boundaries to what is ethically acceptable in potentially new treatment. This, to my mind, is the greatest challenge of all. The use of human embryos to produce stem cells for treating genetic disorders is an example of this ethical dilemma. The possible benefits are obvious; but so too is the fact that manipulation of potential life decreases, at least marginally, our respect for life. Nothing is for nothing.

We are all aware of the slippery slope that can easily take us from promising new treatment to a trivialising of life. The boundaries of what is acceptable are constantly being tested, and it is important that in defining them, and assessing their continuing validity, we use our spiritual heritage and the surprisingly common, ethical values found in our different faiths to give us a fuller perspective on life.

I believe a holistic approach to health is inseparable from a holistic approach to life, which leads to an understanding that it's not health, but how we use it that is all-important.

Sikhs And the Oath, Published in The Magistrate

An oath taken in a court of law, or on a similarly solemn occasion, is a curious mix of law and ritual based on what many would consider a superstitious view of religion.

When a superstitious person is asked to take an oath on a holy book to tell the truth, the whole truth and nothing but the truth, the intended effect is to make him, or her, feel that divine retribution might follow any failure to tell the truth in any statement that follows the oath. Similarly, it is assumed that even the less superstitious would be under increased pressure to tell the truth out of a feeling that a false statement would be disrespectful to the holy book to which they owe allegiance.

On the other hand, a truly religious person would probably be inclined to tell the truth irrespective of any oath. Indeed, such a person might well object to the whole business of oath-taking on the grounds that it is rooted in superstition, and trivialises not only religion, but, by an assumption of constant Divine intervention in the mundane by God himself. This must be the Sikh position. Our Gurus constantly reminded us to keep clear of ritual and superstitious practices. They also taught us that God, the ultimate reality behind all Creation, is beyond our human fallibilities of anger and enmity.

A God that gets angry when a falsehood is told in His name could with equal logic show similar wrath to those who drag his name into the trivia of daily life. In any event, such a view of God is far removed from that of our Gurus' teachings.

As Sikhs, we are required to distance ourselves from all superstition that detracts from true religion, and this must be true of a practice that requires the swearing of an oath on a holy book. Instead of following the superstitious practices of others, Sikhs should exercise their legal right to simply affirm to tell the truth.

This would also help to avoid the many absurdities and anomalies that face a Sikh in taking part in any court proceedings. For example, in Britain, the practice has grown of handing a Sikh a copy of the Japji Sahib, a composition by Guru Nanak, and asking him to swear on the *Guru Granth Sahib* (as if the Japji Sahib and the *Guru Granth Sahib* were one and the same), that in the name of Guru Nanak they swear to tell me truth. Incidentally, though it's not relevant to the main thrust of this paper, Christians swear in the name of God, not Jesus Christ, why Guru Nanak and not God for Sikhs?

182

If Sikhs decide to eschew the oath and assert the right to affirm, we will be joining a growing band of others who would like to see the oath abolished from court proceedings. Since 1968, the Magistrates' Association, supported by the Law Society and the Justice Clerks' Society, has been urging a reform of the law by the abolition of the swearing of oaths. A similar recommendation was made by the Criminal Law Revision in their Eleventh Report (Cmnd 4991 paras 279/281). A solemn affirmation following a reminder of the consequences of perjury, would probably achieve a greater degree of justice than the swearing of oaths, not only for Sikhs but for people of all faiths.

What though of oaths taken outside the court; to swear solemn allegiance to this body or that institution? What should be the Sikh attitude and how binding is such an oath on Sikhs? For similar reasons to those discussed above, Sikhs should refrain from taking an oath that links religion with superstition, and, where appropriate, give a simple pledge of loyalty. But this should not be done lightly and Sikhs should not pledge loyalty to any enterprise or institution with aims contrary to basic Sikh teachings. In the ultimate, an individual's ultimate loyalty must be to his deeply held religious and moral beliefs; something we are reminded of in the following two verses.

All human powers men make pacts with
Are subject to death and decay
I have signed a bond with righteousness
That can conquer the world.

— Guru Granth Sahib, p. 366

We owe allegiance to the State:
But deeper, truer, more
To the sympathies that God has set
Within our spirit's core.

— *James Russell Lowell*

Appendix One
Brief Excerpts from 'Strangers in Our Midst', 1978

Concerns About the Newly-Formed Commission for Racial Equality

In industry and commerce, when things are going a little wrong, it is a fairly common practice for management to order a 'comprehensive restructuring'. The former Race Relations Board and Community Relations Commission were not conspicuous successes in achieving communal harmony, and a comprehensive restructuring was considered desirable. The names of the two vaguely titled bodies previously responsible for promoting communal harmony were combined to bring into being a new body called Commission for Racial Equality (CRE).

The CRE has far greater powers than the RRB and CRC combined. Will it use them wisely to soothe and heal the wounds of extremism and intolerance? Already there is some cause for concern that it is doing little to remove the mists of ignorance and prejudice in which small differences between communities assume exaggerated and frightening proportions.

Need for More Enlightened Debate

A danger to democracy of the 'immigration issue' is that it is all too easy and highly tempting for the aspiring politician, or the cheap vote catcher, to capitalise on fears and misunderstanding, with talk of 'stemming the flow', 'prevention of ghettos' and threats to 'racial balance'. This sort of talk, based on myths and assumptions, is food and sustenance to divisive elements in society, and serves to increase misunderstanding, ready for further exploitation.

The Myth of Race

*Some call themselves Hindus Others call themselves Muslims
And yet man is of one race in all the world*

– Guru Gobind Singh, tenth Guru of the Sikhs (1666–1708)

A racist may be defined as one who seeks to exploit the differences between races. A fair definition at first sight, but a dangerous fallacy lies in the implied assumption that it is possible to divide the human family into a number of distinct groups with their own permanent and separate characteristics.

184

The myth started with an observation that there were groups of people who look different, such as Black, White or Mongoloid. It was then assumed that different appearance must indicate deeper and more significant differences.

In the 1930s, this led to talk of superior and inferior races. Ashley Montagu, in his book, *Man's Most Dangerous Myth*, writes how this theory of a hierarchy of races ran into some difficulty when it was found that the average brain size of a Mongoloid was greater than that of a Caucasoid or White, and that Neanderthal man had a larger cranial capacity than his successful survivor Homo Sapiens. Even worse, an average has little statistical meaning unless accompanied by an indication of spread or deviation from the mean, and this spread of brain size between the different so-called races was found to be so overlapping as to make such measurement totally meaningless.

The whole concept of race or racial difference, based as it is on ignorance and witchcraft science, may have been understandable in an age when there was little social contact between different communities, but in the late twentieth century, when travel and educational opportunities have mushroomed, it becomes totally and obviously meaningless. Today we can see for ourselves in schools and workshops, universities and offices, and in sport and recreation, that those who look different are in no way inferior or less human than ourselves. The renowned scientist Julian Huxley, in his book *Man Stands Alone*, urged that we drop the misleading word race from 'all discussion on human affairs'. We cannot do better than heed his sound advice.

It is sad that RRB, and now the CRE, are continuing to perpetuate this divisive word. Among which races are they trying to promote racial equality? People from the Indian subcontinent vary in colour from black to white; are they considered a homogeneous entity? If not, what are the constituent races? To what race do Turks, Cypriots or Italians belong? It is not only wrong but misleading to use the emotively charged word 'race', when we mean nationality or geographic origin. The CRE, after changing its misleading title, should make it plain that its function is not concerned with rigid and immutable differences between people, but with transient differences arising from different geographical or cultural backgrounds.

Ethnic Groups

All those concerned with the improvement of understanding between those of different background are urged to use instead the term 'ethnic groups', which simply refers to people from different geographic or cultural backgrounds.

Once we remove the fog-producing term 'race', with all its emotive connotations, from the vocabulary of discussion, real issues become infinitely more distinct and far less intractable. The term 'ethnic group' frees us from the false permanence and rigidity of racial difference and allows us to see things as they are. Different ethnic groups, due to geographic or social isolation, do have different cultures and differing social attitudes. To either deny or attach permanence to these differences is simply dishonest. Their existence is neither good nor bad;

it is simply a fact, and the greater the geographic and or social isolation, the greater will be these differences.

Even in Britain today there exist clearly discernible differences in social and cultural attitudes between, say, the inhabitants of London and Yorkshire, or Lancashire and the West Country. We can now see the absurdity of referring in absolute terms to Indian culture, where social barriers and geographic isolation are many times greater. Or, even more absurdly, as is still frequently done, categorising all 'non-whites' as 'blacks' and pretending that we all have similar backgrounds and cultures.

Immigration has brought to Britain not one or two or even half a dozen ethnic groups, but many times that number. Some of these have a great deal in common, while others have much in common with those from the majority community. Ethnic differences, though real, should not be looked at as necessarily divisive features in society; they are superficial, transitory and variable, and their future diminution a certainty. Already we are viewing a worldwide emergence of a youth culture, where young people wear the same jeans and enjoy similar musical tastes to those in distant parts of the world, despite never leaving their own country.

While it is clearly in the interests of all in this country to emphasise the wide areas of common interest and common aspirations, and reduce unnecessary social and cultural barriers wherever possible, any artificial attempts to impose assimilation can only provoke resentment and alienation in both the majority community and minority ethnic groups.

Fallacies in the Pursuit of Equality

We have seen that 'racial' is a discredited term and virtually devoid of meaning. What of its counterpart, 'equality'? The trouble with this word is that, far from it being devoid of meaning, it means all things to all people. To the racial equality fanatic, it often means having obligatory proportions of people from different religions or different ethnic minorities in different spheres of industry and commerce. Such people demand 'positive discrimination' as a means of achieving such quotas. Translated into more normal English, this means selection on the grounds of ethnic origin, rather than ability. Pursuit of such a policy is every bit as unfair as more conventional discrimination based on prejudice and ignorance. Such a policy can only succeed in perpetuating ill-feeling between those it seeks to help and those it proposes to hold back, and it is an insult to the vitality of minority ethnic groups that cannot but make worse the malady it sets out to cure.

Economic or Social Difference

People from different ethnic backgrounds, not surprisingly, have different proportions of their populations in the various socio-economic groups. There's nothing startling or alarming about this; there are considerable differences in socio-economic groupings, even between those living in inner and outer London;

186

that is, different proportions in the managerial, skilled, semi-skilled and unskilled sectors of the workforce. It would be ludicrous to argue that unskilled people in inner-city areas be given skilled and managerial jobs to even out this anomaly. Why then advocate it for those of different coloured skin who come from more widely varying rural and industrial backgrounds?

There is only one sort of equality that is worth pursuing and that is equality of opportunity, which should be independent of both ethnic origin and social and economic background. It is the opportunity for each individual to rise to his or her highest level.

Portrait by Don McCullin at the National Portrait Gallery

With Kawal and Prince Charles

With John Snow

Invitation to No. 10, post-9/11, with a group of Sikhs

With some Sikhs on the HMS Victory, at the invitation of the admiral

At Westminster Abbey

About the Author

Lord Singh of Wimbledon CBE is an internationally recognised journalist and broadcaster and frequent commentator on social and religious issues. He is widely regarded as both the secular and religious voice of the British Sikh community. In 1989 he became the first non-Christian to be awarded the UK Templeton Prize 'for the furtherance of spiritual and ethical understanding'.

Indarjit was named by *The Independent*, a leading British newspaper, as one of 50 people who have made a major contribution to world peace. In 2011 he was made an Independent Peer in the House of Lords.

The Hills of the Peak District

Peak District

A guide to 75 of the best hills of the Peak District.

by

Barry Smith

Published by Where2walk

The Hills of the Peak District

ISBN: 978-0-9956735-4-0

Every reasonable effort has been made by the author to trace copyright holders of material in this book. Any errors or omissions should be notified in writing to the author, who will endeavour to rectify the situation for any future reprints.

Front Cover Photo: Climbing Lord's Seat

Designed and published by Where2walk

Printed by Briggs Brothers, Cononley BD20 8LG

Contents

Summit of Wolfscote Hill

List of the Peaks 75

	Page No	Height (m)	Height (ft)
THE DARK PEAK			
Kinder Scout	14	636	2,088
Bleaklow Head	18	633	2,077
Higher Shelf Stones	18	622	2,041
Grindslow Knoll	14	601	1,972
Black Hill	20	582	1,909
Howden Edge	24	550	1,804
Lord's Seat (Rushup Edge)	28	550	1,804
Back Tor	26	538	1,765
Mam Tor	30	517	1,696
West Nab	20	501	1,644
Lose Hill	30	476	1,562
Win Hill	34	463	1,520
The Tower	36	460	1,509
High Neb	40	458	1,503
White Path Moss	40	457	1,499
Higger Tor	40	434	1,424
Barker Bank	30	426	1,398
Bamford Moor	43	426	1,398
Bridge End Pastures	38	392	1,286
Crook Hill	38	382	1,253
WHITE PEAK EAST			
Bradwell Moor	46	471	1,545
Eldon Hill	46	470	1,542
Chelmorton Hill	48	446	1,463
Sir William Hill	49	429	1,407
Shatton Edge	50	417	1,368
Longstone Moor	51	395	1,296
Harboro Rocks	66	379	1,243
Minninglow Hill	56	372	1,220
Beeley Moor	58	371	1,217
Wardlow Hay Cop	52	370	1,214
Masson Hill	62	338	1,109
Fin Cop	54	327	1,073
Stanton Moor	64	323	1,060
Bolehill	60	323	1,060
High Tor	62	205	673

List of the Peaks 75

	Page No.	Height (m)	Height (ft)
PEAK DISTRICT WEST			
Axe Edge Moor	70	551	1,808
Shutlingsloe	72	506	1,660
The Roaches	74	505	1,657
Ramshaw Rocks	74	460	1,509
Grin Low	71	434	1,424
Hen Cloud	74	410	1,345
Revidge	80	401	1,316
Gradbach Hill	78	399	1,309
Gun	81	385	1,263
The Cloud	82	343	1,125
PEAK DISTRICT DALES			
Hollins Hill	86	450	1,476
Chrome Hill	86	443	1,453
High Wheeldon	90	422	1,384
Pilsbury Castle Hill	92	395	1,296
Wolfscote Hill	94	388	1,273
Carder Low	92	380	1,247
Parkhouse Hill	86	375	1,230
Wetton Hill	98	371	1,217
Ecton Hill	98	369	1,211
Narrowdale Hill	96	367	1,204
Gratton Hill	96	363	1,191
Parkhouse Hill North	86	362	1,188
Wetton Hill SW Top	98	358	1,175
Bunster Hill	101	329	1,080
Thorpe Cloud	101	287	942
NORTH WEST PEAK			
Shining Tor	106	559	1,834
Mill Hill	110	544	1,785
Cats Tor	106	522	1,713
Black Edge	112	507	1,663
Combs Head	112	503	1,650
South Head	114	494	1,621
Mount Famine	114	473	1,552
Chinley Churn	114	457	1,499
Sponds Hill	120	413	1,355
Whaley Moor	121	411	1,348
Coum Edge	118	411	1,348
Teggs Nose	122	382	1,253
Lantern Pike	118	373	1,224
Eccles Pike	117	370	1,214
Kerridge Hill	124	313	1,007

An Introduction to...

This book is a guide to the hills of the Peak District. It identifies 75 of the best hills and details 50 interesting walks, mostly circular, that go over their summits.

The Peak District is in central England at the southern end of the Pennines. A substantial part is in northern Derbyshire, but the area includes parts of Staffordshire, Cheshire, Greater Manchester, West Yorkshire and North Yorkshire. The Peak District National Park is very popular with walkers and has over 10 million visitors per year.

There are many walking books covering Derbyshire and the Peak District, but none lists its hills and routes to climb them. As these hills, together with its Dales and beautiful villages, define the Peak District, I have drawn up a list of the best hills and hopefully demonstrated that any of them can be climbed by a relatively fit and determined walker.

Summit of Revidge Hill

Derbyshire is the dominant County. Out of the 75 hills selected, 52 are contained within or on its county borders. It is one of the great counties of England, made famous by the Peak District National Park, Chatsworth, one of Britain's greatest stately homes, Ashbourne, the home of Royal Shrovetide Football, and the ancient Derbyshire mills, a World Heritage Site centred on Cromford.

The remaining hills are divided between Staffordshire (12 hills), Cheshire (7 hills) and Yorkshire (4 hills). Staffordshire is best known for classic hills such as Shutlingshoe, the Roaches, and Hen Cloud, whilst Shining Tor dominates the views in East Cheshire.

The Peak District National Park stretches from Holmfirth in the north to Ashbourne in the south, from Macclesfield at its western extremity, to Chesterfield and Sheffield in the east. It includes the White Peak and the Dark Peak. The Dark Peak forms an arc to the north east and west sides, and comprises high moorland and gritstone. The White Peak makes up the central and southern part of the Peak District, and is a limestone area with valleys and gorges.

The Hills of the Peak District

How were the hills selected?

I selected the hills on the list by considering all those within the Peak District with a 30m drop or prominence. They are known as TUMPs, see page 140. I have only included those hills that are on access land or can be reached by a clearly defined Right of Way. In order to finalise the list I climbed all the hills, consulted with some more experienced Peak District walkers, removed some hills, and added five hills that are well known and popular, although they have less than 30m prominence. In my view, the result has been a good and comprehensive list of the hills of the Peak District.

The 75 hills selected are listed in full by height on pages 6 and 7. They are also listed at the start of each section. In addition, there are a few subsidiary hills that will be traversed whilst completing the walks. These have less than 30m prominence and are not sufficiently well known to be included in the list.

Hill lists have evolved over the years. Perhaps the best-known hill list in Britain is the Munros, the mountains in Scotland over 3,000ft, of which there were 282 at the last count. Sir Hugh Munro did not define a drop or prominence for each mountain, although it has subsequently been agreed that every mountain over 3,000ft in Scotland with a drop of 500ft on all sides should be included in the list. More recently the Wainwrights have been developed as the main hill list in the Lake District, named after Alfred Wainwright, whose seven volume Pictorial Guide to the Lakeland Fells became well known. There are 214 Wainwrights. More recently the Dales 30 is now the hill walking challenge in the Yorkshire and Cumbrian Dales.

Some of the more recent hill lists have a defined drop on all sides and details of these lists are given on page 140. The best known of these is the Marilyns, the listing of all 1,556 hills in Britain with a 150m drop on all sides. Only eleven people have completed this list.

Summit of Mam Tor

How to Use this Book

The book is divided into five areas. The Dark Peak in the north which includes the north of Derbyshire and parts of Yorkshire. The White Peak East which is all contained in Derbyshire. The White Peak West which includes the far west of Derbyshire and parts of Staffordshire. The Peak District Dales centred on Dovedale. The North West Peak which includes the north west of Derbyshire and parts of Cheshire.

Main Sections

Each section starts with a list of the hills in that section, and a map to show their location. The hills are then divided into walks, in total 50 walks cover the 75 hills. Between one and four pages are devoted to each walk. There is a full description of the walk, photos of places on the walk, details of parking and postcodes where possible, and the distance and difficulty of each walk.

I have graded the walks 1 to 4;

1 is a relatively easy walk, probably only taking an hour or so and mainly on good paths.

2 is a moderate walk, may take 2-3 hours, but not too strenuous.

3 is a longer walk and/or on more difficult terrain.

4 is the for the longest and most strenuous walks, these may take most of the day to complete.

I have asterisked three walks because of particular difficulties, which are explained in the text.

Additional Sections

I have added two final sections, the first is on favourite hill walks in the Peak District written by Martin Summers who has spent a lifetime walking the hills of the Peak District.

I am also indebted to Ed Bradwell who has unveiled the secrets of an activity that I have little experience of, cycling the hill climbs of the Peak District. There are numerous hill climbs that are cycled and raced on a regular basis, including Winnats, the famous road climb near Mam Tor, and the Cat and Fiddle climb from Macclesfield.

I hope you find the book interesting. I believe this is an achievable list of summits, which gives an insight into a remarkable part of Britain.

Safety in the Mountains

The Peak District 75 involve climbing the highest hills in Derbyshire, Staffordshire, Cheshire, and South and West Yorkshire. Whilst there are paths on most of the walks, some areas are trackless, or with only small paths, and it is easy to become disorientated when the cloud comes down. Winter conditions are particularly dangerous; short days, frozen ground and snow slowing progress are typical difficulties.

This book is only intended to be a rough guide to the routes up the best hills in the Peak District. The O/S Explorer Maps OL1 (Dark Peak area) and OL24 (White Peak area) are also needed together with a compass. A GPS can be used as an aid to a map and compass but not as a replacement. Mobile phones can also help but they are easily damaged, run out of battery and it is not always possible to get a signal.

Appropriate clothing should be worn and, if walking on your own, a second person informed of your route and likely return time. In groups always plan for the slowest member of the party. If in serious trouble call 999 or 112 and ask for the Mountain Rescue. These precautions should help reduce any dangers and make the walks more enjoyable.

Access

The hills in this list were all on Access Land or with a Right of Way running over the top of them at the time of going to print. Where there is a Right of Way or a concessionary path going over private land, please stay on the path. Access land is shown on the O/S Explorer 1.25,000 Maps by yellow shading.

Narrowdale Hill from Gratton Hill

Peak District –
Dark Peak

The Dark Peak covers the highest and wildest parts of the Peak District including the high moorland of Kinder and Bleaklow, where the ground rises to over 2,000ft, and the areas around the Derwent Watershed. The area lies in the north part of the Peak District and includes well known and popular spots such as Mam Tor, Stanag Edge, and the three reservoirs, Ladybower, Derwent, and Howden. Twenty hills of the Peaks 75 are located in the Dark Peak.

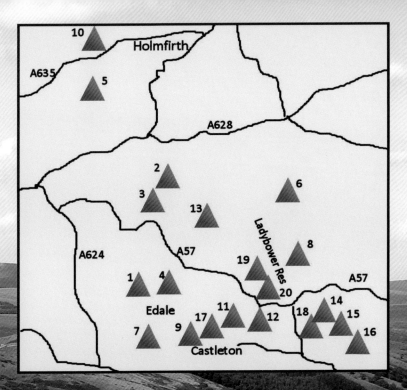

	Page No	Height (m)	Height (ft)	Map Ref
THE DARK PEAK				
Kinder Scout	14	636	2,088	1
Bleaklow Head	18	633	2,077	2
Higher Shelf Stones	18	622	2,041	3
Grindslow Knoll	14	601	1,972	4
Black Hill	20	582	1,909	5
Howden Edge	24	550	1,804	6
Lord's Seat (Rushup Edge)	28	550	1,804	7
Back Tor	26	538	1,765	8
Mam Tor	30	517	1,696	9
West Nab	20	501	1,644	10
Lose Hill	30	476	1,562	11
Win Hill	34	463	1,520	12
The Tower	36	460	1,509	13
High Neb	40	458	1,503	14
White Path Moss	40	457	1,499	15
Higger Tor	40	434	1,424	16
Barker Bank	30	426	1,398	17
Bamford Moor	43	426	1,398	18
Bridge End Pastures	38	392	1,286	19
Crook Hill	38	382	1,253	20

Summit of Mam Tor

Kinder Scout

The classic circuit of Kinder Scout, the highest hill in the Peak District, from Edale.

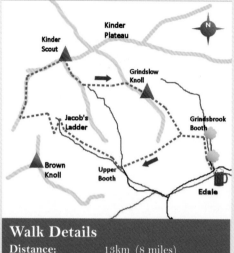

The Hills

Kinder Scout

Kinder Scout is a Marilyn and the highest mountain in the Peak District, the highest point being in the middle of a large expanse of moorland north east of the Trig Point.

Height:	636m (2,088ft)
Summit:	SK 085875
Map Ref:	O/S Explorer **OL1**

Grindslow Knoll

Grindslow Knoll is an attractive peak 2.5km east of Kinder Scout. It lies on the southern fringes of the Kinder plateau overlooking Edale.

Height:	601m (1972ft)
Summit:	SK 110868
Map Ref:	O/S Explorer **OL1**

Walk Details

Distance:	13km (8 miles)
Height to Climb:	440m (1,455ft)
Start:	SK 124853
Difficulty:	4

Walk Summary

Kinder Scout is the highest hill in the Peak District, and the highest in central England. It lies between Sheffield and Manchester, and is part of a high moorland region stretching north over Bleaklow and the Black Hill, both marginally lower than Kinder. It was the location for the mass trespass in 1932.

Partly as a result of this Kinder Scout became open access land soon after the Second World War. Kinder Scout may not be the best summit, but it is the highest and defining hill in the Peak District. The walk outlined is a great walk, highly placed in Britain's favourite walks.

I recommend completing this walk in good weather, not just because that will make for a more interesting walk, but also the Kinder plateau is hard to navigate, particularly in mist.

The Kinder Trespass

On 24th April 1932 the Kinder mass trespass took place. This was an act of wilful trespass by ramblers and members of the young Communist League.

The 'Trespass' arguably led to the National Parks legislation in 1949, the Right to Roam legislation and helped pave the way for the Pennine Way and other long distance footpaths.

Walk Description

The walk starts in Edale, the start of the Pennine Way and a well-known centre for walking. Park at the main car park near Edale Station (postcode S33 7ZQ), and walk north up the minor road for a few hundred metres to the start of the Pennine Way. For the next 5km the Pennine Way is followed. Initially, walk west along the Pennine Way for 2km to Upper Booth. Now the path turns north west and continues to a steep section up Jacob's Ladder. A cairn marks the top of Jacob's Ladder,

Continue west for 600m to the high col between Kinder Scout and Brown Knoll. Now turn north on the Pennine Way to the Trig Point at Kinder Low. However, this is not the summit of Kinder Scout. The high point is 800m north east. Continue north on the path for about 250m, then turn east on a small path which runs to the cairn marking the high point. In clear conditions the cairn can be seen from a few hundred metres away which makes navigation easier. The summit is much quieter than the Trig Point.

Upper Booth   *Trig Point near the summit*

From the quiet summit of Kinder Scout, walk south east towards Crowden Tower. There is a small path but it is not always easy to follow. At Crowden Tower, the main path running along the edge of the plateau is joined. Continue east along the edge of the plateau for 1.5km. There are good views south. Grindslow Knoll appears in front of you and to the right.

Take the path which branches off right and heads directly towards Grindslow Knoll. After a short climb the summit of this spectacular viewpoint above Edale is reached. From Grindslow Knoll a direct descent to Edale can be made by following a large path south east. The easiest route is to follow the wide ridge south then branch left on a path to reach this wide path to Edale.

Follow the path as it descends steeply to rejoin the Pennine Way a few hundred metres to the west of Edale, and a well-deserved drink.

Grindslow Knoll and Kinder Plateau

Bleaklow

A high level walk over the moors and hillside of Bleaklow from Snake Pass.

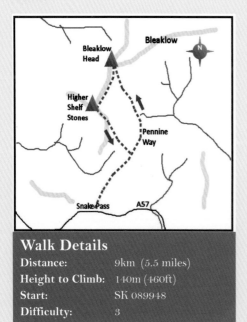

Walk Details

Distance:	9km (5.5 miles)
Height to Climb:	140m (460ft)
Start:	SK 089948
Difficulty:	3

The Hills

Bleaklow Head

Bleaklow Head is a HUMP and the second highest hill in the Peak District. It is only 3 metres lower than Kinder Scout.

Height:	633m (2,077ft)
Summit:	SK 094961
Map Ref:	O/S Explorer **OL1**

Higher Shelf Stones

Higher Shelf Stones is the best summit on Bleaklow Moor. It lies on the southern edge of the plateau. Classed as a Nuttall it is one of only three hills over 2,000ft in the Peak District.

Height:	622m (2,041ft)
Summit:	SK 089948
Map Ref:	O/S Explorer **OL1**

Walk Summary

This is a high-level walk from Snake Pass, never dropping below 1,650ft. The outward journey to the summit of Bleaklow Head follows the Pennine Way. The return via Higher Shelf Stones gives a different perspective of this high and wild peaty moorland.

Summit of Bleaklow Head

Snake Pass with Higher Shelf Stones beyond

Walk Description

The usual start point is the top of Snake Pass at 512m. Parking is usually possible by the roadside but it can be busy at weekends. From here there is only 400ft of climbing to the summit of Bleaklow Head. Follow the Pennine Way which heads north east, with good views of Higher Shelf Stones to the left. Initially the track is good but it deteriorates after a couple of kilometres. Gradually the track turns north west then north as it approaches the substantial cairn at the summit of Bleaklow Head.

From Bleaklow Head summit return along the Pennine Way for 600m to Hern Stones, then leave the Pennine Way to continue just west of south towards Higher Shelf Stones. There is a path but it is indistinct at times as it crosses the peat hags. After about 800m, you will come across plane wreckage strewn across the hillside. From here it is a short walk west to the Trig Point at the summit of Higher Shelf Stones.

The most interesting part of Bleaklow is around Higher Shelf Stones, as there is steeper hillside and views stretching to Manchester. After visiting the Trig Point, return to the crash site. A path goes south east, crossing a burn before reaching the Pennine Way 1km north of Snake Pass.

Black Hill & West Nab

High on the moors between Huddersfield and Oldham, lie the two most northerly summits in the Peak District.

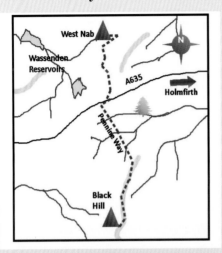

Walk Details

Distance:	11km (7 miles)
Height to Climb:	200m (650ft)
Start:	SE 077076
Difficulty:	3

The Hills

Black Hill

Black Hill is a Marilyn and is often visited as part of the Pennine Way. It is the high point of a flat and wide plateau with considerable peat bog.

Height:	582m (1,909ft)
Summit:	SE 078047
Map Ref:	O/S Explorer **OL1**

West Nab

West Nab is the most northerly summit in the Peak District. The summit is rocky and interesting with excellent views to the north and east.

Height:	501m (1,644ft)
Summit:	SE 076088
Map Ref:	O/S Explorer **OL1**

Walk Summary

Surprisingly Black Hill is the highest point of the historic county of Cheshire. It is now on the border between Derbyshire and West Yorkshire. It is the fifth highest hill of the 'Peaks 75' and one of only five Marilyns, hills with a drop of 150m on all sides. The area surrounding the summit has virtually no vegetation and is very dark, probably giving the hill its name.

The Pennine Way now gives a good route to the summit from the north, and its paved surface allows walkers to reach the top with dry feet in most conditions. West Nab can be combined with Black Hill to give an excellent walk of approximately 11km.

The Pennine Way

The Pennine Way is a National Trail mainly in England stretching 268 miles (431km) from Edale in Derbyshire to Kirk Yetholm, just over the Scottish border. It is one of Britain's best known and toughest long distance walks, declared open in 1965. The record time for completion of the walk is 2 days 13 hours and 34 minutes by Damian Hall in 2020, an incredible time.

The summit of West Nab

Walk Description

There is parking just off the minor road which runs north from the A635 Holmfirth to Mossley road. This is approximately 200m north of the main road so is ideal for combining the two summits. To climb Black Hill first, walk south down the minor road, along the Pennine Way, turn right, then turn left on the Pennine Way. The footpath leaves the main road and heads south towards Black Hill.

Follow the footpath which descends to a stream, then climbs to cross the moorland, before ascending to the summit plateau of Black Hill and its large trig point. It is best to return on the Pennine Way path. There are alternative routes but they involve tackling the peaty moorland without a clearly defined path.

After returning to the car, walk north on the minor road. West Nab is straight ahead and is a more pronounced hill than Black Hill. A path leads up the hill from south, south east of the summit. There is a sign indicating that no dogs are allowed on this hill. The path gives a short, but good climb to the Trig Point, and great views all around. West Nab is the most northerly hill in the Peak District.

Most people do not know West Nab but it is a distinctive hill with an impressive summit area. It is rumoured to have been a place of ancient worship, and is an atmospheric place that feels steeped in history. I suggest walking west along the ridge to Raven Rocks, a distance of just over 600m, before returning south to the minor road.

Black Hill from the A635 near Holmfirth

Howden Edge

A remote summit that can be approached from the north along the Cut Gate path or from Fairholmes car park to the south.

The Hills

Howden Edge

Howden Edge is a TUMP and the County Top of South Yorkshire. It is remote and lonely, situated to the north east of the Peaks.

Height:	550m (1,804ft)
Summit:	SK 188944
Map Ref:	O/S Explorer **OL1**

Derwent Watershed Walk

The traverse from Margery Hill to Howden Edge is part of the Derwent Watershed Walk, a 40-mile circular walk around the water-gathering area of the River Derwent. In the excellent book 'the Big Walks', the Derwent Watershed Walk is described as 'the best, boggiest, bleakest, roughest, toughest, loneliest, wettest parts of the Peak District all brought into a day's walk.

Walk Summary

This area at the north east side of the Derwent Watershed gave rise to some difficulty as to what to include in the list of 75 hills. Howden Edge is the highest hill and the County Top of South Yorkshire. Therefore, it was felt that this must be included and take its place as the remotest hill in the list just beating Horse Stone Naze (below). In my view it is best climbed from near Langsett Reservoir to the north east and this enables Margery Hill to be added. It is a long walk, 17km or over 10 miles, but it is an attractive route and goes over Margery Hill. It is best to ensure clear visibility because route finding would be difficult in mist, and some of the benefits of the walk, the terrain and views, would be lost.

Summit of Horse Stone Naze

Walk Description

The best start point is from a car park just off the A616 which runs from Huddersfield to the M1 just north of Sheffield. The car park is on the east side of the road just south of the junction between the A616 and A628. Walk south for 50m from the car park on the west side of the road, then a minor road goes west. Follow this west for 400m, then go south on a track through the woods. This track passes the east end of Langsett Reservoir before climbing onto Hingcliff Common. This is the Cut Gate Path which continues all the way to Howden Reservoir. It is a good path passing through attractive heathland, and easy to follow.

Continue south along Mickleden Edge and the path gradually turns south west. At grid reference SK 186960, just before the path starts to descend, a lesser path goes off to the left. Follow this south east for 500m to the Trig Point at the top of Margery Hill. From the top of Margery Hill return to the path along the edge. This is faint at

The Cut Gate Path

times, but continues 1.5km to the cairn signifying the summit of Howden Edge. This is the highest point for miles around.

Retrace the outbound route over Margery Hill and along the 'Cut Gate path'. Retracing the outward journey, this excellent path runs north east then north for 6km, and returns to the west head of Langsett Reservoir. Walkers and cyclists usually start appearing as the path nears the Reservoir.

The alternative route to Howden Edge from Fairholmes car park is approximately 16km (10 miles). It follows the track up the east side of Upper Derwent Reservoir and past Howden Dam. About 600m past Howden Dam and close to the end of an inlet, a path goes off to the right, through some woods, then follows the north side of a stream. 2km after leaving the reservoir, there are some grouse butts. Turn right at the grouse butts up the trackless hillside to the summit.

Back Tor

Back Tor lives up to its name with the summit on top of a rock tor which can be climbed.

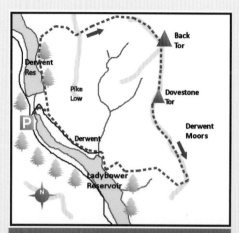

Walk Details

Distance:	14km (8.5 miles)
Height to Climb:	320m (1,050ft)
Start:	SK 173893
Difficulty:	4

The Hills

Back Tor

Back Tor is a TUMP on Derwent Edge overlooking Derwent Reservoir. The Tor is 5 metres high and makes a challenging summit tick!

Height:	538m (1,765ft)
Summit:	SK 198910
Map Ref:	O/S Explorer **OL1**

Reservoirs of the Peak

There are three reservoirs in the Upper Derwent Valley, Howden Reservoir, Upper Derwent Reservoir, and Ladybower Reservoir. During the second World War the reservoirs were used by 617 Squadron for practising Dam Buster raids.

Walk Summary

This is a classic circular walk from Fairholmes car park next to Ladybower Reservoir. It climbs to the top of Back Tor via the summit of Lost Lad, then follows the top of the edge south before descending to Ladybower Reservoir and following the east side of the reservoir back to Fairholmes. Half a day should be allowed for the walk.

The Derwent Dam

Summit of Back Tor

Walk Description

From Fairholmes car park cross beneath Derwent Dam and walk north up a good track. After walking for just over 1km, turn right to follow a path which climbs east through the woods. Continue on the path as it climbs steadily towards Lost Lad hill. Keep left at a fork in the path and continue on the path to the summit of Lost Lad. The summit of Back Tor is straight ahead, 400m to the south east.

On arriving at Back Tor, it is worth walking around the summit tor to find the easiest way up to the summit Trig Point. The best routes appear to be from the south or the east. Whether you climb to the Trig Point or not, the summit is a remarkable spot.

The route continues south along the top of Derwent Edge for nearly 4km. It passes the Cakes of Bread, the Salt Cellar boulder, White Tor and the Wheel Stones. At grid reference SK 198885 there is a good path which descends west to Ladybower Reservoir.

At the side of Ladybower Reservoir a minor road goes north west back to Derwent Dam. Cross beneath the dam to return to the car park and the possibility of refreshments at the café.

Lord's Seat, Rushup Edge

Lying just west of Mam Tor lies the less frequented but impressive summit of Lord's Seat.

Walk Details

Distance:	3.5km (2 miles)
Height to Climb:	140m (450ft)
Start:	SK 123832
Difficulty:	1

The Hills

Lord's Seat

Lord's Seat is a TUMP and the high point of the ridge stretching west from Mam Tor. It is a higher summit than its popular neighbour and looks north across the valley to Kinder Scout.

Height:	550m (1,804ft)
Summit:	SK 112835
Map Ref:	O/S Explorer **OL1**

A 'Bowl Barrow'

Lord's Seat has a well preserved bowl barrow close to the summit. Bowl barrows are funerary monuments generally belonging to the period 2,400 to 1,500 BC. This monument includes a roughly circular steep sided mound with a diameter of 15m by 15.5m and a height of 2m.

Walk Summary

On a warm summer day, it is possible to sit undisturbed on the summit of Lord's Seat, watching hundreds of people going up Mam Tor, just over a mile away. This is an underrated summit on the ridge between the high plateau of Kinder Scout and the Great Ridge from Mam Tor to Lose Hill.

I have suggested climbing Lord's Seat separately because it makes a short and relatively easy walk that can be enjoyed to the full. It could be climbed with Mam Tor or combined with Kinder Scout and Brown Knoll in a long walk from Edale. The summit is also passed on both the Edale skyline walk and the Derwent Watershed walk.

Lord's Seat - Bowl Barrow

Looking north to the Kinder plateau

Walk Description

Park at the Mam Tor National Trust car park (charge). Exit the car park and follow the path north east towards Mam Tor for 200m. When nearly at the high point of the road, cross the road to a path which follows the crest of the ridge, Rushup Edge, west to the top of Lord's Seat. This is a distance of 1.5km along a pleasant ridge with views in all directions. The summit is unmarked but a small cairn is placed in a sheltered spot with a superb view over Edale.

Mam Tor & the Great Ridge

Voted number 10 in the top 100 walks in Britain, this classic walk takes you on a circuit from Castleton including the great ridge from Mam Tor to Lose Hill.

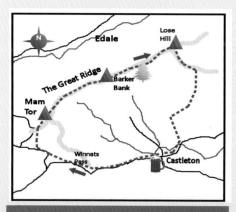

Walk Details

Distance:	11km (7 miles)
Height to Climb:	450m (1,475ft)
Start:	SK 149829
Difficulty:	3

'The Mother Hill'

Mam Tor means 'the mother hill'. It is so called because frequent landslips on its eastern face have resulted in a multitude of mini hills beneath it. The hill is crowned by a late Bronze Age and early Iron Age hill fort.

The Hills

Mam Tor

Mam Tor is a TUMP and probably the most climbed hill in the Peak District. It has a large rock summit and a Trig Point.

Height:	517m (1,696ft)
Summit:	SK 128836
Map Ref:	O/S Explorer **OL1**

Lose Hill

Lose Hill stands at the east end of the Great Ridge. It is a TUMP whose summit lies on a pleasant grassy area .

Height:	476m (1,562ft)
Summit:	SK 153854
Map Ref:	O/S Explorer **OL1**

Barker Bank

Barker Bank is an unspectacular hill towards the centre of the Great Ridge. Although it is usually passed with barely a glance it is a TUMP and therefore worthy of the listing.

Height:	426m (1,398ft)
Summit:	SK139846
Map Ref:	O/S Explorer **OL1**

Walk Summary

This is a very popular Peak District walk and traverses the Great Ridge that separates Edale from the Hope Valley. The route starts and finishes at Castleton and traverses Mam Tor and Lose Hill at opposite ends of the ridge, as well as the subsidiary summits of Barker Bank and Back Tor. The Great Ridge rolls and underdulates from Mam Tor to Lose Hill, with views stretching from Kinder Scout to Stanage Edge. Mam Tor, which means the 'Mother Hill' is the most popular summit in the Peak District, a glorious spot.

Walk Description

Parking is available in the village of Castleton (charge). Castleton attracts a large number of tourists and is popular with walkers. There are pubs, tea shops and accommodation, as well as an information centre, several outdoor shops and a Youth Hostel.

From the car park walk west beside the road to Speedwell Cavern, one of four show caves in the area. Walk west beside the road to the entrance to Speedwell Cavern, and cross to the north side of the road which goes up Winnats. Follow a good path west up steep hillside just north of Winnats Pass. This path bends north west and continues towards Mam Tor. After a further 2km, the road below and just south west of Mam Tor is reached. Now complete the climb up Mam Tor by walking north east on a paved footpath to the fine summit of the 'Shivering Mountain', as Mam Tor is known.

The Great Ridge now stretches out in front of you, 4km of fine walking to the top of Lose Hill, which can be seen in the distance to the north east. Follow the top of the ridge as it descends north from Mam Tor, then bends east to go down to Hollins Cross. Paths lead down from this dip in the ridge, north to Edale and south to Castleton.

Climbing Lose Hill

Stay on the ridge as it climbs gently to the top of Barker Bank, the second of the hills climbed on this walk. The ridge then descends to another col before a short but steeper climb to Back Tor. There is a short descent before the path makes its final ascent to Lose Hill.

Descend south east on a good path for 400m, then take the right fork to continue in the same direction, passing Lose Hill Farm. The path now goes south to a T junction next to Spring House Farm. Turn right to follow the track towards Castleton. A final turn left at Hollowford Road, then there is the the welcome sight of Castleford with its cafes and pubs.

The summit of Mam Tor

Win Hill

Win Hill stands proud and alone, just east of Kinder Scout. It is one of Britain's great small hills.

Walk Details

Distance:	4.5km (2.5 miles)
Height to Climb:	300m (990ft)
Start:	SK 198849
Difficulty:	2

The Hills

Win Hill

Win Hill can be seen as an impressive hill from all its neighbours. The summit is a short ridge above heather slopes and does not disappoint.

Height:	463m (1,520ft)
Summit:	SK 187851
Map Ref:	O/S Explorer OL1

Interesting Fact

Win Hill's near neighbour is Lose Hill, and this prompted a fanciful tale concerning the outcome of an imagined seventh century battle between the forces of Edwin of Northumbria and Cynegils of Wessex. Cynegils forces occupied Lose Hill, but when they advanced up Win Hill, Edwin's forces pushed the boulders off a wall down on them to win the battle.

Walk Summary

Win Hill is the most easterly of the 'golden circle' of Peak District Hills, including Kinder Scout, Lord's Seat, Mam Tor, Barker Bank, Lose Hill, and Win Hill. The walk climbs Win Hill from a point near Ladybower Reservoir to the east.

Climbing Win Hill from the east

Summit of Win Hill

Walk Description

Win Hill can be climbed from Hope to the south west or from Yorkshire Bridge to the east where there is roadside parking. Alternative parking is available at Heatherdene car park near Ladybower Reservoir. This adds 1.5km to the distance of the walk. In my view the ascent from the east is the better route as it gives an interesting circuit, including a walk along Ladybower Reservoir and a direct ascent of the hill.

From the west side of Yorkshire Bridge, walk 50m north along the road, and turn left. Follow a good path up the hillside through woodland.

The ascent is steep and direct. After less than 1km the path emerges out of the trees and the summit is ahead of you, a glorious hill of rocks and heather.

From the summit continue west for 400m, then turn right down a good path which goes north east towards Ladybower Reservoir. The path enters the woods and turns north. After a few hundred metres there is a T junction. Turn right and follow the path east then south east to arrive at Ladybower Reservoir just north of the dam. Turn south and follow the track, then a minor road back to Yorkshire Bridge.

The Tower

An awesome spot and regarded by some as the best hill in the Peak District. Requires a scramble and a good head for heights to reach the summit.

Walk Details

Distance:	8km (5 miles)
Height to Climb:	280m (920ft)
Start:	SK 153928
Difficulty:	3*

Walk Summary

There are two parts to this walk, firstly an approach to the base of the Tower from the north east (my preference), secondly, a steep climb of just over 100ft to the top of the Tower.

Alport Castles

Alport Castles are a landslip feature over half a mile long, selected for geological conservation as one of the most significant landslips in the Britain. The name 'castles' comes from the debris from the landslide, which has produced several gritstone mounds that tower over the valley and look like castles. The largest of these is the 'Tower' which is over 100ft high.

The Hills

The Tower

The Tower is a sharp pointed peak rising just over 100ft from the valley floor. Scrambling is needed to reach the summit. A good head for heights is required on the summit. Some believe this to be the finest peak in the area.

Height:	460m (1,509ft)
Summit:	SK 141914
Map Ref:	O/S Explorer **OL1**

Walk Description

The parking on the A57 Snake Pass road is difficult, therefore I prefer to start at Howden Reservoir to the north east. This gives an easier walk to the area of Alport Castles and a spectacular and sudden view of them. However, cars are forbidden to go north of Fairholmes car park on weekends and bank holidays. At weekends it is probably best to start from the A57 at Alport Bridge. Roadside parking is limited.

Assuming an approach from Howden Reservoir, drive north along Derwent Reservoir. After reaching Howden Reservoir the road goes west. At the most westerly point, it is possible to park and a good track sets off west. After 200m, branch to the left following a sign to Alport Castles. The track goes up the hillside through the trees then after a few hundred metres comes out of the woodland and continues across open moorland. After walking for approximately 2km, the edge of the moorland is reached, and suddenly Alport Castles appears in front of you below the cliff edge.

The Tower from the east

Turn left and follow a path along the top of the cliff for 600m. It is then possible to descend to the Castles and walk west to the bottom of the Tower. A path goes diagonally upwards along the north side of the Tower to reach a flat area on the north west corner below the final 40ft of the Tower. By going right from here, it is possible to ascend to the summit using a route from the south west side through a gully. This final section is a grade one scramble requiring care. It should only be attempted by experienced hillwalkers in summer. It is best to return by the same route.

The Hills above Ladybower

An interesting walk over two contrasting hills, with good views of the high hills of the Peak District.

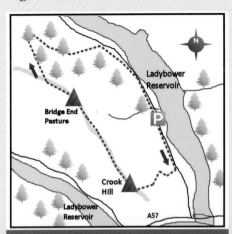

Walk Details

Distance:	7km (4.5 miles)
Height to Climb:	270m (885ft)
Start:	SK 187876
Difficulty:	3

The Hills

Bridge-end Pasture

Bridge-end Pasture is a TUMP lying within farmland north west of Crook Hill. There is a public right of way over the summit.

Height:	392m (1,286ft)
Summit:	SK 176879
Map Ref:	O/S Explorer **OL1**

Crook Hill

Crook Hill is a hill with twin summits situated above Ladybower Reservoir. The northern summit is highest and is a TUMP.

Height:	382m (1,253ft)
Summit:	SK 182872
Map Ref:	O/S Explorer **OL1**

Walk Summary

Above Ladybower Reservoir, and rarely noticed, lie two fine hills, smaller than the surrounding hills but popular with those who know them. They are Crook Hill and Bridge-end Pasture.

As can be seen from the photo below, Crook Hill has twin summits, the higher one is 382m, and the lower and more southerly one is 374m. The lower one is sometimes referred to as Ladycrook Hill. Bridge-end Pasture is an entirely different hill from Crook Hill, and is the only hill on the Derwent Valley skyline that is used for pasture. The walk starts beside Ladybower Reservoir and goes over both summits clockwise, returning beside Ladybower Reservoir.

Twin summits of Crook Hill

Walk Description

Turn off the A57 towards Fairholmes car park and Derwent Dam. Parking is available 1.5km up the road at grid reference SK 187876.

From the car park walk south down the road for 700m, then turn right up a minor road towards Crookhill Farm, a National Trust area. Just before the road goes into the farm, there is a stile on the right, and a path goes through a field to the access land where the twin summits of Crook Hill are found.

It is worth climbing both summits, the northern one is the higher but the southern one is a better summit. Descend north west from the more northerly summit and join a path which heads towards Bridge-end Pasture.

Crook Hill from Ladybower Reservoir

Go north through a gate, and walk north west up Bridge-end Pasture. Stay on the excellent footpath, go through another gate, and continue to the unmarked summit. The high hills of the Dark Peak can be seen all around, from Kinder Scout, to Win Hill and Stanage Edge.

The path descends north west, soon running just above Hagg Side Woods. It is pleasant walking. Approximately 1km from the summit, a track is reached which descends east through the woods and back to the road. Walk south east on a footpath beside the road for just over 1km to return to the car, or take the footpath which runs close to the shore of Ladybank Reservoir. This also leads back to the car park.

The Hills of Stanage Edge

A classic Derbyshire gritstone walk along Stanage Edge, well known for its many and varied rock-climbing routes, followed by the delightful summit of Higger Tor.

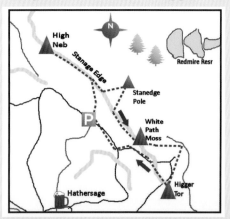

Walk Details

Distance:	13km (8 miles)
Height to Climb:	275m (905ft)
Start:	SK 238837
Difficulty:	4

Walk Summary

The walk described below is a variation of the walk featured in Britain's 100 favourite walks but, in my view better, as White Path Moss and Higger Tor are climbed in addition to High Neb. The Stanage Pole is added to this walk by a short diversion.

The Hills

High Neb

High Neb is a TUMP and by 1 metre the highest point in the area. It lies directly above Stanage Edge.

Height:	458m (1,503ft)
Summit:	SK 228854
Map Ref:	O/S Explorer **OL1**

White Path Moss

White Path Moss is a TUMP at the opposite end of Stanage Edge from High Neb. The Trig Point is spectacularly perched on the summit tor.

Height:	457m (1,499ft)
Summit:	SK 251830
Map Ref:	O/S Explorer **OL1**

Higger Tor

Although Higger Tor does not qualify as a TUMP because its prominence is lower than 30m, it is a well known and popular summit just south of Stanage Edge. Its summit area is shaped like the top of a castle with parapets round the outside.

Height:	434m (1,424ft)
Summit:	SK 257819
Map Ref:	O/S Explorer **OL1**

Walk Description

Start at the Hollins Bank car park 2.5km directly north of Hathersage (post code S32 1BR, charge). Hathersage is a popular spot with great climbing shops, cafes and pubs, and those wanting a longer walk could start from the village.

A path leaves the east end of the car park heading directly towards Stanage Edge in a north easterly direction. After crossing a patch of open ground, go through some woodland, through a gate, then walk north on to Stanage Edge. Turn left and follow the path north west along the top of Stanage Edge for 1.5km to the summit Trig Point of High Neb.

High Neb is the highest point of this vast expanse of moorland, and lies on the county border between Derbyshire and Yorkshire. Return back along Stanage Edge for 1.5km. The Stanage Pole can now be visited by walking 700m east.

Follow a path which runs south west from the Stanage Pole to return to the path along the top of Stanage Edge. After a further kilometre White Path Moss is reached with its Trig Point spectacularly situated on a large rock. Robin Hood's Cave is passed on this section of the walk. There is much to see and good views in all directions.

From the summit of White Path Moss, walk east for 800m on the Sheffield Country Walk (an 85km long distance walk around Sheffield) to a minor road at Upper Burbage Bridge. Higger Tor can now be clearly seen to the south. Walk 100m east along the road, then turn right along a good path that leads directly to the rocky, plateau like summit of Higger Tor. The

Carl Wark Hill Fort

To the south of Higger Tor lies Carl Wark hill fort, a rocky promontory surrounded by cliffs on all but one side, which is protected by a prehistoric embankment. It is thought that the hill fort is of Iron Age origin, dating back to around the 8th to 5th Century BC.

high point is not clearly defined but is probably the large rocks on the south side of the plateau. Take care if climbing these.

From the summit of Higger Tor, follow the path north to the minor road which runs south down to Hathersage. Walk north west across the field on a good path, then follow the road north west past Overstones Farm and turn right up the minor road back to the car. Alternatively, the roads can be avoided by following paths below the cliffs of Stanage Edge.

Stanage Edge

Stanage Edge, famous for its rock climbing, is a well-known part of the Peak District and features in Britain's 100 Favourite Walks at number 35. This walk starts at the Hollin Bank car park and goes to Stanage End at the far north of Stanage Edge, traversing the summit of High Neb. The walk is an out and back walk with the out route above the cliffs and the back route below them

Long Causeway

The Stanage Pole has stood in this spot for hundreds of years marking the border of Derbyshire and South Yorkshire and probably the ancient kingdoms of Mercia and Northumbria. It is on an ancient packhorse route known as the Long Causeway. A new pole was hoisted into place in 2016, replacing the last pole, probably erected in 1915.

The ramparts of Stanage Edge, below High Neb

Bamford Moor

A pleasant stroll to a small cairn on the moors.

Walk Details

Distance:	2km (1.5 miles)
Height to Climb:	90m (295ft)
Start:	SK 215839
Difficulty:	1

The Hills

Bamfood Moor

Bamford Moor is a TUMP close to Stanage Edge and directly above the village of Bamford.

Height:	426m (1,398ft)
Summit:	SK 211847
Map Ref:	O/S Explorer **OL1**

Walk Summary

Bamford Moor lies just above Bamford Village and can be climbed from the village. The route suggested starts from New Road which runs above the village. Starting from here saves 1.5km of walking and 500ft of climbing, compared with starting at Bamford Village. The walk is a straightforward out and back walk.

Walk Description

There is parking by the road at grid reference SK 216839, near the point marked 338m on the O/S Explorer map. Take the left-hand path north up the hillside and after about 15 minutes the high point, a large flattish boulder, is reached.

Many people walk 100m west to the overhanging rock, a popular spot and a great place for taking pictures. The walk can be extended along Bamford Edge, or it can be combined with the walk along Stanage Edge described on page 41.

Evening light, Bamford Edge

Peak District –
White Peak East

The White Peak is a limestone plateau that forms the central and southern part of the Peak District. The eastern section is in Derbyshire, east of the A515, Ashbourne to Buxton road. There are many hills of historical interest including Stanton Moor, Minninglow Hill, and Eldon Hill. Fifteen hills of the Peaks 75 are located in the White Peak East.

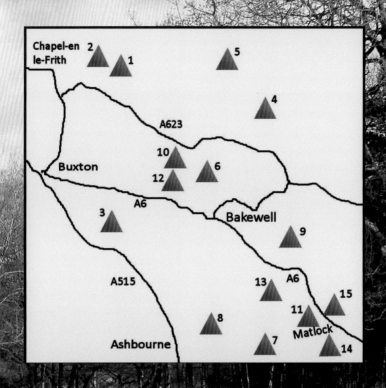

	Page No	Height (m)	Height (ft)	Map Ref
WHITE PEAK EAST				
Bradwell Moor	46	471	1,545	1
Eldon Hill	46	470	1,542	2
Chelmorton Hill	48	446	1,463	3
Sir William Hill	49	429	1,407	4
Shatton Edge	50	417	1,368	5
Longstone Moor	51	395	1,296	6
Harboro Rocks	66	379	1,243	7
Minninglow Hill	56	372	1,220	8
Beeley Moor	58	371	1,217	9
Wardlow Hay Cop	52	370	1,214	10
Masson Hill	62	338	1,109	11
Fin Cop	54	327	1,073	12
Stanton Moor	64	323	1,060	13
Bolehill	60	323	1,060	14
High Tor	62	205	673	15

Nine Ladies Stone Circle

Bradwell Moor & Eldon Hill

An enjoyable walk over the hills south of Mam Tor, with the remains of old mine workings peppered round Eldon Hill.

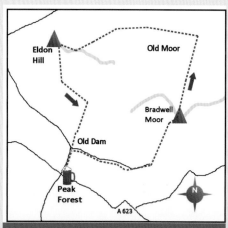

Walk Details

Distance:	8km (5 miles)
Height to Climb:	210m (690ft)
Start:	SK 114795
Difficulty:	3

The Hills

Bradwell Moor

Bradwell Moor is a TUMP with a prominent Trig Point situated close to the Limestone Way. It is the highest hill in this section of the book.

Height:	471m (1,545ft)
Summit:	SK 132801
Map Ref:	O/S Explorer **OL1/24**

Eldon Hill

Eldon Hill is of considerable geological, historical and industrial interest. A large section of the north of the hill has disappeared as a result of quarrying. There is a large cairn on the summit

Height:	470m (1,542ft)
Summit:	SK 116812
Map Ref:	O/S Explorer **OL1/24**

Walk Summary

These two hills give an excellent circular walk from Peak Forest. Bradwell Moor is climbed first then a traverse west leads to Eldon Hill with its old mine workings.

Eldon Hole

It is worth making a short detour to have a look at Eldon Hole which lies 350m south of the summit of Eldon Hill. Eldon Hole is the deepest pothole in the area at 55m deep.

Approaching Eldon Hill

Walk Description

The walk starts at Peak Forest and goes over two hills with good views north to Mam Tor and Kinder Scout. The walk details assume that Bradwell Moor is climbed first. Turn right at Peak Forest if driving along the A623 from the east. It should be possible to park by the side of the road between Peak Forest and Old Dam. Walk north east to Old Dam and turn right along Old Darn Lane. After just over 1km, the minor road reaches the Limestone Way. The Limestone Way is a long-distance walk from Castleton to Rocester (south of Ashbourne).

Follow the Limestone Way north east for 1km. After a stile, a small path goes up the hill to the right. Follow this, keeping the wall on your right, and the summit Trig Point appears ahead. This is the summit of Bradwell Moor.

The Limestone Way

To continue the walk to Eldon Hill with its interesting old mine workings, walk north, rejoin the Limestone Way and continue on this for 1.5km. A good track crosses at grid reference SK 135813. Turn left, and after 200m, carry straight on when the main track goes right. After another 700m a path goes off to the right. Ignore this and carry straight on for another 300m. Now turn left onto Access land, with the summit of Eldon Hill straight ahead.

Continue west up Eldon Hill to the summit cairn. Descend south then east to reach a good track, and follow this south to return to Peak Forest.

Chelmorton Hill

The highest summit in the area gives a short and fairly steep climb from Chelmorton Village.

Walk Details

Distance:	1.5km (1 mile)
Height to Climb:	50m (165ft)
Start:	SK 114702
Difficulty:	1

The Hills

Chelmorton Hill

Chelmorton Hill is a TUMP and prominent summit directly above Chelmorton. It is a short climb from the village.

Height:	446m (1,463ft)
Summit:	SK 114706
Map Ref:	O/S Explorer **OL24**

Walk Description

Chelmorton village is one of the highest villages in England and lies four miles south east of Buxton. When driving to Chelmorton from the west, Chelmorton Hill is clearly visible overlooking the village. It is possible to park on the Main Street at the north end of the village.

After parking the car, walk north east past the parish church of St John the Baptist, which dates back to the eleventh century. Continue to the end of the street. The street turns into a track. There is a gate on the left which gives access to the open hillside and access land. From here a path traverses round the hillside. Follow this for about 150 metres before heading directly up the hill. There are two tumuli on the summit, the westerly one appears to have a cairn on it, but the easterly one looks higher. Descend west to rejoin the path round the hillside and return to the village.

Chelmorton Hill from the west

Sir William Hill

An enjoyable walk with excellent views.

Walk Details

Distance: 3.5km (2 miles)
Height to Climb: 120m (400ft)
Start: SK 224780
Difficulty: 1

The Hills

Sir William Hill

Sir William Hill is a HUMP with an impressive summit. It stands apart from the surrounding hills.

Height: 429m (1,407 ft)
Summit: SK 215779
Map Ref: O/S Explorer **OL24**

Walk Description

'Sir William' Hill was probably named after one of the Sir William Cavendishs (owners of Chatsworth). The hill lies above Eyam, well known because it was badly hit by the Great Plague in 1665/66. Between 50% and 75% of the villagers died and at one stage the whole village was quarantined.

The hill is easily climbed from the east where it is possible to park at the start of the rough road heading west. Walk west up the road and the Trig Point can be seen ahead to the right of the wall. After 600m, there is a stile over the wall on the right. Cross this and walk up the path to the Trig Point. To see more of Eyam Moor, and enjoy an alternative route back to the car descend north from the Trig Point. After 800m there is a Ring Cairn, prehistoric ritual cup marked stone, on a 15m circular mound on the right. Carry on for another 200m, then turn right to follow a path east then south east back up the hill to the car.

Starting the climb of Sir William Hill

Shatton Edge (Burton Bole)

Shatton Edge, sometimes called Burton Bole, dominates the skyline looking west from Hathersage.

Walk Details

Distance:	4.5km (2.5 miles)
Height to Climb:	260m (855ft)
Start:	SK 199824
Difficulty:	2

The Hills

Shatton Edge

Shatton Edge is a TUMP. The summit is unmarked and lies on Abney Moor within access land.

Height:	417m (1,368ft)
Summit:	SK 194807
Map Ref:	O/S Explorer **OL1**

Looking to north to Win Hill

Walk Description

Turn off the A6187 Hope to Hathersage road, drive through the hamlet of Shatton, turn left up the hill and park near some farm buildings being careful not to block access.

Walk south up the minor road, not suitable for vehicles, for just over 400m, then a footpath leaves the road to head up the grassy hillside towards the mast. The path gives a good climb over short grass (to the above gate) and joins a track 50m east of the obvious mast on the hillside.

Turn right to walk along the track past the radio mast. After 800m a gate appears on the left. This gives access to the hillside. Climb up the heathery hillside for 200m to a gate on the right. Go through this to reach the unmarked highest point, near a grouse butt. Return by the same route.

Longstone Moor

A walk to the highest point of Longstone Moor, north east of Monsal Head.

Walk Details

Distance:	6km (3.5 miles)
Height to Climb:	190m (625ft)
Start:	SK 188718
Difficulty:	2

The Hills

Longstone Moor

Longstone Moor is a HUMP with the summit marked by a cairn on tumulus. The summit is an excellent viewpoint.

Height:	395m (1,296ft)
Summit:	SK 189733
Map Ref:	O/S Explorer OL24

Walk Description

Longstone Moor is immediately north of the village of Great Longstone and about 5km (3 miles) north of Bakewell. It is a wide expanse of high moorland, running 6km (4 miles) east to west, from the River Derwent to Monsal Dale. The highest point is a HUMP (hundred metres or more prominence).

Park in Great Longstone and walk north up Moor Lane. One kilometre after leaving the village, a Right of Way appears on the left. Follow this as it climbs the hillside onto the moor. Pass Watershaw Rake 300m after reaching the moor. Shortly after this a path goes west to the summit. The summit is a bowl barrow used for burials in the Bronze Age. Descend west for a short distance to a gate. Turn left to follow a path through another gate. This bends south east and joins a minor road which leads back to Great Longstone.

Summit of Longstone Hill

Wardlow Hay Cop

An impressive hill above Cressbrook Dale.

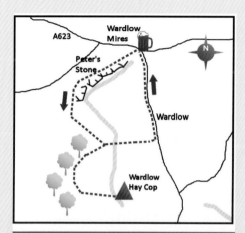

Walk Details

Distance:	7km (4.5 miles)
Height to Climb:	150m (500ft)
Start:	SK 181757
Difficulty:	3

The Hills

Wardlow Hay Cop

Wardlow Hay Cop is a TUMP with a rounded summit and a Trig Point. It is a prominant landmark.

Height:	370m (1,214ft)
Summit:	SK 179740
Map Ref:	O/S Explorer **OL24**

Peter's Stone

Peter's Stone, also referred to as Gibbet Rock, is a circular limestone dome at the northern end of Cressbrook Dale. This is where the last Gibbet in Derbyshire stood. A Gibbet was a gallows used to display the bodies of criminals after execution, and legend has it that it was last used in 1815.

Walk Summary

Driving north from Monsal Head, an impressive rounded hill appears on the left. This is Wardlow Hay Cop, a hill that can be climbed from the south. However, the best route starts from Wardlow Mires on the A623 to the north, and takes in Cressbrook Dale and Peter's Stone.

Approaching Peter's Stone

Walk Description

Park in Wardlow Mires, and walk west along the A623 to a footpath. This leaves the main road just west of the junction between the A623 and A6465 Monsal Head Road. After a few hundred metres, Peter's Stone comes into view, on the hillside to the left. Peter's Stone, also referred to as Gibbet Rock, is a circular limestone dome at the northern end of Cressbrook Dale. Continue on the path down the valley south west past Peter's Stone. The path turns south, and then south east. The summit of Wardlow Hay Cop can now be seen directly ahead. A path goes off to the left climbing the hillside diagonally. Take this path to reach the top of the hillside above Cressbrook Dale.

Wardlow Hay Cop from Longstone Moor

Once above Cressbrook Dale, the path follows the west side of the wall. Continue following this path south west for about 400m, until you see a gate on the left. An additional small gate beyond gives access to the hillside, and a good path leads to the summit Trig Point.

Return to the small gate, turn right and retrace your steps for 400m. Straight ahead and slightly to the right, there is another small gate which gives access to a grassy path sandwiched between two stone walls. This leads east to Wardlow village. At Wardlow village turn left and walk for 1km on a footpath beside the road, to return to Wardlow Mires.

Fin Cop

An interesting walk above and into Monsal Dale starting at Monsal Head.

Walk Details

Distance: 6km (3.5 miles)
Height to Climb: 180m (600ft)
Start: SK 185716
Difficulty: 2*

The Hills

Fin Cop

Fin Cop is a TUMP with a grassy summit next to a wall. Steep slopes drop down to the River Wye.

Height: 327m (1,073ft)
Summit: SK 174709
Map Ref: O/S Explorer **OL24**

Walk Summary

Monsal Head, where this walk starts, is one of the best known viewpoints in Derbyshire. It lies directly above Monsal Dale, the winding River Wye and Headstone viaduct. There is a pay and display car park and refreshments. The asterisk is because of the narrow path beside the wall near the summit of Fin Cop. This becomes overgrown in places during the summer.

Headstone Viaduct

The Headstone Viaduct was built by the Midland Railway over the River Wye in 1863. It was harshly criticised at the time by John Rushkin. However, it is now Grade II listed.

The Weir on the River Wye in Monsal Dale

Walk Description

The walk starts from the northern and smaller car park at Monsal Head. Walk west to the edge of the car park and a path goes downhill towards Ashford and Monsal Dale. After 50m there is a fork, take the left-hand path towards Ashford. Continue south west for 600m, and just before a sign to Ashford, a footpath branches off to the right, between the wall and the drop to the valley floor of Monsal Dale. Follow this footpath west as it makes its way along the right hand side of the wall through trees. This footpath becomes overgrown in places during the summer and brambles grow across the narrow path so shorts are not recommended.

After 800m, the path swings left, still following the right hand side of the wall. After a further 250m the summit is reached at the highest of the broken cairns next to the wall.

Near the summit of Fin Cop

Return by the same route, rejoin the path from Monsal Head to Ashford, and after returning practically to the start, descend to the viaduct above Monsal Dale. This is an optional extra as the hill has already been climbed, but it is worth the additional effort to see more of Monsal Dale. The path descends to the viaduct, arriving just opposite the point where the Monsal Trail goes through a tunnel. Cross the viaduct, turn left, and descend to the north side of Monsal Dale.

Walk west along the north side of the Dale. After 600m a weir is passed. 100m west of the weir, there is a footbridge crossing the River Wye. Cross the footbridge and turn left to follow a path along the other side of the dale.

This path goes east and climbs the hillside to the right. After 800m Monsal Head with its pub and cafe is reached again.

Minninglow

A concessionary path leads to the top of Minninglow, an ancient and mysterious summit surrounded by trees.

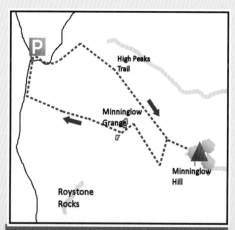

The Hills

Minninglow

Minninglow is a TUMP located in a copse of trees. The summit is an ancient burial site.

Height: 372m (1,220ft)
Summit: SK 210573
Map Ref: O/S Explorer **OL24**

Interesting Fact

Minninglow Hill is the site of a collection of Neolithic tombs dating from around 3,000 BC. The tombs are scattered around a later circular mound constructed in the Bronze Age. The whole site is now crowned by a copse of beech trees.

Walk Details

Distance: 5km (3 miles)
Height to Climb: 60m (200ft)
Start: SK 194582
Difficulty: 2

Walk Summary

This is an excellent circular walk to the top of Minninglow Hill from the car park on the High Peak Trail, just south of Pikehall. The High Peak Trail leads to the foot of the hill, then a concessionary path goes to the summit.

Minninglow from the High Peak Trail

Walk Description

The walk starts from Minninglow car park on the High Peak Trail. Walk east from the car park and cross over a narrow lane. Follow the High Peak Trail as it crosses over fields on a high embankment. This was constructed in the 1830s when the High Peak Trail was the Cromford and High Peak Railway line. The trail turns south east and the summit area of Minninglow, surrounded by trees, is now directly ahead.

After nearly 2km, and just before the trail turns south over a high embankment, the concessionary path appears on your left. This leads directly up the hill through slabs of limestone, to the circle of trees that defines the summit of Minninglow.

Minninglow summit

Enter the woodland to explore this ancient site with its 5,000 year old tombs, and visit the highest point.

Return back down the hill to where the concessionary path left the High Peak Trail, and turn left to cross the Embankment on the High Peak Trail. After 400m turn right to walk north west up a good track, Minninglow Lane. Follow the track north west past Minninglow Grange, then just north of west, as it turns into a minor road. On reaching a junction, grid reference SK 192577, turn right to return to the car park.

Beeley Moor

A walk over rough moorland above Chatsworth, the summit is 900m north west of the Trig Point.

Walk Details

Distance: 3km (2 miles)
Height to Climb: 80m (265ft)
Start: SK 286681
Difficulty: 2*

Walk Summary

Beeley Moor lies on moorland above and to the south east of Chatsworth. The hill lies on land sometimes used for grouse shooting but is access land. The walk is relatively short but the terrain is rough and pathless. At times it is not as easy as it appears on the map.

The Hills

Beeley Moor

Beeley Moor is an isolated TUMP and the high point of the substantial moorland plateau between Chesterfield and Chatsworth.

Height: 371m (1,217ft)
Summit: SK 293687
Map Ref: O/S Explorer **OL24**

Prehistoric Landscape

Beeley Moor is a prehistoric landscape with many protected ancient monuments, including cairns, burial mounds and guidestones. Hob Hurst's House is an unusual Bronze Age burial cairn on Harland Edge, 800m north west of the summit.

A grouse butt on the top of Beeley Moor

Walk Description

The normal route to the summit is from the corner of Beeley Lane (above Beeley) to the south west. This gives a reasonable walk, but with a potentially boggy area about halfway, so it is best completed in dry conditions. From the corner of the road, go through a gate and walk north east on a good track for a short distance. When the track bends left, go through a gate straight ahead, and continue on a small path. This continues north east, just right of the boggy area, with the route marked by stone pillars, similar to cairns. When the path bends right, continue straight towards the steep hillside, Harland Edge.

A lone tree on Harland Edge

Cross a 20m boggy area and continue straight towards two large stones on the hillside. The ground becomes easier, then there is a steep climb to the top of the hill followed by a further 150m of walking on rough terrain to the highest point. The top is unmarked near a grouse butt (see picture opposite).

The walk details assume a direct return to the car. However, a Trig Point can be seen 900m south east in clear weather. To visit the Trig Point, walk south east. There is no path so it is best to keep to the shorter heather where possible. To return to the car from the trig point descend south then walk just north of west below Harland Edge, crossing the bog by the same route as on the outward journey.

Bolehill

A short but interesting walk over this prominent hill between Cromford and Wirksworth.

Walk Details

Distance:	2.5km (1.5 miles)
Height to Climb:	80m (265ft)
Start:	SK 292557
Difficulty:	2

The Hills

Bolehill

Bolehill is a HUMP which gives a straightforward climb from Wirksworth past the spectacular Black Rocks to a flattish summit area.

Height:	323m (1,060ft)
Summit:	SK 294553
Map Ref:	O/S Explorer **OL24**

Cromford Mills

Cromford Mills is the home of Sir Richard Arkwright's first mill complex, birthplace of the modern factory system, and internationally recognised as a UNESCO World Heritage Site. Richard Arkwright developed the first water-powered cotton spinning mill in 1771 and the mill structure is a Grade 1 listed building. The Mill has now been restored and there is a visitor centre with shops, galleries, restaurants and cafes.

Black Rocks

Black Rocks is a small outcrop of natural gritstone which has been a well-known rock-climbing venue since the 1890s. Two climbs are featured in the documentary 'Hard Grit', these are Gaia and Meshuga.

Walk Summary

The area around Cromford and Wirksworth is one of the most scenic and historic in the Midlands. This circular walk passes Black Rocks and the summit of Bolehill, before descending to Bolehill village..

Café at Cromford Mills

Black Rocks

Walk Description

If driving from Cromford or Matlock, turn off the A6 and join the B5036 Cromford to Wirksworth road. After one mile, turn left on to a minor road, signposted to Black Rocks. There is a car park (charge) or there may be parking by the side of the road. From the car park at Black Rocks, follow the track east as it climbs past the cliffs to the summit plateau.

At the summit plateau the path turns to the right and goes south. After 200m the summit Trig Point is reached. Walk past the Trig Point, and after a further 200m the path turns right and goes sharply downhill. The descent takes you back to the road. Walk north west down the road for approximately 600m. When the road turns left, carry straight on under a railway arch (the High Peak Trail runs above the arch), to return to Black Rocks car park.

Masson Hill & High Tor

Steep hill walking to reach the summits surrounding Matlock Bath.

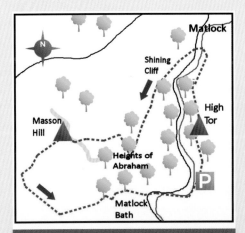

Walk Details

Distance:	8km (5 miles)
Height to Climb:	420m (1,400ft)
Start:	SK 297583
Difficulty:	3

The Hills

Masson Hill

Masson Hill is a TUMP. The high point is at the corner of a small wood above the Heights of Abraham.

Height:	338m (1,109ft)
Summit:	SK 286587
Map Ref:	O/S Explorer **OL24**

High Tor

High Tor is a rocky hill with cliffs rising directly above the east side of Matlock Bath. It is a popular summit usually climbed from the station car park.

Height:	205m (673ft)
Summit:	SK 297590
Map Ref:	O/S Explorer **OL24**

Tinker's Shaft

The Tinker's Shaft was once the main access point to the Great Masson Cavern, a working lead mine in the 17th Century. The shaft was named after Mr Tinker, who first sank it back in the 1600s.

Walk Summary

Matlock Bath has many attractions including the Heights of Abraham Park, Gulliver's Kingdom Theme Park, the Peak District Mining Museum, the Grand Pavilion and the Aquarium. This walk showcases the scenery above the town as well as going over two summits, one on each side of the road which passes through Matlock Bath.

Walk Description

Park in the large car park next to the railway station and walk north to the bottom of the cable car for the Heights of Abraham. Go past the entrance and turn left to climb High Tor, the lowest summit of the Peaks 75 list. The top is a superb spot, directly above Matlock Bath and looking across to the Heights of Abraham and Masson Hill. Giddy Edge runs just below the summit but this is best avoided. Descend north following the Derwent Valley Heritage Way, turn left and cross the river at a footbridge, (SK 297597), to reach the main road through Matlock Bath.

Walk south down the main road for a short distance then walk up a side road (St John's Road). Continue

Matlock Bath and the Heights of Abraham

straight, ascending gradually. Just before Cliffe Cottage, a path goes off to the right beside a wall. Follow this to the Heights of Abraham. After passing the entrance to the Heights of Abraham, follow a tarmac path which zig-zags up the hill, then follow the Right of Way which runs just below the Tinker's Shaft. There is a great view from here across the valley to High Tor.

Continue along the path, then turn right down a track. After 100m the track emerges onto open land. Turn immediately left up a path. Go through a small gate and continue uphill as the path bends right to a stile. Continue to a small wood with a gap in the wall. Go through this and follow the path through the right-hand side of the small wood to another gap in the wall, the summit.

To descend continue following the Right of Way, as it descends south to Ember Farm. Go through Ember Farm and turn left. 30m to your left there is a sign. Follow the path signposted to Matlock Bath, descend steeply through the Wood and follow the sign to the Cable Car and the station.

Stanton Moor

A walk through history and heathland on Stanton Moor.

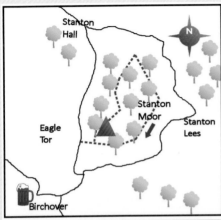

The Hills

Stanton Moor

Stanton Moor is a HUMP. The high point of this heathland moor is denoted by a Trig Point.

Height:	323m (1,060ft)
Summit:	SK 245629
Map Ref:	O/S Explorer **OL24**

Nine Ladies Stone Circle

The Nine Ladies Stone Circle, dating back to the Bronze Age is the best-known site on Stanton Moor. Traditionally, it is believed to depict nine ladies turned to stone as a penalty for dancing on Sundays, and is part of a complex of prehistoric circles and standing stones on Stanton Moor.

Walk Details

Distance:	6km (4 miles)
Height to Climb:	40m (130ft)
Start:	SK 242628
Difficulty:	2

Walk Summary

The Stanton Moor walk is featured in Britain's favourite 100 walks. It is a superb walk, which will be enjoyed by all the family. There are a number ancient sites including the Nine Ladies Stone Circle and the Reform Tower, and many wind-eroded pillars of sandstone, including the Cork Stone.

The Cork Stone on Stanton Moor

Nine Ladies Stone Circle

Walk Description

The walk is normally started by driving east out of Birchover, then turning left past Birchover Stone. Just past Birchover Stone, there is an area to park on the right-hand side of the road (SK 242628).

A path goes off to the right and climbs the hill. After a short distance the magnificent Cork Stone appears.

Turn left at the Cork Stone on a good path heading north east. After 100m, the Trig Point denoting the summit of Stanton Moor comes into view on the right. A short detour from the main path allows this summit to be 'bagged'. Stanton Moor is a HUMP, over one hundred metres prominence. Return to the main path and continue north east to the Nine Ladies Stone Circle.

From the Nine Ladies Stone Circle, a direct return route can be made by heading south across delightful heather moorland and silver birch. Alternatively follow a good path south east which goes round the east edge of the moor passing the Reform Tower. This was built to honour Charles, 2nd Earl Grey, who introduced the 1832 Reform Bill. This path also leads to the south end of the moorland. Turn right to follow a good path back to the Cork Stone and the car.

Harboro Rocks

A short walk to an unusual rock peak.

Walk Details

Distance:	3km (2 miles)
Height to Climb:	60m (200ft)
Start:	SK 252547
Difficulty:	1

Walk Description

This hill lies between Wirksworth and Brassington, a few kilometres north of Carsington Water.

I suggest parking in one of the laybys on the road from Wirksworth to Brassington, about 1.5km south east of the summit (grid reference SK 253546). Join the High Peak Trail and walk north west for just over one kilometre until due south of the summit.

A signpost appears, turn right up a path which winds through the rocks to the summit Trig Point. There are good views in most directions although they are disturbed by a factory just south of the hill.

The Hills

Harboro Rocks

Harboro Rocks is a TUMP at the top of some strange rock formations. It gives a straightforward out and back walk from a convenient road.

Height:	379m (1,243ft)
Summit:	SK 243553
Map Ref:	O/S Explorer **OL24**

The Limestone Cave

Harboro Rocks is a dolomitic limestone hill. Beneath it lies a cave where archaeologists have found evidence of human occupants since the ice age. The author Daniel Defoe reported in his book 'Tour thro' the whole island of Great Britain' that a poor family of seven was living in the cave. The father was a lead miner.

Trig on Harboro Rocks

Harboro Rocks

Peak District –
White Peak– West

To the west of the Derbyshire Dales, in Staffordshire, western Derbyshire, and south east Cheshire, lies an interesting variety of hills. Two of the highest are Shutlingsloe, sometimes described as the 'Matterhorn of Cheshire' and the Roaches, well known for its rock climbing. There are spectacular rock formations round the Roaches and wide, expansive views from the Cloud, in the far west of the area. Ten hills of the Peaks 75 are located in the White Peak West.

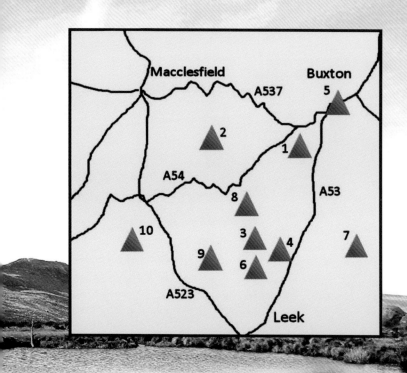

	Page No.	Height (m)	Height (ft)	Map Ref
WHITE PEAK WEST				
Axe Edge Moor	70	551	1,808	1
Shutlingsloe	72	506	1,660	2
The Roaches	74	505	1,657	3
Ramshaw Rocks	74	460	1,509	4
Grin Low	71	434	1,424	5
Hen Cloud	74	410	1,345	6
Revidge	80	401	1,316	7
Gradbach Hill	78	399	1,309	8
Gun	81	385	1,263	9
The Cloud	82	343	1,125	10

On the Roaches

Axe Edge Moor

A high moorland walk just south west of Buxton.

Walk Details

Distance: 4.5km (3 miles)
Height to Climb: 75m (250ft)
Start: SK 033699
Difficulty: 2

Walk Description

Axe Edge Moor is the highest hill in the Peak District south of Buxton. It is worth adding Cheeks Hill to this walk, because just south west of its summit is the Derbyshire/Staffordshire border and the county top (highest point) of Staffordshire.

Park south of the hill just off the minor road which runs between the A53 Buxton to Leek road and the A54 Buxton to Congleton road. A good path leads north from here to the summit of Axe Edge Moor.

Now walk west on another good path for 1km to join the Dane Valley Way (long distance path from Buxton to Northwich). Go south on this path to return to the minor road, 1km north west of the start point.

The Hills

Axe Edge Moor

Axe Edge Moor is a TUMP and the fifth highest summit in the list. It is on high moorland with the best views to the south and east.

Height: 551m (1,808ft)
Summit: SK 035706
Map Ref: O/S Explorer **OL24**

Summit of Axe Edge Moor

To add the highest point of Staffordshire, continue south on a good path with a wall to the right. After 400m the Staffordshire border and the County Top is reached (grid reference 025698). The best return to the car is to walk east for 100m to rejoin the Dane Valley Way, and follow it north back to the minor road a few hundred metres west of where the car is parked.

Grin Low

A short walk through the Buxton Country Park.

Walk Description

Sometimes called Solomon's Temple, Grin Low is Buxton's hill with fine views and an interesting history. Grin Low lies close to the centre of Buxton, at the top of the Country Park next to Poole's Cavern. In 1840 Solomon's Temple was built at the summit, replaced by Grinlow Tower in 1896 by the 8th Duke of Devonshire.

Park at Buxton Country Park car park on Green Lane (post code SK17 9DH, charge) which is also the car park for Poole's Cavern. A path goes uphill through the woods coming out on open land near the summit. Grinlow Tower, previously Solomon's Temple, can be seen just to the east. It is a short climb to the top of the Tower.

The Hills

Grin Low

Grin Low is a TUMP close to the centre of Buxton. It is a straightforward walk from the car park at Poole Cavern to the Tower on its summit.

Height:	434m (1,424ft)
Summit:	SK 054718
Map Ref:	O/S Explorer **OL24**

Buxton Lime Industry

Grin Low was the main location for the early Buxton lime industry between the 17th and 19th Century. Demand for lime grew in the during the Industrial Revolution, and there are widespread remains of over 100 large 'pudding' lime kilns on the hillside.

Grinlow Tower

Shutlingsloe

Shutlingsloe is one of the best hills in the Peak District, its sharp peak dominating views in the western Peak.

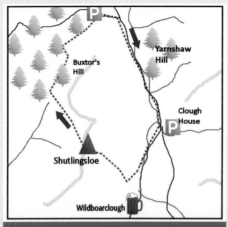

The Hills

Shutlingsloe

Shutlingsloe is a distinctive, steep sided hill near the village of Wildboarclough in Cheshire, sometimes known as the 'Matterhorn of the Peak District'. It is a fine hill, a HUMP (over 100m prominence), and many people's favourite hill in the area.

Height:	506m (1,660ft)
Summit:	SK 976696
Map Ref:	O/S Explorer **OL24**

Walk Details

Distance:	8km (5 miles)
Height to Climb:	215m (710ft)
Start:	SK 987699
Difficulty:	3

Three Shires Head

The Clough House car park is used by some people as a base for visiting Three Shires Head, a walk of about 3km each way. Three Shires Head is the point where Cheshire, Derbyshire and Staffordshire meet (grid reference SK 009685). The packhorse bridge and waterfalls are very picturesque, and are known for wild swimming, although the water is very cold.

Walk Summary

This is a circular walk from Clough House car park, 1.5km north of Wildboarclough. It goes over the summit of Shutlingsloe then traverses the edge of Macclesfield Forest before returning to the start point.

Walk Description

Shutlingsloe can be climbed from the east or the west. The route from the west goes through Macclesfield Forest. The route described is from Clough House car park to the east of the summit, but gives a good perspective of the hill from both the east and west sides. The nearest postcode for the car park is SK11 0BD which is for Wildboarclough village, about 1.5km south of the car park. There was no charge for parking in 2021.

From the car park, leave by the west end and turn left to walk south along the road. After 200m,

Shutlingsloe from Wildboarclough

a path goes off on the right. Follow this through a wood and along the hillside for about 700m, then turn right up a good path which leads directly to the summit of Shutlingsloe (see picture above).

Descend steeply just west of north, and continue on the excellent path as it bends left, then enters Macclesfield Forest. Immediately on entering the forest, turn right on a track which descends north east to a car park at the east end of the forest. From this point follow the road south for 2km back to Clough House car park. Whilst this may sound tedious, the road is generally quiet and on nearing the car park the road runs beside a pleasant river.

Roaches, Hen Cloud, Ramshaw

A classic walk over three rocky and individual summits north of Leek.

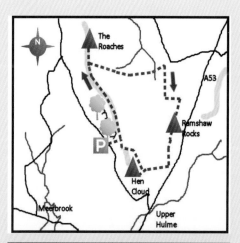

Walk Details

Distance:	13km (8 miles)
Height to Climb:	350m (1,100ft)
Start:	SK 007619
Difficulty:	4

Rock Climbing Legends

Just below the Roaches, the Don Whillans Memorial Hut, also known as Rockhall Cottage, can be seen. Don Whillans was one of the legendary climbers of the 1950s, 60s and 70s, often climbing with Joe Brown and Chris Bonington, making a number of first ascents. He met Joe Brown rock climbing at the Roaches in 1951.

The Hills

The Roaches

The Roaches is a HUMP well known for its west facing cliffs, popular with rock climbers. The Roaches is the defining hill in the south west Peak near Leek.

Height:	505m (1,657ft)
Summit:	SK 001639
Map Ref:	O/S Explorer OL24

Ramshaw Rocks

Ramshaw Rocks is a TUMP with some very unusual rock formations. shown in the photograph on page 77

Height:	460m (1,509ft)
Summit:	SK 020624
Map Ref:	O/S Explorer OL24

Hen Cloud

Hen Cloud is a fine hill. It is a TUMP and a close neighbour of the Roaches. There is rock climbing on its western side but a lovely hill for all.

Height:	410m (1,345ft)
Summit:	SK 009616
Map Ref:	O/S Explorer OL24

Walk Summary

This walk traverses the three great summits in the south west of the Peak District National Park. The walk over the Roaches alone is rated number 53 in the list of "100 best walks in Britain". This walk traverses the Roaches, Ramshaw Rocks and Hen Cloud and is one of the most interesting and varied walks in the Peak District.

Walk Description

There is parking on the minor road which runs north west from Upper Hulme. The walk starts by following the path up to the col between The Roaches and Hen Cloud, therefore it is best to park just west of Hen Cloud or slightly further north. This is a popular spot with walkers and rock climbers so the road can be busy, particularly at weekends.

Start by following the path up to the col between the Roaches and Hen Cloud and turn left to the Roaches. Keep right to ascend above the cliffs and to the east side of the hill. The path is followed north for 2km to the Trig Point at the top of the Roaches. About half way up the path passes the Doxey Pool, said to be home to a malicious mermaid named Jenny Greenteenth.

Approaching the Roaches

Return south along the path for 800m. Before the Doxey Pool is reached, turn left to descend just north of east to the road. Turn right along the road and walk east. After just over 1km a junction is reached. Turn right and walk south for 400m. A footpath now goes left towards Ramshaw Rocks. Follow this, after a few hundred metres it joins the Churnet Way. Continue south on the Churnet Way over Ramshaw Rocks with its magnificent rock formations.

Hen Cloud from Ramshaw Rocks

Walk Description (cont)

After going over the summit of Ramshaw Rocks, descend south to a minor road and turn left towards the A53. There now follows a circuitous route to Hen Cloud where it is best to stick to the path. Walk south down the minor road for a short distance, then walk south down the Churnet Way as it descends towards the A53. Continue following the Churnet Way as it turns right and skirts a farm. The route is marked by posts with the tops painted red. Continue to follow the path as it turns north for a short distance, then a left turn directly towards Hen Cloud.

After a short distance, the Churnet Way leaves to go south. Continue on the path towards Hen Cloud, emerging on a minor road just north of a farm. Turn right u the minor road. Just before another farm, a footpath goes left and crosses a field. After going over a stile the lower slopes of Hen Cloud are reached.

Turn right to walk round to the col between Hen Cloud and the Roaches. From here, follow the path directly to the magnificent summit of Hen Cloud. There are some 'extreme' rock climbing routes on the west side of the summit, and occasionally climbers can be seen attempting them. Return down the path to the col between the Roaches and Hen Cloud and descend west to the car.

Ramshaw Rocks

Gradbach Hill

Visit the Yawning Stone at the summit of Gradbach Hill and Lud's Church on a circular walk from Gradbach.

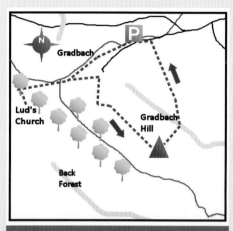

Walk Details

Distance:	7km (4.5 miles)
Height to Climb:	250m (850ft)
Start:	SK 999662
Difficulty:	3

The Hills

Gradbach Hill

Gradbach Hill is a TUMP and close neighbour of the Roaches. Its defining feature is the Yawning Stone, situated very close to the summit.

Height:	399m (1,309ft)
Summit:	SK 001653
Map Ref:	O/S Explorer **OL24**

Lud's Church

Lud's Church is a deep chasm penetrating the rock on the hillside just to the west of Gradbach. It is located in a wood and is over 100m (328ft) long and 18m (59ft) deep. It is mossy and overgrown, wet and cool, even on the hottest days. John Wycliffe, an early church reformer is supposed to have used this place as a secret place of worship in the early 15th Century. It may also have been the setting for The Green Chapel in the medieval poem Sir Gawain and the Green Knight.

Walk Summary

I suggest combining Gradbach Hill with Lud's Church in a circular walk visiting the remarkable chasm of Lud's Church before traversing Gradbach Hill. There is parking and a café at the hamlet of Gradbach. Gradbach is just to the north of the hill and makes a good place to start the walk.

Lud's Church

Walk Description

From the car park just east of Gradbach, walk west along the road for a few hundred metres, then take a right turn to follow the Dane Valley Way, which follows the left hand side of the river past Gradbach. After passing Gradbach, follow the signs to Lud's Church. The path leaves the Dane Valley Way and climbs the hillside in a big zig zag, a distance of about 1km.

After visiting the church, return by the same route to the bottom of the hill and the edge of the wood. Cross to the east side of Black Brook, and follow a sign to the Scout Hut which is at the south end of Gradbach. Turn right at the Scout Hut and follow a Right of Way through a farm. Not long after passing the farm, a marked path goes off to the left and leads to the access land on Gradbach Hill.

Yawning Stone at the summit

On reaching the access land, climb to the top of the edge. A path goes off to the right following the top of the edge and this leads to the unmarked summit of Gradbach and the Yawning Stone.

The top of the Yawning Stone, see below, is marginally lower than the high point of Gladbach so there is no need to climb it, and I advise against any attempt.

To descend, follow a small path north east across the access land. After about 400m, a wall is reached and a stile which allows access on to a Right of Way. This path runs north back to the car park.

Revidge

A pleasant walk from Warslow through copse and heather.

Walk Details

Distance:	5km (3 miles)
Height to Climb:	75m (250ft)
Start:	SK 086587
Difficulty:	1

The Hills

Revidge

Revidge is a TUMP overlooking the hills round Hartington and the Manifold Valley. The summit area is surrounded by heather and is impressive.

Height:	401m (1,316ft)
Summit:	SK 077599
Map Ref:	O/S Explorer **OL24**

Walk Description

Revidge lies between the Roaches and the hills of the Manifold valley. Close to the summit heather blends with small woods, Revidge is higher than the hills to the east so the views in that direction are excellent.

It is best to park near the pub at Warslow. After leaving the village walk west beside the road for 400m. Turn right to follow a path north to Clough Head. Turn left and go west to join a Right of Way. Follow this Right of Way north, and a path goes off to the left to the summit Trig Point.

On the return retrace the outbound route.

Near the summit of Revidge

A simple stroll to one of the five Marilyns in the Peaks.

Walk Details

Distance:	3.5km (2 miles)
Height to Climb:	30m (100ft)
Start:	SK 968609
Difficulty:	1

The Hills

The Gun

The Gun is one of five Marilyns (hills with 150m or more prominence) on this listing. It is also one of the easiest summits to reach.

Height:	385m (1,263ft)
Summit:	SK 970615
Map Ref:	O/S Explorer **OL24**

Walk Description

The Gun lies on Gun Moor at the far south west of the Peak District National Park, to the west of the Roaches and Hen Cloud. At the time of writing the Staffordshire Wildlife Trust was trying to buy Gun Moor as it is the habitat for a number of rare birds including cuckoos, redpolls and snipes. As it is a Marilyn, the highest status of British Relative Hills (see page 140), The Gun is a popular summit for hill walkers.

The Gun is an easy summit to reach, a flattish walk of approximately 650m from the south where parking is possible (SK 968609). There is only 100ft of ascent to the Trig Point.

There is an option to continue the walk north for around 800m before circling back to the Trig Point. This offers an opportunity to enjoy the lovely countryside.

Summit of The Gun

The Cloud

A magnificent hill with a heather covered summit plateau whose distinctive shape can be seen from many miles away.

Walk Details

Distance: 5km (3 miles)
Height to Climb: 200m (650ft)
Start: SK 894628
Difficulty: 2

Interesting Fact

The Gritstone Trail passes over the Cloud and two further hills in the book, Teggs Nose and Kerridge Hill. The Gritstone Trail follows a route over the most westerly hills of the Peak District. It is 56km long with 1,800ft of climbing.

The Hills

The Cloud

The Cloud lies on the border between Cheshire and Staffordshire and is one of only five Marilyns (hills with prominence of 150m or more) in the Peak District area. The summit is on National Trust land.

Height: 343m (1,125 ft)
Summit: SK 904637
Map Ref: O/S Explorer 268

The Cloud

Walk Summary

The walk starts from Timberbrook picnic area and car park just east of Congleton. It is a popular walk to the summit, through trees and then an area of open heathland.

View north from the summit

Walk Description

There is parking at Timberbrook Picnic area and car park on Weathercock Lane (postcode CW12 3PP). From here follow the path east through open grass to a set of steps which leads to the Tunstall Road. Turn left and walk up the road for nearly 200m, then take the track on your right signposted 'The Gritstone Trail'.

Follow this track to a footpath leading off to the left through a stile and waymarked 'Gritstone Trail and Staffordshire Way'. Follow this path uphill through the woods, continuing to follow the Gritstone Trail and the Staffordshire Way. The path emerges on open heathland area.The highest point is the summit of the Cloud. There is a Trig Point and orientation table at the summit with good views in all directions.

Peak District – *Dales*

In the central part of the White Peak, partly in Derbyshire and partly in Staffordsh
lies the Peak District Dales, the best known being Dovedale. The Rivers Dove and
Manifold are the two rivers that form the landscape with the hills lying around them
This section contains some spectacular hills, not particularly high but great to climb.
Particular favourites of mine are Chrome Hill, Parkhouse Hill and the Wetton Hill
There is much to see and do in this area, as well as climb the fifteen hills of the Peak
75 located in the Peak District Dales.

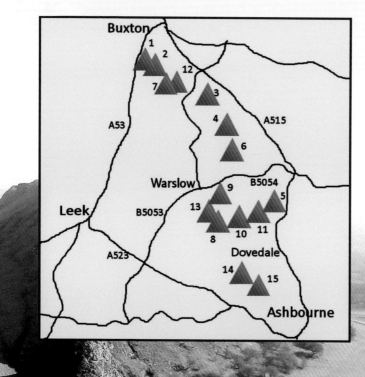

	Page No.	Height (m)	Height (ft)	Map Ref
PEAK DISTRICT DALES				
Hollins Hill	86	450	1,476	1
Chrome Hill	86	443	1,453	2
High Wheeldon	90	422	1,384	3
Pilsbury Castle Hill	92	395	1,296	4
Wolfscote Hill	94	388	1,273	5
Carder Low	92	380	1,247	6
Parkhouse Hill	86	375	1,230	7
Wetton Hill	98	371	1,217	8
Ecton Hill	98	369	1,211	9
Narrowdale Hill	96	367	1,204	10
Gratton Hill	96	363	1,191	11
Parkhouse Hill North	86	362	1,188	12
Wetton Hill SW Top	98	358	1,175	13
Bunster Hill	101	329	1,080	14
Thorpe Cloud	101	287	942	15

Parkhouse Hill from Chrome Hill

Hollins, Chrome & Parkhouse

A remarkable walk featuring the great fin of Chrome and Parkhouse Hills. Chrome Hill is one of the best hills in England under 2,000ft.

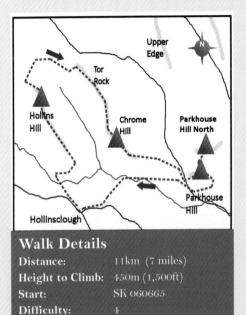

Walk Details

Distance:	11km (7 miles)
Height to Climb:	450m (1,500ft)
Start:	SK 060665
Difficulty:	4

Walk Summary

This walk traverses the length of Chrome Hill and Parkhouse Hill from north to south, two of the best small hills in Britain. Three hundred million years ago, Chrome Hill and Parkhouse Hill were a coral reef, under the sea. There are sheer drops, and nooks and crannies in the rock faces, and it is easy to imagine saltwater life lurking in the crags. Up until 1999, it was illegal to climb Chrome Hill and Parkhouse Hill as both were on private land, but following the Countryside Rights of Way Act in 2000, the summit areas became access land. Later, the Peak District National Park negotiated a concessionary path to access it. The walk starts with Hollins Fell (the highest of the 4 hills) then returns with a magnificent traverse of Chrome and the Parkhouse Hills.

The Hills

Hollins Hill

Hollins Hill is a TUMP with steep eastern slopes and a broad north to south ridge. It is the highest of this set of hills.

Height:	450m (1,476ft)
Summit:	SK 060679
Map Ref:	O/S Explorer OL24

Chrome Hill

Chrome Hill is one of the most interesting of Britain's sub 2,000ft hills. It is shaped like a fin and gives an excellent ridge walk on a good path.

Height:	443m (1,453ft)
Summit:	SK 071673
Map Ref:	O/S Explorer OL24

Parkhouse Hill

Parkhouse Hill is a steep sided and a spectacular peak. It is an extension of the Chrome Hill fin with a steep climb from every direction.

Height:	375m (1,230ft)
Summit:	SK 080670
Map Ref:	O/S Explorer OL24

Parkhouse Hill North

Parkhouse Hill North is a subsidiary of Parkhouse Hill. However it is a distinct hill and a TUMP.

Height:	362m (1,188ft)
Summit:	SK 081673
Map Ref:	O/S Explorer OL24

Walk Description

The best place to start the walk is Hollinsclough in Staffordshire. Walk north west out of Hollinsclough on a minor road. After 200m, a footpath goes off to the right, and drops to a footbridge over the River Dove.

Continue uphill on the footpath past a minor, private road to Hollins Farm. Just after a gate, turn right and follow a concessionary path to the access land at the south end of the summit ridge of Hollins Hill. Once on the summit ridge, a footpath runs north between a wall on your left, and steep slopes dropping down to the right. The footpath leads to the summit tumulus.

From the summit of Hollins Hill, descend west, staying on the access land, reaching the minor road close to Booth Farm. Walk 200m north on the minor road, turn right through a gate and follow a path which goes north east, bending east, and passing north of Stoop Farm.

Parkhouse Hill from Chrome Hill

After passing Stoop Farm, there is a small gate on the right. This is the concessionary path which leads to the great fin of Chrome Hill. The path goes downhill, passing to the left of Tor Rock, and through two gates. Follow the path to the bottom of the hill and the start of the ridge up Chrome Hill. Initially the path goes right keeping below the ridge, but after roughly 100m, it climbs back up to the ridge. There follows one of the best ascents in the Peak District, as the path winds its way up the ridge directly to the summit. From the summit of Chrome Hill continue along the ridge now descending south east with Parkhouse Hill directly ahead.

This is great hill walking country. Go through a gate, and continue on the path to the minor road which goes north through Dowel Dale. There are a number of no parking signs on the grass to the side of the road. The north west ridge of Parkhouse Hill, the next hill on the round, is straight ahead.

Walk Description (cont)

Parkhouse Hill gives a relatively short but steep climb of 350ft. It is a fine hill, a continuation of the great Chrome Hill 'fin'. Although this hill looks impossible to climb direct, there is a route from the left-hand side. The best route to the summit follows a path to the left of the main ridge, and this path turns right to join the main ridge higher up. A more 'sporting' route is straight up the ridge but this is no recommended.

Continue over the summit of Parkhouse Hill and down the east side of the ridge. Parkhouse Hill North is closeby to the north. Near the bottom of the ridge, turn l and head directly towards the col below Parkhouse Hill north. Go through a small gate and climb directly to the summit. Now return to the small gate and descend west to the minor road (or traverse round to the south side of Parkhouse Hill to descend).

After returning to the minor road, walk south down the road for 250m, and a track goes off to the right. Follow this track west, then south west. After just under 2km of walking, you will be back in Hollinsclough.

Hollins Hill and Tor Rock

As noted, Hollinsclough has no pubs or cafes. Possible places close by to stop for refreshments include Longnor and Earl Sterndale. Indeed the walk could be completed from Earl Sterndale, but this would add about 3km to the length of the walk.

Chrome Hill from Parkhouse Hill

High Wheeldon

An interesting walk through an historical part of the Peak District with a steep climb to the summit of High Wheeldon.

Walk Details

Distance:	5km (3 miles)
Height to Climb:	200m (650ft)
Start:	SK 090671
Difficulty:	3

The Hills

High Wheeldon

High Wheeldon is a steep sided TUMP with a history going back 10,000 years.

Height:	422m (1,384ft)
Summit:	SK 100661
Map Ref:	O/S Explorer **OL24**

Walk Summary

High Wheeldon is a distinctive dome-shaped hill which overlooks the villages of Earl Sterndale and Longnor. It is popular with walkers and there are excellent views of the Dove and Manifold valleys. Aldery Cliff, opposite High Wheeldon, is owned by the BMC and contains some excellent rock climbing crags (see opposite).

This is a circular walk from the village of East Sterndale. It traverses Hitter Hill before heading south and making a steep ascent of the northern slopes of High Wheeldon.

Memorial to the Fallen

High Wheeldon was given to the National Trust in 1946 as a memorial to the men of Derbyshire and Staffordshire who died in the War. A plaque at the summit commemorates the presentation, stating that the hill was presented 'in honoured memory of the men of Derbyshire and Staffordshire who fell in the Second World War'.

Walk Description

Park in the village of Earl Sterndale, and walk to the pub, the Quiet Woman. From here a path goes south west leading to access land and the summit of Hitter Hill. There are good views of the fins of Chrome Hill and Parkhouse Hill from this summit. Follow the path (signposted to Longnor) as it descends south to a track.

Turn left and follow the track south east past the farm at Underhill, then turn left at Green Lane and head directly towards High Wheeldon. At the road, turn left and immediately cross the road to a path which heads up High Wheeldon. The track climbs initially, turns right and continues to a wall, then turns left and climbs steeply up the hill. Overall, this is a steep climb of 155m, over 500ft, but a magnificent way to reach the Trig Point. From the Trig Point walk east down a path towards some buildings. Before leaving the access land turn left to descend north west to the road on a good path. Follow the road north west for just over 1km back to Earl Sterndale.

Aldery Cliff opposite High Wheeldon

Pilsbury Castle & Carder Low

A walk over the two summits north of Hartington.

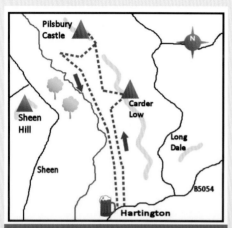

The Hills

Pilsbury Castle Hill

Pilsbury Castle Hill is a TUMP directly above the hamlet of Pilsbury. A quiet, minor road passes south of the summit.

Height:	395m (1,296ft)
Summit:	SK 121640
Map Ref:	O/S Explorer **OL24**

Carder Low

Carder Low is a TUMP lying north of Hartington. It is a classic White Peak summit with grassy slopes and limestone rocks protruding through the grass.

Height:	380m (1,247ft)
Summit:	SK 130626
Map Ref:	O/S Explorer **OL24**

Walk Details

Distance:	11km (7 miles)
Height to Climb:	260m (850ft)
Start:	SK 128604
Difficulty:	3

Walk Summary

Pilsbury Castle Hill and Carder Low lie just to the north of Hartington. This circular walk goes over both hills on the way out and comes back along the valley. Starting and finishing in Hartington means refreshments are available at the beginning and end of the walk.

The hills are just to the east of the River Dove so both hills are in Derbyshire. Across the valley, on the Staffordshire side, Sheen Hill can be seen which is exactly the same height as Carder Low. Access to this hill is unclear so it has been excluded from the list.

On the path to Carder Low

Village of Hartington

Walk Description

Walk 100m east from the centre of Hartington, then walk north along the road, which passes the church, for 800m. When the road bends to the right, a footpath leaves the left side of the road and traverses the hillside past the western slopes of Carder Low and nearly the whole way to Pilsbury Castle.

Follow the path for 1.5km along the side of the hill over stiles and through gates. When you are east of Carder Low, on access land, head directly east up the hillside to the summit. There are substantial gaps in the wall, which enable an easy route to the summit.

From the summit of Carder Low, return to the footpath, and carry on north for over 1km to a minor road which goes west towards Pilsbury. From the minor road, ascend north west over access land to the summit of Pilsbury Castle Hill. Keep left of the wall. Return to the minor road, then follow the road downhill to Pilsbury, and continue through the Hamlet.

From Pilsbury the gated road is followed for 4km back to Hartington. It is a quiet road, with very few cars, so gives a pleasant walk close to the River Dove.

Wolfscote Hill

An interesting walk from Hartington up Beresford Dale to this fine summit looking down Dovedale.

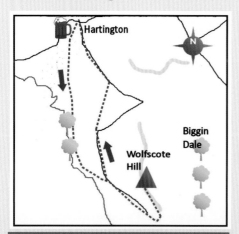

The Hills

Wolfscote Hill

Wolfscaote Hill is a HUMP with a Trig Point at the summit. It has fine views south down Wolfscote Dale and Dove Dale.

Height:	388m (1,273ft)
Summit:	SK 137583
Map Ref:	O/S Explorer **OL24**

Walk Details

Distance:	8km (5 miles)
Height to Climb:	180m (600ft)
Start:	SK 127603
Difficulty:	2

Wolfscote Dale

Wolfscote Dale is a beautiful limestone dale between Hartington and Alstonefield. The walk through it is about 4km, quieter than Dovedale but just as attractive. There are caves in the limestone at Wolfscote Dale. These could, at one time, have been the homes for the many wolves that were reputed to live in the Dale.

Walk Summary

This hill lies on National Trust land above Wolfscote Dale. It is a fine summit qualifying as a HUMP (more than 100m prominence). Wolfscote Hill lies to the south of Hartington, formerly known for cheese making. Hartington lies just to the east of the River Dove, which forms the border between Derbyshire and Staffordshire. The walk goes through Beresford Dale on the way to Wolfscote Hill and returns along rarely used minor roads back to Hartington.

Walk Description

Parking is available in the car park on the south west side of Hartington (charge). Cross the road and walk a few metres towards the centre of the village, then take the path signposted to Beresford Dale from next to Hartington Farm Shop. Follow the path south through the fields into Beresford Dale. Go through Beresford Dale and continue south towards Wolfscote Dale where the path crosses to the east side of the river. Continue for 300m, then I suggest taking a short detour of a few hundred metres to have a look at Wolfscote Dale, a beautiful limestone dale between Hartington and Alstonefield.

Walk Description (cont)

Return to the entrance of the Dale, and turn right on a path which climbs towards Wolfscote Grange. On reaching the minor road turn right and bear left past the entrance to Wolfscote Grange. Continue south until 400m past Wolfscote Grange. Wolfscote Hill lies on the National Trust land to the left. Turn left through a gate and follow a track which ascends to the Trig Point.

Return to Wolfscote Grange, then follow the minor road north. Carry straight on at a byway, continuing north back to Hartington.

Wolfscote Dale

Narrowdale & Gratton Hills

Two fine hills climbed from Alstonefield.

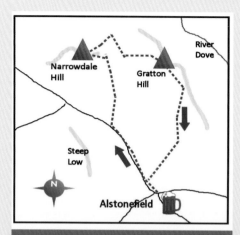

Walk Details

Distance:	8km (5 miles)
Height to Climb:	200m (650ft)
Start:	SK 131557
Difficulty:	3

The Hills

Narrowdale Hill

Narrowdale Hill is a TUMP with an unmarked summit. It has a steep north eastern flank but with gentler, grassy slopes to the south.

Height:	367m (1,204ft)
Summit:	SK 123573
Map Ref:	O/S Explorer **OL24**

Gratton Hill

Gratton Hill is inevitably twinned with Narrowdale Hill but it is marginally lower. It is a TUMP with a cairn marking the summit.

Height:	363m (1,191ft)
Summit:	SK 132572
Map Ref:	O/S Explorer **OL24**

Approaching Narrowdale Hill

Walk Summary

Just to the west of Wolfscote Hill lie two fine hills filling the ground between Wolfscote Hill and Wetton Hill. Both hills are on access land with a narrow strip of access land running between them, so they are best climbed together.

Narrowdale Hill and Gratton Hill could be combined with Wolfcote Hill by a long walk from Hartington, but I suggest climbing them from Alstonefield to the south, where there is good parking.

Walk Description

From the car park at Alstonefield walk 1km along the road which runs north west towards Hulme End and Hartington. When the road bends to the left, take the footpath on the right which heads north through fields towards Narrowdale Hill. Continue north on the path with a wall on the left (see picture opposite). This path eventually leads to Hartington. The summit of Narrowdale Hill can be seen ahead and to the left. When the wall ends, make a direct ascent to the unmarked summit.

Return to the footpath and continue north for about 200m. A path goes off to the right and descends to the valley floor. Take this path. Once at the valley floor, pick up the Right of Way going south. After 300m, the track goes through a gate onto access land. Once past the gate a direct ascent of Gratton Hill can be made.

Narrowdale Hill from Grafton Hill

There is a small broken cairn at the summit. It is worth spending a few minutes looking at the view if the weather is good. Dovedale is to the south and Wolfcote Dale is directly below to the east.

Descend gently south east along a broad ridge to pick up a minor road which heads south towards Alstonefield. After walking down the road for 600m, a track goes off to the right and leads directly back to Alstonefield

Ecton and Wetton Hills

A walk over the open hillside of the Wetton Hills and the old copper mines of Ecton Hill.

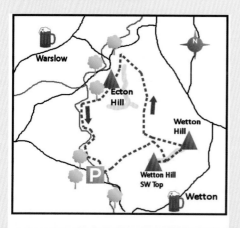

Walk Details

Distance:	11km (7 miles)
Height to Climb:	335m (1,100ft)
Start:	SK 096561
Difficulty:	3

Copper Mines

Ecton Hill's geology gave rise to it being the source of high-grade copper ore. The mine was most active during the 18th Century. Under the ownership of the Dukes of Devonshire, great investment was made in new mining technology to exploit the rich copper deposits within the hill.

The Hills

Wetton Hill

Wetton Hill is a HUMP with a smooth grassy summit. This hill has excellent views to the east and is marginally higher than its namesake to the south west.

Height:	371m (1,217ft)
Summit:	SK 113566
Map Ref:	O/S Explorer **OL24**

Ecton Hill

Ecton Hill is a TUMP with a Trig Point at the summit. There is plenty of evidence of old copper mines on its slopes.

Height:	369m (1,211ft)
Summit:	SK 100580
Map Ref:	O/S Explorer **OL24**

Wetton Hill SW Top

Wetton Hill South West Top is a TUMP with a rounded grassy summit. It is lower than its namesake but arguably the better summit.

Height:	358m (1,175ft)
Summit:	SK 105563
Map Ref:	O/S Explorer **OL24**

Walk Summary

These three hills give a great walk in an interesting part of the Peak District. The Wetton Hills are popular with walkers. The area around Ecton Hill has a history of mining. I suggest starting this walk near the Wettonmill tea room in the Manifold valley, where parking is available. The walk suggests including all three hills in one walk, however they can easily be completed in two shorter walks.

Walk Description

prefer to climb the two Wetton Hills first. Walk east on a path from Wettonmill, and climb a minor hill to join the old Leek and Manifold Railway. This is now a walking route. Follow this path north east through the valley for 1km. On reaching a house, turn right across a footbridge to the open hillside of the Wetton Hills. Follow a path which climbs the hillside to the col between Wetton Hill and the South West top. Although the South West top is slightly lower than the east top it is designated as a separate hill. Climb the South West top first by a short and steady climb west to the summit.

Thor's Cave

About 1.5km from Wettonmill lies Thor's Cave, one of the best known sites in the area. Thor's Cave is a gaping void in the rock high on a limestone crag above the River Manifold. Early Victorian archeologists were the first to discover that this many-chambered cavern, named after the Norse god of war, provided a home for our Stone Age Ancestors. Thor's Cave can be reached by following the Manifold Track for 1.5km south from Wettonmill, then a stairway from the track.

Return to the col from the summit of the South West top, and traverse the hillside east to the main top. This summit overlooks Narrowdale Hill, Gratton Hill, and Wolfscote Hill. From the summit of Wetton Hill, descend west to a minor road at Manor House. Follow this west then north past the Back of Ecton. Walk north down the minor road for a further 1km after passing the Back of Ecton. When the road takes a 90-degree bend to the right, carry straight on along a Right of Way. This goes north west up the hillside to the Ecton copper mine engine room.

Ecton Hill engine room

Walk Description (cont)

After passing the old engine room climb south to the summit Trig Point of Ecton Hill. Continue south west on a footpath which follows the edge of the wide ridge above the Manifold Valley. This is magnificent walking with old copper mines appearing and wide views in all directions. Go through a small gate and follow the concessionary path for 200m to another gate in the wall.

Go through this gate and follow the concessionary path with the wall on your left. After a few hundred metres, a sign signalling the return to access land appears. Go through another two more gates/stiles and then descend gradually to avoid a fence directly ahead. Once below the fence a track descends to the Manifold Trail below. Follow the Manifold Trail, an old railway track, south for 800m to Dale Farm, then Wettonmill.

The Manifold Trail runs 13km from Hulme End just north of Ecton to Waterhouses, a village on the A523, Leek to Ashbourne road.

Café at Wettonmill

Bunster Hill & Thorpe Cloud

An iconic walk over the twin sentinels of Dove Dale and across the stepping stones.

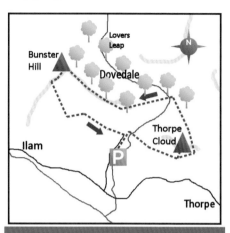

Walk Details

Distance:	5km (3 miles)
Height to Climb:	350m (1,150ft)
Start:	SK 146509
Difficulty:	3

The Hills

Bunster Hill

Bunster Hill lies directly above Ilam and Dove Dale. The summit is in a small wooded area.

Height:	329m (1,080ft)
Summit:	SK 142517
Map Ref:	O/S Explorer **OL24**

Thorpe Cloud

Thorpe Cloud is a TUMP and one of the most popular hills in the Peak District. It has a steep, rocky summit and is often combined with the stepping stones over the River Dove.

Height:	287m (942ft)
Summit:	SK 152510
Map Ref:	O/S Explorer **OL24**

Dovedale

Dovedale is owned by the National Trust, and annually attracts a million visitors. The valley was cut by the River Dove and runs for 5km (3 miles) from Milldale in the North to the wooded ravine near Thorpe Cloud and Bunster Hill in the south. In the ravine, a set of Stepping Stones cross the river, and there are two caves known as the Dove Holes. The walk up the Dove to Milldale, returning by Hall Dale, is featured in ITVs top 100 walks in Britain.

Walk Summary

Bunster Hill towers above Ilam and, with Thorpe Cloud, is one of the twin sentinels which guard the south side of Dovedale. Thorpe Cloud is a very popular hill, and is one of the most climbed hills in the Peak District. The suggested route below goes over both hills, starting at the large Dovedale car park, near the Izaac Walton Hotel.

This is not a long walk but contains two relatively steep climbs, the ascents of Thorpe Cloud and Bunster Hill. It also crosses the Dove Dale Stepping Stones.

Walk Description

The walk over Thorpe Cloud and Bunster Hill starts at the car park in Dovedale near Ilam (postcode DE6 2AY, charge). Walk north east for a short distance down the west side of Dovdale and turn right over a footbridge. Follow the path which runs along the south side of Thorpe Cloud, then turn left to ascend the hill from its east side. Thorpe Cloud is a magnificent small hill and normally there are many walkers at the summit.

Return down the east side then turn left to traverse round the north side of the hill to the Stepping Stones (see opposite). This is a popular spot where the river turns at right angles and the Stepping Stones allow people to cross to the other side, assuming the river is not too high.

Cross the Stepping Stones, or if the river is too high (unusual) walk down the east side of the Dove to cross the river at the footbridge used on the outward journey. Having crossed the stepping stones, walk south west for 150m to find a faint footpath which goes steeply up the hillside to the right. Climb this footpath and bear left to follow the ridge of Bunster Hill. After walking up the ridge for about 800m, a gate into a small wood is reached. Go into the wood and the summit is unmarked, about 50m ahead. This is a quiet spot, in complete contrast to the summit of Thorpe Cloud.

Return to the edge of the wood, go through the gate, turn right and traverse round the top of the access land, going over two stiles. Now turn left and descend the steep hillside to reach a path along the bottom of the access land. Turn left to return to the car. park.

Thorpe Cloud from the east

Dovedale Stepping Stones

Peak District –
North West Peak

The north west Peak is the area closest to Manchester, and often you will see the outlines and skyscrapers of Manchester from the top of the hills. The summit of Shining Tor is higher than any point in the Peak District outside the Dark Peak. The hills range from the high moorland summits of Shining Tor and Black Edge to the local and historical summits of Teggs Nose and Kerridge Hill. The area stretches north to Glossop and west to Macclesfield. Fifteen hills of the Peaks 75 are located in the North West Peak.

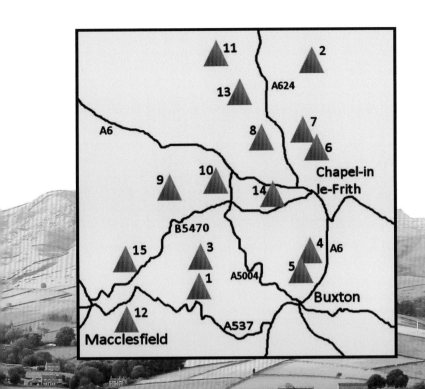

	Page No.	Height (m)	Height (ft)	Map Ref
NORTH WEST PEAK				
Shining Tor	106	559	1,834	1
Mill Hill	110	544	1,785	2
Cats Tor	106	522	1,713	3
Black Edge	112	507	1,663	4
Combs Head	112	503	1,650	5
South Head	114	494	1,621	6
Mount Famine	114	473	1,552	7
Chinley Churn	114	457	1,499	8
Sponds Hill	120	413	1,355	9
Whaley Moor	121	411	1,348	10
Cown Edge	118	411	1,348	11
Teggs Nose	122	382	1,253	12
Lantern Pike	118	373	1,224	13
Eccles Pike	117	370	1,214	14
Kerridge Hill	124	313	1,007	15

South Head and Mount Famine

Shining Tor & Cats Tor

A fine high level ridge walk leading to the highest summit in the western area of the Peak District.

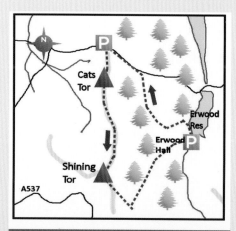

The Hills

Shining Tor

Shining Tor is a Marilyn and the highest summit in the western Peak. Its summit lies on the Cheshire/Derbyshire border.

Height:	559m (1,834ft)
Summit:	SK 995737
Map Ref:	O/S Explorer **OL24**

Cats Tor

Cats Tor is a subsidiary peak of Shining Tor. It is a TUMP and lies on the wide ridge to the north of Shining Tor.

Height:	522m (1,713ft)
Summit:	SJ 995759
Map Ref:	O/S Explorer **OL24**

Walk Details

Distance:	11km (6.5 miles)
Height to Climb:	350m (1,150ft)
Start:	SK 013748
Difficulty:	3

Walk Summary

Four miles west of Buxton lies Shining Tor, the highest and best-known hill in the western Peak District. It is often climbed from the Cat and Fiddle to the south, but this route from Errwood Reservoir, over Foxlow Edge and Cats Tor, is an outstanding high level ridge walk, with a paved footpath all the way from Cats Tor to Shining Tor. The walk is varied and interesting and, in my opinion, one of the best walks in the Peak District.

Pym Chair

Just below and north of Cats Tor lies Pym Chair car park. Local legend tells that Pym Chair is the place where a highwayman called Pym robbed passers by on the packhorse route. Alternatively Pym may have been a preacher who offered sermons! Take your pick.

The valley floor is dominated by two reservoirs, Errwood Reservoir and Fernilee Reservoir, fed by the River Goyt. The high moorland is a Site of Special Scientific Interest. Heather is the main plant but the heathland also has native grasses, rushes, sedges and shrubs.

Walk Description

Park at the Errwood Hall car park approximately three miles west of Buxton (closed Sunday and Bank Holidays but alternative parking available nearby). Walk out of the entrance of the car park and turn left to go over Shooter's Clough Bridge. At the north end of the bridge, turn left to follow a path through the woods. This path climbs the hillside bending right to head north out of the woods and onto the access land.

Continue climbing gently on a good path which goes over the top of Foxlow Edge. Foxlow Edge is a fine ridge but does not have sufficient prominence to qualify for the main list.

The path now drops down to the minor road which climbs from Errwood Reservoir to the car park at Pym Chair. On reaching the road, turn left and follow

a roadside path north west for 800m. Just before the high point of the road is reached, a path goes off to the left. This follows the wide ridge of Cats Tor and Shining Tor. Cross the road and follow this path south.

View from Shooter's Clough Bridge The path rises slowly and, after 800m, it passes over the summit of Cats Tor. The path is now paved all the way to Shining Tor, keeping feet dry even in the wettest weather. This is a magnificent highway with views in all directions, to the west Macclesfield and the Staffordshire and Cheshire plains, to the east the Upper Goyt Valley.

After descending gently from Cats Tor for 1km, the path starts the ascent of Shining Tor, turning slightly right as it makes its final journey to the summit, with the Trig Point through a small gate, and over the border to Cheshire.

From the summit continue south east on the path towards the Cat and Fiddle for 800m. Go through a gate and turn north east to descend to the car park at Errwood Reservoir.

Looking north from Cats Tor

Mill Hill

A visit to the quiet summit of Mill Hill, one of the first summits on the Pennine Way.

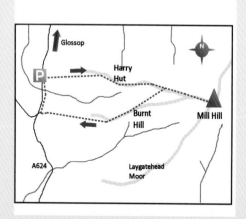

The Hills

Mill Hill

Mill Hill is a TUMP lying on the Pennine Way between Kinder Scout and Bleaklow. It is a quiet summit, mainly frequented by Pennine Way walkers.

Height:	544m (1,785ft)
Summit:	SK 061904
Map Ref:	O/S Explorer **OL1**

Walk Details

Distance:	7km (4 miles)
Height to Climb:	150m (500ft)
Start:	SK 034909
Difficulty:	2

Plane Wreckage

Near the summit of Mill Hill and on the route of the walk lies the wreckage of a US Liberator which crashed on Mill Hill in 1944.

At the same place there is a plaque commemorating a member of the Kinder Mountain Rescue team who died here in 2016.

Walk Summary

Mill Hill is a bare, domed summit on peaty moorland on the Pennine Way. Just to the south west the steep northern slopes leading to the Kinder plateau tower above it.

Mill Hill could be climbed by following the Pennine Way south from the top of Snake Pass, a total height rise of just over 100ft in 4km. However, a more interesting and circular route starts from a parking area just off the A624, 3km south of Glossop. From here a path leads east to the summit of Mill Hill, passing the Trig Point at the top of Harry's Hut and the wreckage of a US Liberator. The return can be varied by traversing Burnt Hill.

Walk Description

Start from the parking area, just off the A624, 3 km south of Glossop. Go over a stile and follow a good path east through heather moorland, with only skylarks and grouse for company. After just over 1km, the summit Trig Point of Harry's Hut is reached. The prominence of this hill is insufficient to qualify for the Peaks 75 listing, but it is a pleasant spot with good views. Continue just south of east on the path. After a few hundred metres the path joins a good paved path. Continue east on this path and the wreckage of an old US Liberator is passed. Soon after passing this the quiet summit of Mill Hill is reached.

The route back can be varied by following the excellent paved path all the way back to the A624. A 20m diversion from the path enables the summit of Burnt Hill to be ticked off, but this has insufficient prominence to qualify for the main list. On returning to the A624, walk north for some 600m by the roadside to return to the car. There is a path by the roadside for most of the route.

Summit of Mill Hill

Black Edge & Combs Head

A substantial walk round the edge of a large grouse moor, on access land, just north of Buxton.

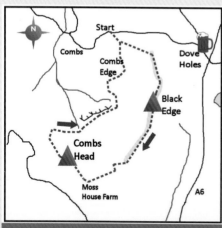

The Hills

Black Edge

Black Edge is a TUMP and by a small margin the highest point on the moor. A Trig Point marks the summit.

Height:	507m (1,663ft)
Summit:	SK 063770
Map Ref:	O/S Explorer **OL24**

Combs Head

Combs Head is an unassuming hill at the southern end of Combs Moss. It is the unmarked high point of a wide expanse of moorland and qualifies as a TUMP.

Height:	503m (1,650ft)
Summit:	SJ 041757
Map Ref:	O/S Explorer **OL24**

Walk Details

Distance:	13km (8 miles)
Height to Climb:	300m (1,000ft)
Start:	SK 052786
Difficulty:	4

Walk Summary

Just north of Buxton lies an area of high moorland with access, much of it above 1,500ft, called Combs Moss. Combs Moss is a privately owned grouse moor (a request is made not to bring dogs), with a shooting hut and grouse butts. The highest point is the Trig Point at Black Edge, 1,663ft, which lies on the edge of the National Park. It is best to start the walk from just north of Castle Naze hill fort where there is a gate and access to the hillside. The walk then does a complete circuit of the moor in a clockwise direction, crossing both summits.

Grouse butt near Black Edge

Castle Naze

Castle Naze is the site of a prehistoric hillfort. The fort is over 2 acres with a triangular layout. It is believed that the fort was built during the Iron Age, and reconstructed during medieval times. Buried remains were uncovered of pits, workshops, and foundations of buildings.

Walk Description

There is parking in an extended layby just west of the start point on the minor Cow Low road running west from Dove Holes. From the gate walk steeply up to the Castle Naze iron age hill fort, and turn left to follow a path running east then south east along the edge of the hillside. The path goes along Short Edge before turning south and continuing to the Trig Point of Black Edge. From here it would be possible to return to the start, and climb Combs Moss from Buxton.

If you are adding Combs Head to the walk, continue south west along the edge for nearly 3km. Buxton is directly to the south, and towards the end of this stretch, the cross at the top of Corbar Hill comes into view. The path turns right following the inside of the wall and continues north west. After just over 1km, the unmarked summit of Combs Head is reached. It is possible to 'cut the corner', from Black Edge but this is not recommended as there is no path and the terrain is poor.

The return journey follows the path along the edge around the west side of Combs Moss (a distance of roughly 6km). It would be possible to reduce the distance by cutting the corners if time is pressing, but the walk is best completed by following the edge round and back north to Castle Naze hill fort.

An alternative way of completing both hills, and also visiting Corbar Hill (not included in this listing because the drop is only circa 20m), is to start at Buxton. The route involves an out and back section of nearly 6km to Black Edge, but overall is marginally shorter.

Park in Buxton, there is parking by the side of the A5004 as it climbs the hill going north west out the town (Grid Reference SK 051739). From here follow a path which goes east then north through Corbar Woods. When the path emerges from the woods the summit of Corbar Hill with its cross is straight ahead. From the summit of Corbar Hill go north west then north over access land. After just under 1km, the path which circuits Combs Moss is reached.

Turn right and make the lengthy return journey to Black Edge, then walk north west to Combs Head. After climbing Combs Head, return south east 200m to a gate which allows access to Midshires Way below, and an easy return to the car, which is south east down Midshires Way along the road.

Chinley Hills

An interesting walk covering an historical part of the Peak District and visiting three summits with good views.

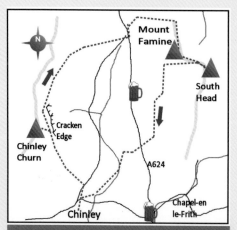

Walk Details

Distance:	12km (7.5 miles)
Height to Climb:	435m (1,430ft)
Start:	SK 039826
Difficulty:	3

Peak Forest Tramway

The Peak Forest Tramway runs through the south side of Chinley. This was an early horse and gravity-powered industrial railway opened in 1796, and remained in use until the 1920s. It was used to carry limestone from the vast quarries around Dove Holes down to Buxworth, and much of it was then taken by boat to Manchester along the Peak Forest Canal.

The Hills

South Head

South Head is the highest hill in this group and lies only 2km west of Brown Knoll and the Kinder group. It is a TUMP with a substantial cairn at the highest point.

Height:	494m (1,621ft)
Summit:	SK 061846
Map Ref:	O/S Explorer **OL1**

Mount Famine

Mount Famine is a TUMP lying on an interesting ridge close to South Head. The summit is unmarked.

Height:	473m (1,552ft)
Summit:	SK 056849
Map Ref:	O/S Explorer **OL1**

Chinley Churn

Chinley Churn fills the ground north of Chinley. The actual summit is 700m north of the Trig Point, reflecting the size of the area of high ground. Chinley Churn is a HUMP.

Height:	457m (1,499ft)
Summit:	SK 037844
Map Ref:	O/S Explorer **OL1**

Walk Summary

The village of Chinley is surrounded by hills, including the three hills mentioned above and Eccles Pike, a fine rounded summit owned by the National Trust. The hills above can be climbed in a circular walk from Chinley or from the high pass between Chinley and Hayfield, at Chinley Head. The walking over Mount Famine and South Head is delightful and the two summits are quickly bagged.

Walk Description

The walk starts by ascending Chinley Churn from Chinley. There is roadside parking near the station (postcode SK23 6AZ). Cross the railway bridge at grid reference SK 041827, and turn right up the minor road. After about 200m, a path ascends the hillside to the left. Take this and climb the hillside to reach the track which goes to Peep-O-Day. Turn right to follow this track north east then north west, and finally north. At all times the track stays below the crest of the wide ridge of Chinley Churn. After 2km, there is a small gate. Go through this and follow a small path 100m up the hillside to the left to reach the crest of Chinley Churn and its summit, which is 700m north of the Trig Point.

Descend back to the track and continue north to a gate at grid reference SK 041849. Turn right to follow the lane down to Peep-O-Day farm and the A624 road to Hayfield. Cross the main road and turn left. After 100m turn right on to a

lane which goes north east to the Pennine Bridleway. Go straight over the Bridleway and continue for another 250m until the path starts to go downhill. Turn right and follow the path directly towards Mount Famine. This is straight ahead with South Head behind to the left.

Summit of South Head

There follows a beautiful stretch of hill walking as the ridge of Mount Famine is crossed followed by the descent to the col between Mount Famine and South Head. A short climb leads to the summit of South Head, the high point of the walk. There are good views of Kinder Scout to the east and Chinley Churn and Manchester to the west.

Descend back to the col, and continue west for 200m, then turn left through a gate. A path descends just west of south. After 1km, a minor road to a farm is joined. Continue on this to the A624, Hayfield to Glossop road, cross this and and follow the path towards Chinley. The path goes west then south west, under the railway and emerges 400m east of the start.

Mount Fawnie from the col with South Head.

A great viewpoint above Chinley and Whaley Bridge.

Walk Details

Distance:	6km (3.5 miles)
Height to Climb:	155m (510ft)
Start:	SK 038826
Difficulty:	2

The Hills

Eccles Pike

Eccles Pike lies between Chinley and Whaley Bridge. It is a HUMP with a regular flow of visitors, being easily reached via the minor road to the south.

Height:	370m (1,214ft)
Summit:	SK 035812
Map Ref:	O/S Explorer **OL1**

Walk Description

Eccles Pike is an isolated hill between Chapel en le Frith and Whaley Bridge, and just south of Chinley. It is a HUMP (hundred metres prominence) and can be climbed quickly from the minor road running just south of the hill. However, I have described the route from Chinley which offers a better perspective of the hill.

Park close to the station in Chinley, and walk south through Chinley village. Just after crossing a bridge over the A6, turn right up Eccles Terrace. At the end of the terrace, a footpath goes south to Back Eccles Lane. Turn right onto the lane and follow it west for a few hundred metres past Eccles House. There is a gate on the left which allows walkers onto the National Trust land. Either ascend Eccles Pike directly, or follow the track which zig zags up the hill. From the summit descend east for 500m on a footpath, then take the byway which descends north to Back Eccles Lane. From here rejoin the outward route back to the station.

Summit of Eccles Pike

Cown Edge & Lantern Pike

A lengthy walk from the pretty village of Rowarth over two contrasting summits.

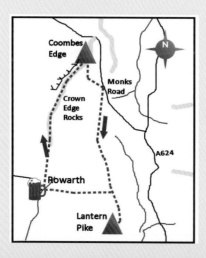

The Hills

Cown Edge

Cown Edge forms a long ridge just south west of Glossop. It is a TUMP with the summit marked by a small cairn on the top of a ruined wall.

Height:	411m (1,348ft)
Summit:	SK 021920
Map Ref:	O/S Explorer **OL1**

Lantern Pike

Lantern Pike is a TUMP just north of Hayfield. It lies on National Trust land and has a viewfinder on its summit..

Height:	373m (1,224ft)
Summit:	SK 026882
Map Ref:	O/S Explorer **OL1**

Walk Details

Distance:	13km (8 miles)
Height to Climb:	275m (900ft)
Start:	SK 012892
Difficulty:	3

Walk Summary

These hills lie just south of Glossop, and close to the western edge of the Peak District. They can either be combined in a long, but not difficult walk from Rowarth car park, or climbed separately (which is quicker but less interesting).

Cown Edge is a large and distinguished hill, a long ridge with the north end overlooking Glossop, and with a number of interesting rock formations.

Cown Edge

Cown Edge is a large curved ridge often mistaken for an old quarry. In fact the unique edge was the result of a large natural landslide. The instability of the edge makes it unsuitable for quarrying.

Lantern Pike is also a fine hill, owned by the National Trust and a short climb from the Pennine Bridleway. Using the Pennine Bridleway is the best way to link the hills.

Walk Description

There is a car park in the picturesque hamlet of Rowarth (SK22 1EF). Rowarth also has two pubs. From the car park, walk north east and pass through most of the hamlet. A footpath sign appears, turn left and walk through a narrow gap between two houses. Ascend north, and carry straight on at a crossing of paths. Soon the wide ridge of Cown Edge is reached.

After 2km, the path crosses a bridleway. Carry on north east for a further 1km to the high point of Cown Edge, a small cairn on top of a wall. Now retrace the outbound route for a short distance and bear left on a path to Rocks Farm. At Rocks Farm turn left towards the road. Just before reaching Monks road a path goes south to the Pennine Bridleway. Follow the Pennine Bridleway south for 3km. At one point, the most direct route is along a path rather than the Bridleway.

Approaching Cown Edge

The summit of Lantern Pike is now directly ahead. Just before the Bridleway passes the east side of the hill, a path goes off to the right. This ascends the hill directly to the summit viewfinder. Return to the Bridleway and retrace the route for 600m along the Bridleway. A path goes off to the left and heads west. After 1.5km the New Mill Inn at Rowarth is reached.

Sponds Hill

A short, high-level walk along the Gritstone Trail to the grassy summit of Sponds Hill and an uninterrupted view over Manchester.

Walk Details

Distance: 3km (2 miles)
Height to Climb: 60m (200ft)
Start: SK 970792
Difficulty: 1

The Hills

Sponds Hill

Sponds Hill is a TUMP on a grassy hillside. The viewpoint marks the highest point. This lies 400m south of the Trig Point.

Height: 413m (1,355ft)
Summit: SK 971799
Map Ref: O/S Explorer **OL1/24**

Walk Description

A few kilometres west of Whaley Bridge lies the pleasant, grassy summit of Sponds Hill, with views all round as Sponds Hill is the highest point in the area. It lies just off the Gritstone Trail. The Gritstone Trail is a 56km (35 miles) trail along the west side of the National Park, mostly just outside it, although this section near Sponds Hill is within the National Park.

Drive to a minor road which leaves the B5470 Macclesfield to Whaley Bridge road 2km south west of Kettleshulme. Drive a few hundred metres up the minor road to where it meets the Gritstone Trail. It is usually possible to park by the side of the road. Walk north up the Gritstone Trail, a good track to a viewpoint. This is the highest point. It is marginally higher than the Trig Point which can be seen 400m to the north. However, I recommend continuing to the Trig Point for the clear, uninterrupted view of Manchester it offers.

Sponds Hill viewpoint

Whaley Moor

n unassuming summit, lying between **Whaley Bridge** and **Lyme Park**.

Walk Details

Distance:	5km (3 miles)
Height to Climb:	140m (450ft)
Start:	SK 997820
Difficulty:	2

Lyme Park

Lyme Park consists of a mansion house surrounded by formal gardens in a deer park. The house is owned by the National Trust and is the largest in Cheshire, with a deer park covering 1,359 acres. In the grounds are a refreshment kiosk, a coffee shop and a restaurant.

The Hills

Whaley Moor

Whaley Moor is a HUMP with an unmarked summit close to a wall. It is a short climb through access land from the Right of Way which connects Whaley Bridge and Lyme Park.

Height:	411m (1,348ft)
Summit:	SK 990821
Map Ref:	O/S Explorer **OL1**

/alk Description

nergetic walkers can add this hill to Sponds Hill by continuing north for 2.5km from Sponds Hill, hen turning right on a footpath which leads east to the access land on which Whaley Moor is located.

The route suggested starts to the east of the hill, 2km outside Whaley Bridge. Drive up Whaley Lane from Whaley Bridge and there is parking near a small wood. Walk north west up the road for 200m, and turn left along a track signposted o Lyme Park. The track goes south, then turns west and goes over a footbridge. Continue for another 500m, and turn right up the hillside after going through a gate.

Follow a small path up the steep hillside. The path keeps disappearing and there s some tussocky ground to cross, awkward underfoot, before the summit. The ummit is next to the corner of a wall. Return by the same route.

f using public transport, it is possible to climb this hill from the station at Whaley Bridge. Walk up Whaley Lane to the point where the footpath to Lyme Park leaves he road. An alternative descent route can be found past the reservoir.

Teggs Nose

A walk over an historic hill on the edge of the Peak District National
Park near Macclesfield.

Walk Details

Distance:	5km (3 miles)
Height to Climb:	180m (600ft)
Start:	SK 950733
Difficulty:	2

The Hills

Teggs Nose

Teggs Nose is a TUMP at the high point
of an old quarry. There is a viewfinder on
the summit with views to the east over old
quarrying equipment. The higher hills of
the Peak District are beyond.

Height:	382m (1,253ft)
Summit:	SK 948726
Map Ref:	O/S Explorer **OL24**

Walk Summary

*Teggs Nose lies just outside the National
Park on the Cheshire Gritstone Trail, a 56km
long distance path from Disley in Cheshire to
Kidsgrove in Staffordshire. This walk starts at
the Visitors' Centre and follows the Teggs Nose Trail to the reservoir just south of Teggs Nose. The
return to the visitors' centre is via the summit.*

Walk Description

Park at the Visitors' Centre for Teggs Nose Country Park (charge) where there
is also a café. It is worth picking up a leaflet at the Visitors' Centre. This has a
good map of the Country Park. I recommend following the Teggs Nose Trail,
deviating off the route just before the Quarry Exhibition, in order to visit the
summit.

From the car park at the Visitor Centre take the track south east then south
downhill. Walk south past Clough House Farm and into the woodland. Carry
on past the reservoir, then turn right to cross the dam wall of the reservoir.
Ascend the slopes to the south end of the summit area of Teggs Nose, then turn
right and continue north towards the quarry exhibition. Just before the quarry
exhibition items, turn left to ascend to the top of the quarry, then turn right to
walk over the summit of Teggs Nose. From
the summit walk north to return to the
Visitors' Centre.

A detour can be made to view the old
quarrying equipment below the summit of
Teggs Nose.

Interesting Fact

Quarrying took place at Teggs Nose as
early as the 1500s and continued until
1955. The park's quarrying history and
some of the machinery used lie just below
the summit.

Looking east from the summit of Teggs Nose

Kerridge Hill

An interesting hill on a long ridge and climbed from the attractive Cheshire village of Bollington.

Walk Details

Distance:	4km (2.5 miles)
Height to Climb:	170m (560ft)
Start:	SK 937775
Difficulty:	1

The Hills

Kerridge Hill

Kerridge Hill is a TUMP lying above the Cheshire village of Bollington. It has an impressive summit ridge with the Trig Point and highest point at the south end.

Height:	313m (1,007ft)
Summit:	SK 942759
Map Ref:	O/S Explorer **OL24**

Walk Summary

Kerridge Hill lies just east of the Peak District National Park. It is climbed from Bollington. This allows the full summit ridge to be traversed from White Nancy to the Trig Point. Bollington lies on the Macclesfield Canal, part of the Cheshire Ring, and the mills and wharfs of the canal are explored in Sally Bailey's guide to the Cheshire Ring (volume two).

White Nancy on Kerridge Hill

Bollington from Kerridge Hill

Walk Description

Park on the south east side of Bollington just north of White Nancy which can be seen on the hillside above. Walk up one of the paths which climb the hill to White Nancy from Bollington. This is roughly 500m. White Nancy is a popular spot for picnics when the weather is good. Continue south along a fine ridge, with the quarry on your right, and good views of the higher Peak District hills to your left.

The path goes directly south through a couple of gates, and along a pleasant and relatively flat ridge. After just over 1km the path makes the final climb to the Trig Point and highest point of Kerridge Hill.

My Favourite Walks

"I have lived close to the Peak District all my life and have loved walking its hills with many different companions.

The 'official' O/S list below contains some fine walks in the area including one of my personal favourites, Mam Tor.

The 2018 Favourites from the Ordnance Survey and Ramblers

The Peak District has six entries in the list of Britain's 100 favourite walks. This list was created by a survey of thousands of walkers by the Ordinance Survey and The Ramblers, and revealed in 2018.

Five of the walks are included in this book with some changes to include all the summits.

The hills around the Manifold and Dove Valleys

The coutryside around the Manifold and Dove valleys is one of my favourite parts of The Peak. Between the villages of Hartington and Hulme End to the north and Wetton and Alstonfield to the south lies a cluster of fine hills and some of the best walking in the area. Wetton Hill rises steeply above the village which gives its name, with Ecton Hill to the nor▉ and Narrowdale Hill, then Gratton Hill and finally Wolfscote Hill running across the Dove Valley. Wolfcote Hill stands proudly on the east banks of the river Dove, but Wetton Hill enjoys greater prominence and commands the other hills from its 371m elevation.

Uniquely among the group, Wetton Hill has two summits, standing half a mile apart and ea▉ very worthy in its own right. The higher summit lies to the east and offers fine views in all directions, while the western summit is 13m lower but on many maps is misleadingly name▉ "Wetton Hill", suggesting that it represents the highest point. Some of the best views can ▉ gained from the small spur a few hundred yards further west, from where the Manifold Vall▉ meanders away in either direction below.

A walk along this wonderful valley can be coupled with the high-level route over Ecton Hil▉ and Wetton Hill (8 miles in all), perhaps including lunch at Hulme End or Wetton – or a pa▉ lunch at the spectacular vantage point on the Tor above Thor's Cave, itself an essential det▉ for exploration. The Tor is an exposed precipice and care should be taken.

by Martin Summers

Wetton Hill from Thor's Cave

Another of my favourite routes in this area is a great round of 20km (12 miles) going south from Hartington. Early on, the route leads through the peaceful col between the Narrowdale and Gratton Hills, from where both can easily be summitted over access land. Continue to Alstonefield, then turn for home at Milldale to follow the beautiful Dove upstream through the Wolfscote and Beresford Dales. My first sighting of a kingfisher was on this peaceful stretch of river. Towards the end of a full day, at the foot of Biggin Dale the decision to leave Wolfscote Hill for another time can be readily agreed!

I discovered one of the finest views of the Dove Valley hills purely by chance one June evening when I detoured off the A515 just before the left turn to Alstonefield to discover an easy stroll to the top of Moat Low. Although part of the higher Tissington Hill which guards the eastern banks of Dovedale, Moat Low enjoys a commanding position of its own at 343m, just half a mile from the main road. The lane is marked 'gated', but there are no obstacles before Moat Low Farm is reached, and from there a footpath reaches the top in just a few minutes.

With the setting sun beyond, the group of trees on Moat Low provides a stunning frame for the view north-west to the row of peaks from Wetton Hill across to Wolfscote Hill. As Moat Low is also a Bronze Age burial site, a few minutes of quiet solitude to appreciate the panorama feels appropriate.

Wetton, Narrowdale and Gratton Hills from Moat Low

My Favourite Walks (cont)

Eccles Pike

Eccles Hill with Rushup Edge beyond

Eccles Pike is the lowest of three fine Humps which surround the small town of Whaley Bridge, but The Pike is my favourite. It punches well above its weight by dint of its shapely symmetry and wonderful 360 degree panorama from a very distinctive summit.

Along with Whaley Moor to the west and Chinley Churn to the north, Eccles Pike completes an excellent round of these three hills and a very satisfying day's walking. Navigation is a major part of the day with the choices between footpaths and tarmac in the valleys dependent on personal choice - and the time available, as Barry and I almost found to our cost one November day.

After parking in Whaley Bridge, we set off past the near-infamous Toddbrook Reservoir and soon reached open ground with the upper reaches of Whaley Moor lying ahead in heavy mist. The poor visibility led us to roam the high ground for over half an hour to ensure we had attained our first objective. We later encountered a similar problem on Chinley Churn, where we must have walked at least an extra mile to exhaust all summit possibilities. The Trig Point offers no guidance as it is some distance from the top, and also on private land.

The challenges of route-finding on the day were not restricted to poor visibility, however. Our second difficulty lay in the sheer number of practical obstacles between the three hills. The crossings of railway lines (two), rivers (three) and roads (numerous) meant I was glad to have spent the previous evening planning what I hoped would be the optimal way to navigate these hazards. On a dull late autumn day, we certainly didn't have much time for u-turns!

Whilst the first two summits were not easy to pin down in the conditions, there was no such difficulty on Eccles Pike, which has good paths leading to the top, including one which is only a few minutes stroll from the Eccles Road running over its southern flank. There is no ambiguity on this fine peak, with marvellous views across to our earlier conquests – Whaley Moor and Chinley Churn, then over to Kinder Scout, Rushup Edge to the east and Combs Moss beyond the reservoir to the south.

by Martin Summers

The gentle descent back into Whaley Bridge is a joy, with a choice of footpaths eventually leading past the cricket ground, where the final overs can offer a pleasant diversion towards the end of a long summer day. There was no such luxury that day for Barry and me, as we reluctantly hastened from the top of Eccles Pike in the rapidly gathering twilight.

The Whaley Bridge Three Peaks may be too grand a title, but The Whaley Bridge Round certainly makes for a wonderful day – and next time, a long sunny summer's day!

Mam Tor

The Shivering Mountain from Lose Hill

Winnats Pass and Mam Tor

This Derbyshire Peak is famous for many good reasons. At 517m, Mam Tor stands proudly at the head of the Hope Valley, its spectacular face shaped by a landslip in the 1970s which caused the collapsed A6187 to be diverted through the dramatic Winnats Pass and gave the hill its colloquial name 'The Shivering Mountain'.

The fine summit enjoys glorious vistas across both the Hope and Edale valleys and the classic view along The Great Ridge leading to Lose Hill, with Win Hill beyond.

Many superb walks can be designed to start from this great hill and along The Great Ridge before returning along either of the valleys. In the Hope Valley, Castleton offers a variety of excuses for a long lunch before the return leg. Fortified by refreshment, additional interest can be added by either picking up the entrance to Cave Dale behind the village, or climbing out over the pasture beyond Peak Cavern and taking a route over access land above Winnats Pass for a fitting finale to the day.

Cycling over the Hills

In this section, Ed Bradwell talks about the challenges of cycling round the Peak District, and in particular some of the great hill climbs which are popular with cyclists.

Ed has spent many days cycling round the Peak District and has completed all the hill climbs. It is a sport he loves. He comments on his favourite climbs including two well-known cycle climbs of the Peak District, Winnats and the Cat and Fiddle, and the endurance required in what is a tough sport.

Cycling towards the Cat and Fiddle

Hiking requires endurance and a threshold for pain. One's feet, toes, legs, back and neck can all become sore after a long hike in the hills. I open up with these words having spent my childhood and early adult life hiking with my father on the high hills of Britain and abroad. Road biking also requires endurance and a threshold for pain, and the bike can be unrelenting and unforgiving. Both fell walking and cycling climbing are wonderfully free activities and Manchester, where I live, is a hotspot for both activities. I am very fortunate to be able to spend my spare time doing both.

Ed Bradwell, a local expert

Bike riding has changed over the years in both popularity and equipment. Sir Bradley Wiggins winning both Le Tour de France and Olympic gold for the time-trial in 2012, propelled the sport into the minds of many keen amateur athletes. Bike shops and brilliantly marketed gear popped up everywhere, making bike riding the new trend. I found myself being sucked in and once I moved to Manchester in 2013, I found myself with a basic road bike, helmet and trainers. I had the luck to live close to a friend who was in the same position. Within weeks we were venturing further and further from our Manchester postcode into the local hills.

I consider myself fairly fit, but when I attacked my first proper climb in the peaks, I never knew what hit me. I was in the lowest possible gear the bike provided, struggling and shuffling around in my seat. Standing or sitting, high cadence or low cadence. Anything I could do to get myself up the climb.

This first climb was one of the more popular climbs within the Peak District and is known as the 'Brickworks'. It does not seem long compared to an Alpine climb, but professional cyclists from all nationalities regularly comment on British road bike climbing. They are of constantly varying gradients, poorer road quality and more often than not, slightly damp. These are all factors making life more difficult, thus appealing.

The brickworks is 2.68 kilometres long, with an average gradient of 5.9%, some towards 15%. It runs from near Bollington (see Kerridge Hill) to close to the start point for Sponds Hill. Having done it close to 100 times with many different people, it is often considered, especially to Cheshire and Manchester bike riders, as the 'gateway' to the Peak District. Once you have summited, you can see Manchester in the far distance in one direction, and the peaks as far as the eye can see in every other direction. From this point on, it is decision time. One can return down the hill back to safety or immerse yourself in constant gradients grinding down your energy levels. One must never forget every hill from that point requires a similar hill again, to get yourself back out, but the rewards are fantastic.

Cycling over the Hills

In June 2010, an author called, Simon Warren published a book called, 100 Greatest Cycling Climbs. Very briefly, the author created a list of 100 of Britain's climbs. Not necessarily the toughest or longest, but a fine selection throughout the country, to make the list appealing to everyone. Having climbed 21 of them, I can assure you, none have been easy, but all have been rewarding in their own right.

Approximately 5km from my house is located my nearest '100' climb. Swiss Hill is only 502 metres long, but the average gradient is 13% and has a max gradient of 17%. Swiss Hill is a beautifully enclosed cobbled road surrounded by luscious trees. With houses relatively close, you are not completely cut off like many other climbs available. However, the cobbles for most of the time are sodden damp making them very slippery. Once you start the climb, there is no hiding onto smoother surfaces and standing up on the bike is nigh impossible. Your body weight generally needs to be planted on the saddle over the rear wheel making steep climbing even more difficult. There is the temptation to stand up and 'dance' on the pedals, however before you know it, your rear wheel will be skidding and you'll be going nowhere. Your only option therefore will be to unclip your cleats and fail the climb. No walking is allowed on a road bike. If and when one summits the climb, I can guarantee your heart rate will be near max and you will be begging for it to stop towards the top.

Swiss Hill is a mere 502 metres long and from there, if you point yourself in an easterly direction you will find yourself near Macclesfield. From Macclesfield there is a classic, '100' climb, the Cat and Fiddle. It is over 11.3 kilometres long with an average gradient of 3%. It would be defined as close to an Alpine or Pyrenean climb on paper due to its length. In my opinion this is a slight misdemeanour. Midway there is a section that is relatively flat and even downhill. This drastically reduces the total average gradient, but gives a very welcome rest.

From Macclesfield there is an aggressive start for 1 kilometre or so with an average gradient of close to 10%. Once clear of the hustle of upper Macclesfield, it eases up to allow the rider to settle into a steady cadence and wattage before it ramps up again close to 7 or 8%. Sway your way up the smooth road and before you know it, when looking left you are, what feels like, miles above the town skyline and climbing out of the trees and into the peaks. Continue the climb at a pace you feel comfortable with, taking in the views and close to half way you will find a circular stone with a written sign stating, 'Welcome to the Peak District'. It is very welcome as you have made good progress and know the top is approaching. Near the summit, you are greeted by Shining Tor, then at the summit by the second highest public house in England, The Cat and Fiddle. It has been closed in recent years, but now it has re-opened and you can purchase cakes, coffee or for the brave, a dram of whiskey.

Ed Bradwell, a local expert

Snake Pass

ccording to the 100 Greatest Cycling Climbs book there are seven located within the
eak District. Having completed them all, I must mention Winnats Pass, next to Mam
'or. A quick google image search of Winnats Pass and it will not take long to appreciate
1e beauty of this climb. Located deep within the Peak District and close to Castleton,
is a classic. Simon Warren rates the climb as an 8/10 in difficulty, which compared
) the Swiss Hill rating of a 5/10 means you know it is going to hurt. With a distance
f 1.7 km and an average gradient of 12% it does not seem so bad. However, the max
radient is listed as 20%, which at the time you hit that part, your heart rate is pumping
ut of your chest. It has to be approached out of Castleton and the build-up quietens the
eloton.

Cycling over the Hills

Chit chat reduces, people take in an energy gel or there is the nervous laughter at what is to come. Some people even dispense water from their bottles to lessen the load. Many climbs throughout the peaks go relatively unnoticed and you just get on with it. Winnats Pass requires full effort at a minimum and usually it is a race to the top. May the strongest rider win. It is widely considered as cattle grid to cattle grid from bottom to top respectively. However, the lead up to the lower cattle grid is a small climb in itself, which for me already requires the lowest gear. Once you hit the grid, your GPS will often remind you the segment has started. I would say even a professional rider would not need a beep from the computer to tell you the suffering is well under way. From then, you hit the harsh gradient and try to get into the groove.

Top of Winnats Pass

Ed Bradwell, a local expert

There is no point racing as there is still so far to go. If your colleague has left you for dead, there is a chance they will have gone too early. Limit your loss, stick to your power and have faith you will catch up after they explode. After 500 metres or so, the view is spectacular, but once you meander right, the view opens up even more. You are deep in the gorge with stunning sleep slopes all around you and you have the final kilometre to go. Stand up, sit down, whatever feels comfortable to get you up. Ramblers will often be there. Even they are impressed and will clap encouragement. Eventually, you make it past the cattle grid to the top and discuss with your mate (who is often waiting for me) how tough it was.

You will find many people cycling the hills of the Peak District, some completing time trials on the classic routes of Winnatts and the Cat and Fiddle, but most just enjoying a day out and testing themselves on these challenging hill climbs, getting off the bike when necessary. Within the peak district there are countless climbs varying in length, gradient and beauty. Just when one thinks they have completed their local area a new climb segment pops up.

I was 'bimbling' about near Trentabank Reservoir, in the Macclesfield Forest and close to Shutlingsloe, 'The Matterhorn of the Peak'. I decided to cycle a road which I had not noticed before. The road looked like a possible way through the Forest gaining access to the Peak District. After a few hundred metres, the road curved left into the Forest and flattened out. Just ahead, all I could see was a wall. The road had no turns, no white lines and was barely wide enough to accommodate a car. The surface worsened with loose gravel etched in places and large potholes, but maybe still passable.

The gradient steepened and steepened until I had no choice, but to drop to the lowest gear and stand on the pedals. Sitting was not an option and fortunately with a newly purchased rear cassette, I had access to one extra gear. My casual recovery ride converted quickly into a max heart rate test and pure survival to reach a summit in an unknown distance. I plodded on at walking pace with very tempting thoughts of turning back and losing. However, I was determined to fight it. Eventually the top appeared with glorious views, a well-earned descent and a good gulp of water. I have since learned the climb is titled, 'Charity Lane'. It is not a top 100 climb, but is within the list of official, north west climbs with a maximum gradient of 18.3%.

Hills of the Peak District by Height

	Hill	Area	Height (m)	Height (ft)	Prominence (m)	Listings (see page 140)
1	Kinder Scout	Dark Peak	636	2,088	497	M,H,T,N,CT
2	Bleaklow Head	Dark Peak	633	2,077	128	H,T,N
3	Higher Shelf Stones	Dark Peak	622	2,041	20	N
4	Grindslow Knoll	Dark Peak	601	1,972	15	
5	Black Hll	Dark Peak	582	1,909	165	M,H,T,D,CT
6	Shining Tor	North West Peak	559	1,834	236	M,H,T,D,CT
7	Axe Edge Moor	White Peak West	551	1,808	84	T,D
8	Howden Edge	Dark Peak	550	1,804	62	T,D,CT
9	Lord's Seat (Rushup Edge)	Dark Peak	550	1,804	62	T,D
10	Mill Hill	North West Peak	544	1,785	32	T,D
11	Back Tor	Dark Peak	538	1,765	67	T,D
12	Cats Tor	North West Peak	522	1,713	38	T,D
13	Mam Tor	Dark Peak	517	1,696	62	T,D
14	Black Edge	North West Peak	507	1,663	98	T,D
15	Shutlingsloe	White Peak West	506	1,660	133	H,T,D
16	The Roaches	White Peak West	505	1,657	123	H,T,D
17	Combs Head	North West Peak	503	1,650	41	T,D
18	West Nab	Dark Peak	501	1,644	50	T,D
19	South Head	North West Peak	494	1,621	38	T
20	Lose Hill	Dark Peak	476	1,562	85	T
21	Mount Famine	North West Peak	473	1,552	44	T
22	Bradwell Moor	White Peak East	471	1,545	50	T
23	Eldon Hill	White Peak East	470	1,542	20	
24	Win Hill	Dark Peak	463	1,520	145	H,T
25	Ramshaw Rocks	White Peak West	460	1,509	32	T
26	The Tower	Dark Peak	460	1,509	35	T
27	High Neb	Dark Peak	458	1,503	107	H,T
28	Chinley Churn	North West Peak	457	1,499	127	H,T
29	White Path Moss	Dark Peak	457	1,499	34	T
30	Hollins Hill	Peak District Dales	450	1,476	62	T
31	Chelmorton Hill	White Peak East	446	1,463	63	T
32	Chrome Hill	Peak District Dales	443	1,453	61	T
33	Grin Low	White Peak West	434	1,424	48	T
34	Higger Tor	Dark Peak	434	1,424	15	
35	Sir William Hill	White Peak East	429	1,407	123	H,T
36	Barker Bank	Dark Peak	426	1,398	34	T
37	Bamford Moor	Dark Peak	426	1,398	49	T

Log of climbs

Date Climbed	Companions	Weather	Other Details

Hills of the Peak District by Height

	Walk	Area	Height (m)	Height (ft)	Prominence (m)	Listing (see page 140)
38	High Wheeldon	Peak District Dales	422	1,384	35	T
39	Shatton Edge	White Peak East	417	1,368	55	T
40	Sponds Hill	North West Peak	413	1,355	72	T
41	Whaley Moor	North West Peak	411	1,348	105	H,T
42	Crown Edge	North West Peak	411	1,348	85	T
43	Hen Cloud	White Peak West	410	1,345	62	T
44	Revidge	White Peak West	401	1,316	40	T
45	Gradback Hill	White Peak West	399	1,309	43	T
46	Longstone Moor	White Peak East	395	1,296	108	H,T
47	Pilsbury Castle Hill	Peak District Dales	395	1,296	38	T
48	Bridge End Pastures	Dark Peak	392	1,286	37	T
49	Wolfscote Hill	Peak District Dales	388	1,273	102	H,T
50	Gun	White Peak West	385	1,263	168	M,H,T
51	Teggs Nose	North West Peak	382	1,253	36	T
52	Crook Hill	Dark Peak	382	1,253	33	T
53	Carder Low	Peak District Dales	380	1,247	58	T
54	Harboro Rocks	White Peak East	379	1,243	65	T
55	Parkhouse Hill	Peak District Dales	375	1,230	53	T
56	Lantern Pike	North West Peak	373	1,224	91	T
57	Minninglow Hill	White Peak East	372	1,220	45	T
58	Wetton Hill	Peak District Dales	371	1,217	132	H,T
59	Beeley Moor	White Peak East	371	1,217	89	T
60	Eccles Pike	North West Peak	370	1,214	135	H,T
61	Wardlow Hay Cop	White Peak East	370	1,214	53	T
62	Ecton Hill	Peak District Dales	369	1,211	82	T
63	Narrowdale Hill	Peak District Dales	367	1,204	71	T
64	Gratton Hill	Peak District Dales	363	1,191	50	T
65	Parkhouse Hill North	Peak District Dales	362	1,188	36	T
66	Wetton Hill SW Top	Peak District Dales	358	1,175	40	T
67	The Cloud	White Peak West	343	1,125	177	M,H,T
68	Masson Hill	White Peak East	338	1,109	55	T
69	Bunster Hill	Peak District Dales	329	1,080	24	
70	Fin Cop	White Peak East	327	1,073	96	T
71	Stanton Moor	White Peak East	323	1,060	110	H,T
72	Bolehill	White Peak East	323	1,060	104	H,T
73	Kerridge Hill	North West Peak	313	1,007	71	T
74	Thorpe Cloud	Peak District Dales	287	942	79	T
75	High Tor	White Peak East	205	673	47	T

Log of climbs

Date Climbed	Companions	Weather	Other Details

Relative Hills (what are they?)

Up until 1992, all hills were defined mainly by height, and lists were compiled on the basis of height. The key heights are 3,000ft, used for the listing of Scottish Munros, and 2,000ft, the height required to be classified as a mountain.

In 1992 Alan Dawson published his book, the Relative Hills of Britain, in which he lists the 'Marilyns', all the hills in Britain with a prominence of 150m. There are 1,556 of these. Following this came the HUMPs, all hills in Britain with a 100m prominence, and most recently, the TUMPs, all hills in Britain with a 30m prominence.

The concept of Relative Hills allows hills lower than 2,000ft to be included in lists. Some of these lower hills are great hills to climb. Many of us have been up Mam Tor and Thorpe Cloud in Derbyshire but they were not included on any list until the TUMPs were listed in 2013.

The TUMPs listings make it easier to define and put together a list of local hills, and I am indebted to the hill bagging community for all the work they do in determining heights and prominence of the hills around Britain. If you are interested in finding out more about Relative Hills, I suggest visiting the websites www. rhsoc.uk (the website for the Relative Hills Society) and www.hill-bagging.co.uk (the website which gives details of every hill in Britain with a prominence of over 30m). The Relative Hills Society welcomes new members and subscribers.

Terminology

M = Marilyn, any hill in Britain with prominence of 150m or more
H = HUMP, any hill in Britain with prominence of 100m or more
T = TUMP, any hill in Britain with prominence of 30m or more
N = Nuttall, hill in England or Wales over 2,000ft with a prominence of 15m or more
D = Dodd, any hill between 500m and 599m with a prominence of 30m
CT = County Tops.
Tor – this is a large, free-standing rock outcrop that rises abruptly from the surrounding land.

ibliography

'S Explorer Map OL1 – Dark Peak Area

S Explorer Map OL24 – White Peak Area

e Relative Hills of Britain - Alan Dawson

ore Relative Hills of Britain - Mark Jackson

lls of the Peak District and Surrounding Area – Rob Pollitt

ak District – Mountain Climbing Logbook

y Walks in the Peak District – Norman Taylor and Barry Hope

ak District Walks to Viewpoints – Chiz Dakin

e Dales 30 - Jonathan Smith

tain's Best Small Hills – Phoebe Smith

) Greatest Cycling Climbs - Simon Warren

Top of Higher Shelf Stones

About the Author

Barry Smith

Barry has been climbing mountains for over 50 years. Although an accountant by trade he has alwa had a passion for the mountains. Family holiday. in the Lake District were his grounding but it wa not till his early 30s that a strong interest became lifetime addiction. The change came when he start visiting Scotland regularly.

For 30 years he visited every corner of Scotland, completing all the Munros, Corbetts and many smaller hills in that magnificent walking country He was then able to put together an entirely new walking challenge "The Top 500 Summits in Britain and Ireland", complete with a detailed boc full of excellent photography and personal anecdot

With the trips to Scotland becoming harder (due t creeking knees and long journeys) he looked closer home for his mountain fix. Based in Loughboroug the Peak District became his obvious area of choi It was on the many trips to the area that he felt th was a need for a more detailed look at the mounta and hills. The result was the "75 Hills in the Pea District."